RETURN TO

The

Big Fancy

RETURN TO

The Big Fancy

FREEMAN HALL, author of *Retail Hell*

Adamsmedia
Avon, Massachusetts

Published by
Adams Media, a division of F+W Media, Inc.
57 Littlefield Street, Avon, MA 02322. U.S.A.
www.adamsmedia.com

ISBN 10: 1-4405-3677-5
ISBN 13: 978-1-4405-3677-9
eISBN 10: 1-4405-4174-4
eISBN 13: 978-1-4405-4174-2

Printed in the United States of America.

10 9 8 7 6 5 4 3 2 1

Interior illustrations © istockphoto.com/123rf.com

This book is available at quantity discounts for bulk purchases.
For information, please call 1-800-289-0963.

★ ★ ★

The events and characters portrayed in this book are based on my past experiences. Names, places, dialogue, and situations have been changed to protect the victims and keep the asshats from suing. Any resemblances to real people, places, or companies are purely coincidental and any complaints should be sent directly to my Shoposaurus. (Though I have to tell you she usually eats complainers, so if you're a corporate executive, I would advise you to take a deep breath and just relax into the tale. Maybe you'll learn something.)

★ ★ ★

For my sister Billee Burchett and her wife Michelle Quevedo.
I could not have come this far on my journey without the love,
support, and spiritual guidance of such two amazing women.

Contents

2ND QUARTER

Dancing for The Big Fancy Man: Corporate Ridiculousness 97

3RD QUARTER
Super Seller Blood on the Sales Floor *147*

4TH QUARTER

Season's Beatings! It's Not Over Till the Bloodsucker Buys Something 213

INTRODUCTION:

Happy Black Thanksgiving
from My Retail Tic

"You stupid idiot, don't you know how to do anything right?" said the prune-faced old lady to the grocery store cashier. "I suppose that's why you're a clerk—you're too dumb to go to school and get a real job."

I was standing in a checkout line at my favorite neighborhood Ralphs grocery store (#198), where I know all the peeps who work there and the hag that said this was right in front of me. Unfortunately for her, her sudden outburst and belittling tirade was one movie I'd seen way too many times.

Looking like she just crawled out of Middle-earth, the crotchety old biddy continued to berate the cashier, who had waited on me countless times. I knew for a fact she was very good at her job. So why did Crotchety get her granny panties all in a bunch?

Because she was trying to use a coupon that wasn't scanning. Probably because she bought the wrong item, or she didn't buy it at all, who knows?

"Ma'am, she's doing the best she can to try and help you," I ever-so-politely pointed out. "There's no need to call her names. It's a problem with your coupon. It's not her fault."

The hag turned to me with hackles raised and said, "Excuse me, do you work here? I'm a customer and this is none of your business."

When cashiers are humiliated like this, surprisingly, most customers say nothing. I was not one of those customers.

Crotchety was going down.

"It becomes my business when you treat the people in my favorite store like second-rate human beings," I replied heatedly. "I don't work in retail anymore and now I talk *back* to the customers. This nice girl has been here for years and probably waited on you many times. Stop being such a huge bitch and leave."

Crotchety's mouth started to quiver. She turned away from me to leave while angrily mumbling how she was going to call the cops on me.

Go right ahead! I will be happy to get arrested for calling you a bitch in the defense of any grocery store cashier!

My Retail Tic had been set off.

★

While most people have normal nervous tic disorders relating to spasmodic muscular movement, my little hair-raiser rears its angry tic head whenever I bear witness to a scene like that one. I have no doubt that I'm overcome with this affliction because of a life spent slaving away in service-oriented jobs. My tic began to grow as a teen working newspaper and flower delivery, fast food, flea markets, and movie theaters. As I reached adulthood, a fetish for fashion led me to the life of a department store sales associate for nearly twenty years.

When I eventually clawed my way up out of retail hell after decades of entrapment, I felt the need to create a place where service-industry workers could gather—and Retail Hell Underground was born. It features photos of two of my coworkers (who are the characters Cammie and Jeremy in this book) and me wearing skull masks and retail costumes; I went for a *Tales from the Crypt* theme because we all felt dead in retail. I might have escaped retail, but my friends were still in deep and couldn't show their names or faces or they would have been fired by their stores. The website became a place where thousands of service workers and retail people all over the world could tell their stories, rant, and laugh about the craziness of it all. Many of them took on secret identities also so they could tell their tales and have a voice. Retail Hell Underground became known as RHU to its beloved readers and voices. Soon after that I wrote a book called *Retail Hell*, humorously chronicling my beginnings as a handbag (that's *handbag*, not purse) salesman at The Big Fancy Department Store. Running a blog for service people to bitch on and promoting a book of my past retail nightmares ensure I never forget my hell.

But I think it created my Retail Tic.

Unfortunately, my Retail Tic can't be cured and usually requires speaking out—or else medicating with Xanax or Jack Daniels.

My Retail Tic can be activated in any number of ways.

Sometimes it's a shopping cart left somewhere it shouldn't be left, or rejected merchandise dumped in an area of the store where it doesn't belong—like a pair of socks tossed in the freezer with the Lean Pockets. I once stopped a man at a grocery store and handed him an empty carton of Eggo Waffles in the family size. I had just picked it up off the floor. Apparently his wife sent him in with an empty package so he'd buy the right Eggo product. Once he found it, I watched the piggy toss the empty carton as if the litter fairies were right there to catch it. He gaped at me, speechless, when I said, "Sir, I believe this is yours. I just watched you drop it."

My Retail Tic will also fire up when I encounter rudeness at places like Whole Foods Market. I had to loudly ask a group of mannerless healthy people to move their asses so an older woman could get by with her cart. Rudeness doesn't care whether you're shopping at Kroger or Whole Foods—it's equal-opportunity, and it's everywhere. And one time when I was leaving Costco with my sister, some entitled customer tried to line-cut. We got into it because she felt she had the right of way even though she wasn't in a lane. "You don't get to create your own lane, lady," I snapped, cutting her off with my cart.

Last month the woman who gives me a buzz cut at Supercuts told me about a customer she had who wanted a discount on a $5 blow dry. And then another lady told her that she felt my gal had pushed her into a shampoo, so she was using the tip to pay for it! Her only sin had been to ask the customer if she wanted a shampoo. She did her job, with no hard selling. If she hadn't asked she probably would have gotten whined at as well.

It's freakin' Supercuts, bitches!!!! You are not at José Eber salon!

And if I had been there, I would have told them that.

★

By the time the holidays roll around, my Retail Tic is always a festering, furious mess.

Most of that comes from editing the stories on my website, but recently when major stores got into a war over opening times for Black Friday and decided to open at midnight, or to simply stay open on *Thanksgiving Day*, not only did my Retail Tic detonate, I'm sure it shot fire out of its sore holiday ass and was more disgusted than it had ever been before.

During my retail career many of my Thanksgivings were ruined. That's the price retail workers pay to work, so we sort of expected it and figured out a way to enjoy the holiday anyway. But like so many others in the service industry, I would make the most of my Turkey Day by spending it with friends or in extreme homesick cases flying out to my family in Reno and back again just for the day! People who work in retail can't even do that now.

When do they get Thanksgiving? In the break room? On the Sunday before? Are they supposed to have Thanksgiving breakfast?

The corporations don't care. And neither do the customers.

The sad part about all this Black Friday Thanksgiving bullshit is that the year when stores decided to force their employees into working on Turkey Day also happened to be the same year Occupy Wall Street began and the "99 percent" slogan reverberated across the media. There was uproar on RHU about stores staying open and ruining Thanksgiving for so many, and I ranted about it myself. In fact, many other media outlets questioned the greedy desperate opening times initiated by executives.

And do you know what happened the day retail people lost their Thanksgiving?

Black Friday came and went with great fanfare. And apparently the Occupiers and the rest of the 99 percent all went shopping on Thanksgiving Day, because stores had the best Black Friday increases they'd seen in years.

No one cared about the humans missing their holiday. Shoppers had to get that cheap TV, and they were being herded like cattle to Black Friday Sales.

Store executives chose the opening times, and the shoppers flooded into stores with bellies full of turkey dinners, while retail people ate turkey jerky and potato chips in the break room.

Whether we work in retail or not, we are all under the thumb of corporate America controlling what we do and, in this case, how we shop.

We're all just dancing for the man.

So now I have another Big Fancy Department Store tale to tell you. You see, a long time ago in a Retail Hell galaxy far far away, I escaped from The Big Fancy . . .

And then I had to go back. . . .

This story takes place a few years after Y2K and September 11. Technology was on the rise, but we had not yet been gifted with iPads, smartphones, or high-definition TV. There was no texting, and Facebook had not been hatched yet (two things many of us couldn't live without today!).

Mine is the tale of how a department store becomes dehumanized by corporate greed and technology inciting salespeople to behave unethically just to keep their jobs.

And the scary thing? The Big Fancy is every store.

And the people that shop there and work there are the people you find in any mall.

I call the customers of The Big Fancy *custys*, a term that originated on my website years ago. The thieves are NATs (Nasty-Ass Thieves) and annoying coupon shoppers like that bitch are called Discount Rats.

You get the picture.

So buckle up, hold on, and get ready to scream while you're LOLing. This is going to be one Big Fancy roller coaster ride you won't soon forget.

LET THE

Sharking Begin

Satan's Super Deal

My favorite bloodthirsty custy, Lorraine Goldberg, is ransacking The Big Fancy like it's a Louis Vuitton Outlet Center and everything's a dollar. With a hunger for fashion and a mouth like a truck driver, Lorraine is the spitting image of a six-foot-plus Rick Perry in Jackie O drag. "I'll buy this whole motherfucking place!" she howls. Saliva drips from her mouth as she fondles a pair of Ellen Tracy slacks, then deems them a "hideous fucking color" and returns them to the rack. I wave my magic wand, calling forth all things gorgeous. Lorraine goes wild, piling one thing after another into my open arms . . . blouses, slacks, dresses, and even expensive granny panties. I have become her human shopping cart and I pray it will all ring up to a million dollars. Lorraine eyes a designer sweater with beaded playing cards and shrieks in a distinctly public-orgasm way, "Ooooohh-hhh, yeeeesss! This little bitch will bring me luck in Vegas!" The buying frenzy continues as the Shoposaurus clomps down The Big Fancy main aisle. Suddenly she spots the kind of fuel for her shopping addiction that could burn down a city. Lorraine comes to a roaring halt in front of Shoes, steam rising from her nostrils, her chest breathing heavy. Some new Ferragamo Lillaz shoes have arrived in a piss yellow color. Her eyes light up like a robot about to unleash a laser death stare. Here comes the firestorm: "Fraaaaayman! Oh my God! Yelloooooooow! I want four of these cock-suckers!!" I try to control Lorraine's giant tower of clothing and accessories, but she has bought too much, and it begins to tumble . . . sweaters with playing cards and yellow-bowed shoes are raining down on me . . .

"Woohooooo, Burbank!"

What the . . . ?

"Oooh yeaaaaaaaaaaaaah . . . "

What the hell *is that?*

It sounds like a prehistoric bird is going in for the kill. Where am I? Land of the Lost?

"Waaaaaake up, Burbank! It's time to get *super*!! Woohoooooooo!"

Unfortunately, I knew exactly where I was.

Stuffed into a cheap plastic folding chair at The Big Fancy department store. All of the merchandise tables and fixtures of men's sportswear had been temporarily moved aside to make room for hundreds of chairs facing a portable stage adorned with cheap party-store football-theme decorations. From two huge speakers the rap classic "Jump Around," by House of Pain, threatened to shred eardrums. I was just one of over two hundred sales-zombies looking disheveled, dismantled, and half awake at 7 a.m. We were not jumping around to House of Pain; we were paralyzed, clutching our coffee cups as if they were life-support IVs.

"Yeeeeeeeeehaaaaaaaaw yaaaaaaaaaaaay, Buuuurbank! Are you readyyyyyyyy!"

And that bloodcurdling *Jurassic Park* sound?

It was erupting from my store manager, Suzy Davis-Satan. Okay, so her last name isn't Satan, it's Johnson. I added Satan because even though she has the face of Strawberry Shortcake and the voice of a Playboy bunny, pretty much everyone in the store saw her as Lucy-fer wearing designer pumps. Today, however, Satan wasn't wearing pumps. Since it was the big Super Seller rally, she had decided to perform her MC duties in a pair of hideous, crystal-covered high-top sneakers and a blinding oversized orange and blue football jersey that sagged to her knees. Suzy Satan was on some kind of sugar high, running up and down the stage doing a mix of Frankenstein lunges and nerdy rapper moves.

"It's kick-off time, Burbank!!! Yaaaaaaaaaaaaay!!" bellowed The Big Fancy's own pterodactyl manager. "Who wants to be a Super Seller? Jump around! Jump around! I want to hear you clapping, Burbank!! Woohooooooooooooooooooo!"

Satan was joined by three jumping henchmen all infected with the cheerleading virus and all wearing matching Day-Glo jerseys: HR Manager Tammy (known as Two-Tone Tammy for her backstabbing ways), Store Operations Manager Brandi (a condescending baby-talking droid model), and Customer Service Manager Richie (known as Ass for his being an . . . well I'm sure you get that one!). Collectively they were quite hilarious: a trio of pasty white suburban bitches in their flabby forties moving like geriatric Black Eyed Peas.

I failed to get any enjoyment out of the spectacle, and I didn't want to jump around—I wanted to kill myself.

Scratch that. I'd shoot the fucking rally speakers before doing myself in.

My nightmare in question was The Big Fancy's annual powwow to promote the yearlong Super Seller contest encouraging salespeople to shred each other like taco cheese while vying to devour sales from as many custys as possible. The big prize for the selling war? A 31 percent store discount for an entire year.

Why thank you, Big Fancy! Stick a tail on me and call me a dumbass—I am all ready to sell my soul for a prize that can only bring me joy if I spend money at your store. That's your awesome, heartfelt reward for my hard work. You guys are too kind!

Many Big Fancy worker bees coveted the employee discount prize, which jumped from 20 percent to 31 percent when Super Seller status was achieved, but I wasn't one of them. (Though I had no trouble spending like a Kardashian and maxing out my Big Fancy credit card every week.)

And the odd percentage number was puzzling. Was Mr. Lou (The Big Fancy CEO and owner) too cheap to go for 50? Was 31 his favorite number? Maybe a psychic told him a weird discount was the only necessary table scrap he needed to throw at the starving employees of his company?

Whatever the reason, I'd received the discount prize before, both as a manager and a salesperson. (Managers automatically got the 31 as an incentive to shop and dress the part in Big Fancy duds.) It might have been addictively fun at times, but when you're a poor bitch and your salary is hovering around $28,000, the last thing you should be doing is calculating how much you'll save on a pair of $500 Gucci boots. You still can't afford them!

I wanted to cry.

At the moment I seriously hated life. My ass ached from the plastic folding chair, and the large Coffee Bean latte I had in my hand was turning my stomach into a Category 4 hurricane. This dismal mood wasn't directly The Big Fancy's fault, but the necessity of returning to work there was a constant reminder that I had failed at my dream: screenwriting.

After leaving The Big F the first time and vowing never to go crawling back, there I was again, a Big Fancy kewpie doll bouncing around behind a glass counter, schlepping out designer handbags for a pittance of pay. I felt washed up and beat, like a pissed-off, couldn't-give-a-shit Al Bundy wanting to shove my hand down my pants and zone out in front of the TV. My life had become just as miserable as his. I was back in a shitty retail job barely making enough money for rent, food, Internet, and my moviegoing addiction. In the last few years, the prices of everything had gone up—our salaries had not. Instead The Big Fancy liked to extol the increase in prices as the best way to get an increase in our salaries. "Just sell more and there's no limit to the amount of raises you can give yourself." Yes, that was every Big Fancy executive's ridiculous answer to the plight of their economically strapped salespeople.

Sell more.

Seriously? Do they really have their business heads that far up their designer suit asses? If I could sell more, I wouldn't have to live off my credit cards, borrow money from relatives, eat unhealthy frozen foods, and get disconnection notices on a regular basis! If I could sell more, I'd take a two-month vacation to Hawaii and write a new screenplay while drinking mai tais on the beach! I'd have a new flat-screen TV and I'd be dining at Mr. Chow in Beverly Hills. Come the fuck on, guys! Sell more?

Corporate bullshit aside, like millions of other people with career dreams, I had to suck it up and do a job I hated but was very good at. And the fact that I could do it blindfolded chased by hungry sale zombies, made it all the easier to end up dancing for The Big Fancy Man. I needed a job and they needed another shark on the sales floor.

Time to cry like a brat, curl up into a ball with a bottle of Jack Daniels, and drink until I give myself alcohol poisoning.

The only thing that made the soul-sucking situation barely livable was the two women sitting on either side of me: Maude and Cammie. I don't think about it much, but when everything in my life goes to shit, I can always count on good friends and family to be there.

My handbag manager was a woman in her sixties I'm calling Maude. She looked like actress Bea Arthur and had the same strong, witty, passionate personality that her characters were famous for. Maude was a self-made woman with passion, conviction, and a dry sense of humor. She was a fighter, having raised and put three kids through college after an ugly divorce with a cheating douche bag. Maude once told me that Elton John's song "I'm Still Standing" saved her life. When she first interviewed at The Big Fancy some fifteen years prior, the HR manager who ended up hiring her asked her, "I see you were a housewife. How 'bout we start you in an area you're familiar with, like the restaurant?"

"I cooked for twenty-five years," Maude replied, "and I don't want to do that anymore! No, thank you."

Maude accepted a position on the receiving dock. Not the most glamorous position in the store, but her athletic body helped survive it and her newfound freedom gave her strength to build the skills that helped her claw up The Big Fancy's ladder to management. Several stores later, she ended up in Broken-Down Burbank—a sad nickname many called our store—with what some were saying was a broken-down crew. Not only had she begged me to help her with The Big Fancy madness, but she recruited my BFF girl Cammie as well.

Yawning and trying to look mildly interested, the small-framed black-haired girl in her thirties nestled in closer to my arm, catching secret catnaps under her dark Chanel sunglasses. It was my duty to keep Cammie upright during the meeting. They have been known to put her to sleep in seconds.

Like Maude, I met Cam at The Big Fancy—but when I was hired. She was one of the women who helped me transform from a "purse"-saying idiot to a handbag-touting expert! A cross between lovable Zooey Deschanel and badass Christina Ricci, Cammie was the girl next door with edge and heart. She was a blast to be around.

Cammie, like me, had become another Hollywood statistic: Her acting career had stalled, with crappy agents only able to book her work as an extra and a stand-in. Fed up with the acting life, she accepted Maude's invitation, dyed her infamous golden locks blue black, and fell into brooding mode. We must have guzzled hundreds of twelve-packs together.

"Are Satan's shoes really sparkly, or am I still drunk from last night?" muttered Cammie, as groggy and confused as if she'd just woken up.

It was going to be a long meeting.

Like she was Snow White on Fox News, for the next half hour Suzy covered every detail of the Super Seller contest, adding brain-fart motivational statements at will: "Life is hard and gets harder if you don't make your selling goals here at The Big Fancy. But when you do we reward you like no other store!" Satan brought out several male managers who did a scary-ass cheerleader drag skit, lip-syncing to En Vogue's "Lady Marmalade." Following that train wreck was an airhead lingerie executive attempting to compare selling at The Big Fancy to football and Brett Favre. The brain-numbing speeches were followed by a guest appearance by the Gestapo (Maude's collective name for Suzy's henchmen Tammy, Richie, and Brandi), who whined their way through the announcements.

Next up was Suzy's earsplitting rendition of "Scream out your goal!" Cammie whispered something about beating Suzy with her plastic chair. Suzy bounced around the room, forcing each department to shout out their Super Seller goal for the year. After Maude, Cammie, and I croaked out our hefty goal of $325,000, rasping like field mice with laryngitis, the jitters set in and my head began to pound. I never should have drunk that mocha latte chaser after the can of diet Rockstar I'd swilled on my commute in.

Shaking like I needed a cigarette, I slept with my eyes open and waited for it to end.

★

Reaching home some four hours late I felt like The Big Fancy Bullshit Bus had run me over. And then decided to back up a few times. . . . I collapsed in exhaustion onto the bed and quickly slipped into a restless midmorning slumber. The noise from the godforsaken

Super Seller meeting and Suzy's prickly voice jackhammered my head like an irritating TV commercial jingle turned up to 11.

Darkness swept over me. My eyes lost the battle for daylight.

Then came the faint sound of a conch shell in the distance, which morphed into an electronic humming . . .

We're not in L.A. anymore, are we, Toto?

A blank page materializes.

Like in so many of my dreams and nightmares, a screenplay had decided to write itself. I may have been a tortured and depressed writer at the time, but I was born with a cinematic eye. That moviemaker mind never stops unraveling the fantasy world in my head—no matter how fed up I've been as a writer.

Letters begin forming Courier font words . . . to the soundtrack of an old typewriter.

A script!

RETURN TO THE BIG FANCY PLANET OF THE APES

An original screenplay by FREEMAN

Down at the bottom on the left corner:

Revised a trillion times. Final fucked draft.
January 10, 2020.
Represented by my balls.
Produced by my ass.
Authenticated by my middle finger.

Then those famous screenplay words appear.

FADE IN:

This is followed by a screenplay magically writing itself because that is the last fucking thing on earth I want to do right now even though I think about it constantly.

INT. A MAN'S HOT, MUSCLED, HAIRY CHEST GLISTENING WITH
SWEAT—ESTABLISH
CUT TO:
INT. SPACESHIP—DAY

Astronaut FREEMAN awakes from a bump on the head to
the tantalizing sight of the most perfect chiseled man-
chest of all time. Of course it belongs to Astronaut
stud HUGH JACKMAN, bearded and clad only in a loincloth
made out of shredded spacesuit. Next to him is a hot
young CHARLTON HESTON, also bearded and wearing a
spacesuit thong—the difference is that Chuck looks
crazier than Nick Nolte's mug shot as he peers out the
portal window mumbling about killing him some monkeys.

> FREEMAN (narrating)
> When I came to and saw Hugh's stunning man-chest
> up close, I was hoping I had stopped breathing so
> he would be forced to give me mouth-to-mouth. But,
> sadly, that didn't seem to be the case. Our ship
> had been headed to the GaGa Quadrant for a big
> dance party celebration. It was clear we didn't
> make it and had inadvertently landed on some
> smelly backward shithole of a planet.

> HUGH
> I've got bad news, mate. We freakin' crashed on
> Planet of the Apes. We're in the parking lot of
> a Big Fancy Ape Store and it doesn't look good.
> They're hiring. And dude . . . we're surrounded
> by apes on Segways! Maude and Cammie were captured
> when we crashed. I heard they were taken to The
> Big Fancy cantina to serve as wenches for the
> Gorilla Generals.

> FREEMAN
> OMG NO! We have to rescue them! (narrating)
> Serving rude, smelly male orangutans is a fate
> worse than death for Cammie and Maude!

> HESTON
> This is what happens when you give up your guns!
> The Beasts inherit the earth!

FREEMAN (to Hugh)
Did Chuck take his meds? Where's Kanye?

HUGH
Our boy K was the first to get caught. But you
know Kanye . . . he won't dance for any ape. I
heard they sent him to work in the sanitation
department.

FREEMAN
Poor Kanye! We have to rescue him too!

HESTON (crazed)
If I can get my hands on a goddamn gun, I'll
rescue Kanye *myself*! I'm comin' for ya, Kanye
. . . watch out, you dirty stinking apes . . .
here comes Chuck!

Sexy young Heston goes full-on apeshit. Grabs a piece
of metal from the wreckage, pretending it's a machine
gun. He runs YELLING out into the parking lot like a
drunk redneck Braveheart, his handsome bearded face
transforming into psycho Charlie Manson's twin brother.

EXT. BIG FANCY PARKING LOT—OUTSIDE SPACESHIP—DAY

The spaceship is surrounded by an army of Ape soldiers
on Segways with waiting nets.

HESTON
No one is taking my gun, goddammit! I'll kill all
you monkeys!

A maniacal Heston runs SCREAMING right into their
waiting ape hands.

EXT. SPACESHIP—DAY

HUGH
Okay, mate, as soon as I clear a path, you make a
run for it. I'm Astronaut Hugh!

EXT. BIG FANCY PARKING LOT

Hugh and Freeman bolt. Hugh FIGHTS with an amazing combination of martial arts and dance, thanks to his theatre background and Wolverine training. He flies through the air SINGING.

For a moment it looks as if Hugh and Freeman have a chance.

Out of nowhere fast-moving souped-up Segways with giant monster-truck wheels appear, carrying Gorilla Generals Tammy, Brandi, Richie, and Suzy.

Tammy, Richie, and Brandi surround Hugh and TAUNT him, asking over and over if he's gay. Hugh gets very mad and starts to CRY, causing him to lose his macho fighting gusto. A pink glittery net jettisons into the air, engulfing Hugh and immobilizing him. The Beasts close in.

> FREEMAN (narrating)
> Before I can even attempt to run or yell to Hugh,
> *It's okay if you are straight, I still love you*,
> the worst Ape of them all is buzzing right in
> front of me.

Riding a tank-style Mercedes Segway and dressed in a purple militaristic high school band uniform, Gorilla Suzy gazes at FREEMAN like he's the lunch special of the day.

> GORILLA GENERAL SUZY
> What a fine specimen! The custys will love you.
> You will dance for me, won't you little human?
> Make me millions? *Get him in the net!*

General Satan chortles into a scary howling screech, reminiscent of Suzy's rally cry. As the net covers his face, FREEMAN screams and the world goes black.

Noooooooooooooo!

I jumped up into the air like there was a tarantula in my bed. The creepy Big Fancy day-mare had given me quite a scare. The apes were going to bust down the door at any moment, I was sure of it, but I was still freakishly turned on by Hugh, Chuck, and Kanye risking their hot shirtless bodies to save me. I made a bold decision: to hell with laundry and day-off chores. Not after that monkey trip.

I called Cammie, and she was in the same place; The BF had seeped into her plans, ruining lunch and a shopping trip to Chinatown. She came over that night and we inhaled a twelve-pack of Dos Equis while watching *Battle for the Planet of the Apes* (definitely one of the worst from the ape series). Before long we were both droopy-eyed and fighting Mr. Sand-ape. The last thing Cammie said before the big gorilla carted her off to dreamland was, "This fucking sucks . . . it's like apes in high school . . . what the fuck, dude . . ."

I couldn't have agreed with her more as I nodded off . . . *and so is The Big Fancy . . . it's just like high school. . . .*

Fast Times at Big Fancy High

I never thought I'd see the day, but there it was.

A line to climb Mount Fancy.

It was nearly 6 P.M. and a mass of people had assembled on the sidewalk in front of the towering employee entrance of The Big Fancy. I knew they were temporary backup for all of us salespeople. Tonight was inventory, the most hated noncusty event of all who work in retail.

If I could have pulled any magic out of my ass to avoid it, I would have, because counting and recording The Big Fancy's merchandise was one late-night party no one wanted to attend. Sadly, showing up for inventory was mandatory. I'd been through so many of these merchandise-counting sessions, as a salesperson and a manager, that they were more of a brain-melting nuisance than anything, but I was at least willing to be there to help Maude. I'd never had any problems conducting my inventories, but tonight was different: The Big Fancy was going high tech. We were armed with electronic devices that looked like Star Trek phasers with screens and keyboards on top of the guns. There would be no more writing—only scanning barcodes with our scan guns and entering quantity amounts. Whenever store trainer Brandi overheard the term "scan gun," she'd snippily correct us: "It's a handheld, not a gun."

It looks a like space gun to me, Brandi! When do we get to start shooting things? I'd like to start with the loudspeaker.

Gone were the days of writing on paper with sharp pencils, when inventory takers' handwriting would be criticized by Satan screaming over the PA five hundred times a day, "Any inventory sheets with loopy 2s, sailboat 4s, or snowman 8s, and you will be sent back to your department for a recount!"

Satan's bullying never did any good. Even if they were trying to change their snowman ways or not doodle a 4 that looked like it was sailing to Catalina Island, people write like they write. They'd try to make their snowman 8 into an acceptable skater 8, but when you've been raised by a snowman it's hard to become a skater just like that. One year after my department finished, we were told that Two-Tone Tammy had rejected a bunch of my sheets because of my sailboat 4s. She'd quickly spotted a bunch of sailboats, several snowmen, and something she called a flowering 5.

How about I show you what six ways till Sunday looks like, Tammy?

I imagined all the things Tammy could do with her flowering 5s, and did not bother to recount. I'd still beaten Lingerie and Jewelry, the two worst departments in the store, to the inventory finish line.

★

As I reached the inventory flash mob in front of the employee entrance, I saw it was the same as every year; a freaky mash-up of odd people who might easily end up being nightmares for any stressed-out manager, including Maude. There were salespeople's relatives and friends who were attending as a favor, entitled high school students forced into raising money for Disneyland, and country club moms and their entitled daughters seeking debutante ball fundage. And no inventory would be complete without the scary Skid Row–looking bums, drunks, and druggies.

We all know what they needed to raise money for.

Next to the door was a check-in table being manned by Calindy, an HR assistant whom I knew and loved because she had saved me so many times when I was a manager. Calindy was proof that not all HR people are evil ogres like Two-Tone Tammy. Helping her check in the temps was Steve from Security, a lazy blob who couldn't catch Betty White if she were stealing the store. I said hello to Calindy and nod-smiled to Steve because he's been such a jerk so many times.

One of the physical things I hated the most about The Big Fancy waited for me next as I pushed a button on the door's side. The familiar clicking sound announced that I could open it and enter. If the inventory victims wanting their extra cash thought counting was going to be no fun, wait till they found out what was behind the employee entrance door.

Eight flights of stairs.

That's right. I had to give them their own paragraph. Eight flights of fucking stairs were climbed by us Big Fancy employees before each shift and descended at the end of each shift. It was a massive stairwell from hell, and I called it Mount Fancy. Managers and execs had mall-entrance privileges and didn't have to climb eight flights of stairs. If you were a sales-peon, the only way to avoid it was to obtain a doctor's note saying Mount Fancy could kill you. How a company thinks it's perfectly fine to make their designer-clad employees go up and down eight flights of stairs every day is beyond me, but they do. Big Fancy CEO Mr. Lou was heard to have said he made sure stores were built with stairs so employees could get exercise before they came in to work. The last time I saw Mr. Lou, a short chunky bullfrog of a man, he could have used a few stair laps.

Get those froggy legs up, Mr. Lou! Feel the burn!

While Mount Fancy was a pain in all of our asses (and feet, knees, and hips), I'd gone through plenty of drama in the stairwell as a salesperson. When I became a manager I didn't have to scale the great mountain, but upon my return as a salesperson/unpaid department assistant, the no-stairs perk was not available. "You will have to start taking the stairs," Two-Tone said in her Gestapo voice. "Suzy has clamped down on people trying to sneak in through the mall. There is a reason we have an employee entrance."

And I'm sure that reason is so you can keep busy with injury claims and lawsuits. I'd like to see you haul your fat ass up and down Mount Fancy every day, Tammy! You'd end up in the ER!

Like all the other selling minions of The Big F, I had no choice but to grab hold of the rail and haul my retail-weary body up a shitload of carpeted steps.

Mount Fancy was vast and had roomy platforms in between staircases, so Suzy, Tammy, and Brandi regularly used it as advertising for Big Fancy propaganda. Suzy once told me she decorated Mount Fancy to "educate and inspire."

I call it drill and brainwash.

The climb up The BF summit on inventory night was the usual workout. Normally I felt like an Egyptian slave scaling the Sphinx, but in dress clothes. Tonight, however, I was happily adorned in street clothes, and the tennis shoes made all the difference with each usually heinous step. The momentary thankfulness I felt for The Big F's allowing me to don appropriate foot gear lasted all of thirty seconds as my attention moved from my feet to the pain in my eyes.

Mount Fancy's visual assault started on the first platform. A massive bold banner sprawled across it, screaming: "Super Sell Yourself! Sell Big or Go Home!"

I'll be happy to go home, Suzy. I'd make more money super selling myself on Santa Monica Blvd. No refunds or exchanges!

An explosion of tacky, leftover, party-store football decorations had been strewn about the platform. The Big Fancy's infamously strange wall mirror that always made you look fat and bestowed the corporate bullshit signage, "Through These Doors Walk the Most Important People in Our Company," had been covered up with Super Seller paraphernalia, including posters listing departmental goals and other eyesores.

Going up the next staircase was a real fright the first time. Many of my coworkers had complained about the scary mannequin dressed like a Harajuku hooker robot holding a sign that warned, "The future is coming with Client Capture! Don't forget to capture every customer!" but nothing had been done about it. I battled the urge to push the creepy thing down the stairs and light it on fire.

On another platform we were reminded that making mistakes at the register was a no-no: "Don't Be a Noncompliance Fool, Be a Compliant Winner!"

I couldn't help but chuckle, thinking what the teens, country club wives, and druggies would think of the goings-on at The Big Fancy.

Don't you want to work here now? I'm sure they are hiring! They love all kinds of people.

I cringed when I passed the platform for New Accounts, which had a football theme going on, with another huge banner that said: "The Big Fancy Credit Bowl: Will You Win or Lose?"

A giant poster showed each department's progress and who was winning and who was losing. The winners got to keep their jobs and the losers were sent to a training class run by creepy Richie. The thought of it sent chills down my spine.

I don't need to write a horror movie, I'm living SAW VI: Retail Massacre.

I didn't look for my name. I had been losing The Big F credit bowl for a while and was awaiting my sentencing.

As I got closer to the top, the walls were lined with awful portraits of salespeople. A few were crooked, a couple were scratched, and one had even been violated with a pen. These were The Big Fancy's current Service Super Stars: sales associates who had gone above and beyond for custys. I was one once. This was the reward for having your blood drained by a Big Fancy custy: a silver bowl (that I eat cereal and drink whiskey out of), a 31 percent store discount for a year (which kept me constantly over the limit on my Big Fancy credit card), and your picture on a wall.

Whenever I climbed with Cammie, we had a good laugh over these photos and talked smack about the Service Super Stars with shark history.

"Jen in Designers told me that whore steals holds," she said about someone named Sandy with six years of service. "She looks like a Pekingese in a St. John suit."

The pictures looked like they'd been shot in a photo booth at Walmart, but there was no way to ignore them. I'd be out of breath and nearing the top of Mount Fancy. My legs would be about to give out. Pain and sweat would make everything seem like it was in slow motion. And the faces would stare at me from the walls, many of them looking like strange animals in designer wear.

Next up were the Super Sellers.

It was the same thing here: another wall of bad portraits with fake smiles. Cammie and I passed the time noting resemblances to dogs and cats and filling each other in on the dirt while we panted our way up yet another flight. A guy named Donald from Men's Suits was no longer there. "That bitch got fired for stealing his custy's credit-card numbers!" Cammie told me once. "I guess that makes him a Super Doucher!"

As much as I'd wished she'd get canned also, Sherry's dreadful portrait always caught my eye. She looked like a WWE wrestler in a Kate Gosselin wig (Brunette Edition).

Oh, and she was also a lying, manipulative, soulless, sale-stealing android.

How did I know all this?

Because I had to work with the super-douching shark in heels!

Sherry wasn't just any shark. If you were going to compare her to the most famous movie sharks of all time, she'd be that mechanical one that doesn't die no matter how many times you try to blow it up. It just keeps coming back hungrier. With her protruding brow and jutting chin, Sherry could have been the sister of the henchman Jaws in the James Bond classic movie *The Spy Who Loved Me*.

Again, you just add a wig, and voila! Sherry's twin!

A strapping six-foot-tall, dark-haired European woman in her mid-forties, my sharky coworker's life details were a mystery beyond the basics: Her husband owned a small construction business, they had two kids, and she could kick your ass (or die trying). Sherry was nicely dressed and tastefully made up, but she kept to a clinical professional look that matched how she interacted with everyone on the crew. Her total focus was on getting as many custys as possible, no matter who had been helping them; she had a long, bloody, tear-stained history of sharking—a retail term for stealing sales or unethical selling. Everyone loathed working with Sherry, and we called her Sharky because she was definitely the department's Great White.

Sharks and douchers aside, there was always one photo on the wall I didn't mind seeing: Maude's. It was her fifth year going for Super Seller in Handbags. Although Maude understood how Cammie and I felt about The Big Fancy, and she supported our dreams like a mother, she also loved The Big Fancy and all it had to offer. It was her career, and she loved selling to people. She just didn't love the Suzy Davis-Johnson high school politics and cartoonishness.

Maude also hated all the new technology flooding into The Big Fancy. More and more work was done on the computer. The merging had begun. Ticket stickers, schedules, stock balancing, and a bunch of other managerial hell stuff had all moved to the computer. It was good for The Big Fancy but bad for Maude. Even the new silent registers made her nervous. She preferred the noise the printer made ringing up a huge sale and the old pen and paper schedule days.

Maude's pic was near the end of the last hellacious staircase, and her face always gave me the strength to get up that last step on the terrible steel mountain.

★

After walking through the door of Mount Fancy into the hallway that leads into the heart of the store, there was a temptation that could either make your day or ruin it. And if you had any care in the world about becoming a Super Seller, you'd give in to this temptation immediately.

Facing the security window was "the numbers" wall. The place where managers and salespeople stopped to check the previous day's numbers. Large binders held figures by store, department, and salesperson.

I shouldn't have, but I did. I checked my employee number, 441064.

$1,578 in sales. $1,672 in returns. Total sales: –$94.

Fuck, why did I even look? Gee, thanks, ladies. What'd you all do yesterday, empty your closets? Was it the great Super-Return Bowl? I'm sure Sharky Sherry gave you great service.

And that must have been what happened, because I then looked up Sherry's number, and sure enough, she'd had a nice cool two-grand kind of day with low returns.

Sharky bitch.

Seeing a negative day on those reports was always hard to take whether you were salesperson or manager. I knew it was going to be bad. January was the start of many negative days after the big sales of November and December. The positive of my seeing negative results was Maude. She made Suzy pay me hourly to help her do inventory with the stockroom. Satan had tried to persuade Maude that helping out was part of my duty as a salesperson and to the team.

Good try, Satan.

And just like in the movies, when you think about the devil, there she was. As I walked down the hallway leading into the store,

I couldn't help but glance at Suzy Davis-Johnson's office. Like most department stores, the store manager's office was spacious and had a hallway window. If the blinds were pulled, someone was getting fired. If they were open with the door shut, that meant a meeting.

Through the window I spotted Satan behind her giant desk laughing with her henchwomen, Brandi, Tammy, and Stephanie the store secretary, who was an annoying, robotic bitch whom I had gone many rounds with, both as a salesperson and manager. The sight of female bonding in Suzy's office was not so strange, but what made me almost wet my pants with laughter was that all four women were wearing the same outfit: white blouses with black sweaters wrapped loosely around their necks like high-society dames attending a luncheon after going yachting or playing fucking doubles tennis at the country club. The Gestapo looked scary and ridiculous at the same time—an *SNL* skit you want to laugh at even though you're not sure it's all that funny. God help The Big Fancy.

All hail Suzy, mein Fancy Fuehrer!

As I wove my way past Customer Service into the heart of the floor and to the escalators that would carry me down to the Handbag Jungle, I began passing people I knew. Cute Benjamin, a snazzily dressed associate from Men's Designers; Danusha, a friendly server in the Café; and Mike, one of the few dudes from Ladies' Shoes who wasn't a shark. Because I had once been a manager and I'd worked there for so long, I knew a lot of people. That was the great thing about working in a department store. There were always more people you liked than didn't. And there was always someone to make you laugh or complain to about how bad things were.

Tonight was a little unique. The dress code for the big counting party was casual, so I saw everything from expensive jeans to ripped sweats to baggy pajamas (aka lounge wear).

Gee, maybe I should have worn a white shirt with a black sweater nestled around my neck and nothing below but a jock strap and combat boots! (Barf.)

As I stood on the escalator and looked out over the first floor, and Handbags, there was definitely a buzz and energy in the air, with everyone running around in clothes that would deliver them straight from inventory hell to bed.

I spotted the Handbag department in the distance, and it looked old and run-down. I felt sad and frustrated. Not only were the salespeople rummaging for good shit to sell, but our fixtures were ancient and out of date, many of them broken and so dirty you couldn't clean them. The weary wallpaper on the back wall was a hideous 1970s paisley print you might find in any granny's bedroom. And our handbag selection was haphazardly horrible too—schlocky, with not enough of the bags women wanted.

Many of us called the store Broken-Down Burbank because it was like The Big Fancy chain's stepchild, the one they forget to buy new clothes for and to groom regularly. Suzy, Mr. Lou, and all the other Big Fancy execs, buyers and merchandisers included, were quick to criticize our performance and impose strange expectations, but the buyers and execs were not so quick to remodel us and fill us up with the popular new handbags they had stocked in their Hollywood, Pasadena, and Valley Village stores. Burbank would remain stalled and junky, a heap of rust getting pushed down the Super Seller highway by its devoted managers and salespeople.

As soon as I stepped off the escalator I was attacked by Jabbermouth Virginia, a chatty old lady custy who was one of the Regulars. A retired bank teller and a nutball, Virginia had a mouth that didn't stop, and she could suck the blood out of you for hours. She did buy something every now and then and ate regularly at Big Fancy's Restaurant. "I'm having a colonoscopy tomorrow," she blurted out to me without saying hello. "You ever have one of those?"

I can't worry about colons now, Virginia, I've got counting to do!

Virginia had some of the strangest TMI greetings I'd ever heard. Nothing shocked me anymore. I just replied, "No I haven't! Sorry to hear that, Virginia, gotta run; it's inventory day! Bye!"

Running away from Jabbermouth, I approached the Handbag Jungle. Linda Sue, Sherry, and Dok were standing behind the cash wrap—the counter—laughing. Typical. Maude had told everyone to keep checking bags and wallets to make sure everything had a ticket, but they weren't doing shit. Having been a manager at The Big Fancy, I saw things differently now. Even though retail was my hell, and I'd much rather be on a movie set or at the computer, I still gave 100 percent to The Big Fancy and its custys, and I was totally devoted to Maude.

I had barely taken two steps onto the carpet when Dok rushed me like a wild native with a shrunken head in her hand. Only instead of a head she was gripping a used handbag.

"Suzy return this!" she cried, scrunching her face and holding out a filthy Kenneth Cole bag with a broken strap. "What we do? Bitch use! Where we count?"

No one could understand Dok completely. She was a Thai woman in her thirties who spoke English poorly (or pretended to), yet she was able to sell like the wind. Dok's name was pronounced "Doc," which was confusing in English. We'd say to a custy, "Dok will help you!" And the custy would look confused for a moment and then ask, "You have a doctor in Handbags?" Then Dok was quick to explain, "My full name Dok-rak. It mean 'pretty flower' in Thai."

But Dok-rak was anything but pretty—inside or out. Even though she herself had a fat round face and pudgy body that she often shoved into skintight designer dresses, Pretty Flower preferred not to be in the presence of anyone who was ugly, fat, or odd looking. "I not wait on her. Too fat; look like a whale. You go," she would be known to hiss at a colleague. Other times, Pretty Flower would scrunch up her face and say about another Big Fancy salesperson, "Oh she so ugly, how she work MAC counter? Who buy lipsticks from a horse?" Although Dok professed not to go near fatties or uglies of The Big Fancy, inevitably she had to if she wanted sales. I could always tell when Pretty Flower was uncomfortable and wilting while helping someone she hadn't chosen; she'd get pushy and shower the custy with compliments: "You buy. It very nice," Pretty Flower would say to a fat woman with a pony tail and bad skin, "It work for your look. Make you more beautiful."

Cynical and lazy Dok annoyed us all, especially Maude. Her stock reply to any question was to nod her head in a "yes" manner and say, "Uh-huh, uh-huh, yes, yes." After the five trillionth time this got really old—especially if you'd asked her a non-yes-or-no question. If there was an argument over a sale in the stockroom, she resorted to crying while repeating, "Uh-huh, uh-huh, yes, yes."

Before I could tell Pretty Flower where to put the returned bag, she walked away, saying something to herself I probably wouldn't understand. Dok had a habit of asking a question and then walking away before you could tell her the answer.

As if waiting her turn, Coworker Nightmare Number One was suddenly in my face wanting advice, waving a bunch of wallets like she was a Discount Rat with sale coupons.

"Some girl from Teens just brought all of these back," whined Linda Sue. "I think they were in her holds or something! I don't know what to do with them!"

A day did not go by where Maude didn't say, "Linda Sue is a blister on my ass!" Linda Sue was the employee tumor in Maude's ass.

In her late fifties, Linda Sue looked more like she should be a cashier at a liquor store, rather than a salesperson of The Big Fancy. Her lack of makeup, disheveled clothes, and overall dumpiness matched her volatile personality. She lived to whine and complain about everything. Linda Sue had a husband who worked for the city and an annoying daughter, and both of them had the hobby of calling to consult with her about their dramas. The phone never stopped ringing in the Handbag Jungle, and half the time it was Linda Sue's family. This pissed Maude off royally and caused major tension. In return, Linda Sue was insanely jealous of Maude's sales figures, calling her a shark because Maude—the better salesperson—often outsold her. Linda Sue hated Maude from day one, and I doubted it would ever change. There had been many showdowns before I arrived, and Linda Sue was not happy when I walked in the door. She was cold and snippy with me, most likely because I was a triple threat to her: younger, a former manager, and a friend of her hated boss.

I knew Linda Sue and I would not be movie pals.

She was still standing there holding the returned wallets and looking like she had indigestion. "They belong in the trouble box Maude made for last-minute issues," I informed her. *No wonder Maude gets frustrated with her.* We had all been told about the box; I'd even been standing next to Linda Sue when Maude showed it to us. Linda Sue had been through just as many inventories as I had. She should know what to do.

But as usual, Linda Sue was playing stupid, so she replied, "Are you sure? I don't want to get in trouble if that's not where they're supposed to go. She's in a mood today. I guess I'll put them in the box. Hope I don't get yelled at."

Oh, I'm sure you'll have no problem yelling back, you condescending whore.

Linda Sue loved to play the game with me where she'd ask my advice and then negate it.

Right then Maude appeared, backing me up. "That's exactly where they go. Please go put them there."

As Linda Sue waddled off to the problem box with her wallets, Maude showed me the stickers with barcodes that I would help her place on fixtures once the store was closed. Suzy was very adamant about not seeing inventory stickers when the store was open. She had an inventory mantra: "We must look gorgeous at all times!"

As gorgeous as Broken-Down Burbank can look.

While Sherry was doing what she did best, which was ring people up, scoring herself a cheap evening bag sale in the process, the rest of us checked bags and wallets to make sure they had tickets. Not surprisingly, Dok found a missing ticket from an area that had been designated to Linda Sue.

"Linda Sue!" Maude said in a raised cracking voice that often got her in trouble. "You told me you checked the LeSportsac!"

"Don't dump that on me, Maude. Someone else must have stuck it on there. You always blame me for everything!"

Before Maude could respond, she spotted Suzy and her sweater-clad henchwomen heading for the handbag counter.

"Aw shit, the Sweater Gestapo," she quipped.

"They just need to add swastika golf caps!" I replied, watching them glide toward us like ghosts.

When the scary threesome came up to the Corral counter, Maude didn't hold back: "Did you three plan the black sweaters, or was it an accident?"

Brandi giggled, Tammy cracked a smile, and Satan replied, "We thought it would be fun! Easy for everyone to spot us tonight if we're needed. We're the sweater girls!"

I wanted to tear off her sweater and strangle her with it.

The Gestapo was making department rounds to see how the managers were doing and to check on inventory supplies.

"I could use an extra gun," Maude said.

"It's not called a *gun!*" admonished Brandi, "It's called a handheld, and we don't have any extras at the moment."

As Brandi and Maude had it out over the handheld *scan guns*, I tried to slip away, but to my dismay, Satan followed me down the counter slithering next to me like she was Nagini, the scary snake from the Harry Potter movies.

"I can't tell you how thrilled I am to have you back at Burbank," Suzy hissed seductively, giving me the chills. "I'm expecting *amazing* things out of you, Freeman!"

So happy for you, Satan! I'm expecting to end up in therapy and on meds!

"Thanks, Suzy," I replied, breaking out into a sweat.

It might be better to run through the mall doors and not stop till I see the ocean.

"I have to tell you straight up, Freeman," said Satan, sounding like one of the good ol' boys, "Maude's crew is a mess and I'm looking for some winners to throw in the mix. I'm counting on you to help her turn things around. Besides, you're better off with us! The movie business is tough. I have several family members who tried to become actors and writers and movie people, but they all failed and had to go back to what they were good at doing. It's about accepting who you are really and shining your light on the world."

I tried not to vomit right in her face. WTF? Why was she saying all that to me? I got that Suzy was trying to tell me she appreciated my abilities at The Big Fancy, but we all know the truth of what happens in the end.

Devoured whole, chewed up, and then spit out—cast aside like garbage. Thank you for all your years of dedication and hard work at The Big Fancy!

If Satan's fake praise wasn't enough to make me set my inventory scan *gun* to "kill" and point it at my head, she had to help me push the trigger by adding, ". . . and you can always go back to management, my friend! I know I'd like to have you on my team again. Just give me the word and I'll find a place for you!"

My brain suddenly filled with vomit.

"If I can help it, he's not going anywhere!" Maude chimed in with a wink. I knew she appreciated my bringing my managerial experience to the floor, along with my flair for handbag merchandising, which she hated doing.

As the Gestapo wandered off to harass Hosiery, Cammie entered the department, shoulders slumped, looking just as stressed-out as Maude, but for different reasons. "I just had the twelve-hour *CSI* shoot from fucking hell! They had me making out with some sweaty, stinky, gross, old fat dude in a hundred-degree tent while a snake killed us. I need a shower. I'm so fucking done with extra work!"

As Cammie tried to calm down and get into inventory mode, the colorful helpers were pouring off the escalator on to the main aisle to be dispersed to departments. "Those people are going to help us count?" she said. "They look like they're in search of free sandwiches."

The store was finally closed, and the metal mall door near our department began its noisy descent downward. Maude prepped for a quick meeting before the count. Suddenly, the PA came alive with Satan's piercing voice.

"Happy Iiiiiiiiiiiiiiiiiiiinventory, Everyone!"

As glass shattered everywhere, she continued the audio assault by using her *American Idol*–reject singing voice, which had tortured all of us before. "Haaaaaaaave I told you lately that I love yooooou . . . Burbaaaaank . . . I love yoooou because you are not going to make any mistakes toniiiiiiiiiiight, Burbaaaaank!"

"Did she take her meds today?" Cammie looked up from checking Coach tickets.

"I think she's eating them like candy!" Linda Sue laughed loudly at her own joke.

"That was for you, Burbank!" announced Suzy in a more normal high-pitched tone. "And welcome to all of our guests tonight! I'm Suzy, the store manager. A big thanks for all our family and friends helping out. I know my beautiful husband and three kids are here! Hi, Ralph! Jenna and Jon! So are we ready, Burbank? Ready to count? S-l-o-w-l-y and correctly? I know you are! And that's why I love you! But since we have a nifty new electronic device for our inventory, tonight we are doing things differently! We are a team and we will work as one until the last item is counted in this store!"

Oh, God, what is she saying? Should I run for the mall doors now?

"When you have been officially excused by your department manager and you are cleared by Tammy's Team and not needed elsewhere, you will be given a special exit pass and be allowed to leave. Steve will be at the door checking passes, and no one will be allowed out without one."

"That fat fuck won't be stopping me," I heard Cammie mumble under her breath.

We were under lockdown.

Big Fancy High had just turned into Big Fancy Prison.

★

Inventory *gun* scanning went off without much drama, except for Linda Sue forgetting to laser a shelf of Cole Haan bags and Maude temporarily bursting into flames over it. Everyone wanted to go home, and we were all scared we'd be sent to another department.

"No way in hell am I counting fuckin' panties!" announced Cammie. "I'll go to Jewelry."

"I go help my friend Barb Cosmetics. She nice," said Dok.

"If they get to pick, then I want Jewelry too . . . ," chimed in Linda Sue, "but I think I really need to go home because I pulled my back out scanning the shelves."

Maude looked like she was gonna kill Linda Sue, who loved to play victim to get out of doing work and used whatever injury she could conjure up.

Cammie was right.

The Big Fancy had gone all penitentiary on our asses, but it was still just like high school. Suzy was the control-freak principal, and all her henchmen, including Security, were the staff. The managers were like teachers, and some were evil—condescending Jasmine in Cosmetics and backstabbing Kevin in Men's Shoes. Others were friendly and amazing, like my Maude; Gwen the Hosiery manager; Joanna from Plus Size; and Bill, the Men's Sportswear manager. The melting pot of salespeople personalities made up the student body, from crazy and lazy to angelic and fun. Some of them were sleeping together while others hated each other and got in fights. And the students of this wacky weird school were all graded on what they got out of the custys.

I considered writing a script about it, but at the moment all my screenwriting dreams were pretty much dead. Writing my name on toilet paper seemed painful. I had just been through the Hollywood washing machine: thoroughly rinsed and spun, and now left to hang out and dry up in a department store.

When I left The Big Fancy the first time I worked there to become a rich and famous screenwriter, it was done with great fanfare and hope—many of my coworkers threw a party, and my friends and family were thrilled that I was going to do what I love. The hope was not that I'd return to a Big Fancy career as a Super Seller. But in real life, Hollywood endings rarely happen.

I had gone through several shitty managers back then, including a militant hothead I called The General. I ended up with a manager named Liz, the best manager I ever had (until Maude). She was fair, hardworking, and fun, and her ability to intuitively know what custys wanted made her a Big Fancy star. Liz embraced my screenwriter dreams but also appreciated my dedication and taught me a lot about the handbag world. When she was promoted to regional buyer, I took over as manager. I celebrated my promotion by going through a whole new level of Big Fancy hell. Liz was always there to support me until I finally decided to take the jump from handbag salesman to screenwriter. She moved her way up The Big Fancy executive ranks, and sadly, one day, after so many years of passionate support and success, Liz was spit out. She was another human casualty of The Big Fancy, of American corporate greed.

If you leave The Big Fancy on your own, you should count yourself lucky. I had written screenplays with a girl who also worked for The Big Fancy, Alison of the Café, and we'd written an action-adventure script that somehow found its way to a producer. We both thought our screenwriting careers had taken off and big bucks were on the way, but what we found was rewrite hell and a script-killing dead end. My friend moved to New York City to pursue the stage, I fell into a depression, and I eventually found my way back to The Big Fancy. Instead of film openings, I was attending Big Fancy inventory parties.

Our inventory crew was growing restless and argumentative. Our complaints—about the possibility of being sent to other departments and being held prisoner in the store—had reached a crescendo, with

Linda Sue loudly declaring that she didn't think it was legal for them to hold us, when the department phone rang.

Maude picked up because lowly workers were not allowed to use Big Fancy's phones during inventory. As she listened, her inventory-war-torn face grew wearier and grayer by the second. The news was not good. The system had dumped several departments' inventories, and ours was one. Everything needed to be recounted. It was going to be a late night. The Sweater Gestapo was on the way.

So much for technology making everything easier! F'd in the A by a computer!

Maude looked like Big Brother had beat the shit out of her. Cammie yelled, "Fuck me! Are you serious?" Linda Sue started bitching up a storm. Dok shook her head and sat on the floor. And Sherry just stood there stone-faced like she always did.

"I need a bottle of bourbon and a gun," cried Maude.

I wished I could get them for her.

Star Trek phasers or not, inventory still sucked.

Queen of the Discount Rats

"Hello, Freeman," said Mrs. Green, clutching the giraffe Kate Spade satchel she'd bought for 50 percent off—at the expense of almost getting Cammie fired.

Every time I saw the sun-weathered, overly made-up OC-housewife-looking whore waltzing around the store and showing off her furry Spade like a trophy, I wanted to yank it off her shoulder and beat the bitch's blond-highlighted head with it. Over and over.

This is for Cammie and all the other poor souls you've tortured at The Big Fancy. Take that, you Discount Rat from hell!

"Hi, Mrs. Green," I replied, suddenly feeling sick to my stomach.

I knew what the evil custy wanted.

"Mark said you would have my credit slip ready," said Mrs. Green, with a pinched, cold expression.

The Mark she was referring to was Mark Sutherford, The Big Fancy's West Coast President. He was a personable, good-looking, thirty-something guy who made me nervous. Not because he was one of The Big F's big executives, but because he was married, and his wife was also a Big Fancy Exec . . . and when I was a manager I'd happened to see him stumble out of a gay leather bar a bunch of friends and I were going into.

Oops! Oh, hey, Mark! How's the crowd tonight? Did you find a hot leather daddy?

It made for an odd moment as he pretended not to see me, even though we were close enough to make out. After that fateful night, whenever I saw him on the sales floor or during walk-thrus with Satan, he did a great job at playing it cool. I, on the other hand, forgot how to speak words and put sentences together.

I was glad I hadn't had to take Leather Boy's call about Flo Green. Maude had handled it, telling him we were on great terms with Mrs. Green and it had been an oversight; everything was fine. After that we were kissing Flo's ratty ass and ringing up her 50 percent off pronto.

"I hope the blond hag rots in hell." Maude had handed me the paperwork, pissed about all the drama Flo had caused and annoyed to have another return against the department's already anemic numbers.

Mrs. Green was truly an awful woman, loathed by pretty much everyone in the store. Her cruel, entitled ways left salespeople in tears—girls *and* boys! She expected ankle-licking, dictator-like attention and treated all of the salespeople like lowly servants, talking down to them and ultimately demanding a discount on whatever she wanted. Everyone knew her in Customer Service as the "Green Nightmare" because she complained so much and her situations were often ridiculous. Some were allowed to call Mrs. Green by her first name, Flo; these chosen few included Satan and the sweet personal shopper Kari (who experienced many fitting-room nightmares with her). But if you were a peon salesman like myself you got the same uppity speech she gave to everyone: "You will address me as Mrs. Green."

Nice to meet you too, Mrs. Green! My name is Mr. Fuck Off, and that's how you can address me!

So how does a vile rodent get the staff of an entire department store to drop to their knees?

With a $50,000 Big Fancy credit line.

In the greedy eyes of Suzy Davis-Johnson, Mrs. Green was a "Big Spender" and a custy she was going to please at any cost. So what if she made salespeople cry? When Mrs. Green had chastised a girl in Children's for not giving a discount on a regular priced shirt that another custy had accidentally thrown on the sale rack, Satan told the salesgirl, "You should have told her yes."

Although Suzy was a believer, the rest of us weren't. And the proof appeared in the mouse turds as I pulled up Flo's Big Fancy account in Customer Service. (Account access was a perk of my being a former manager and having friends in Customer Service.) Maude and Dina checked her out with me, and sure enough, Flo wasn't spending anywhere near 50K. In fact she wasn't even in the thousands. This Discount Rat had a credit-card balance of $567.34, and only $41 at the MAC counter had been charged in the last month. And looking back at her purchases throughout the year, *everything* had been on sale. This not-so-heavy-hitting custy was saving serious dough. She wasn't giving Satan wet dreams of an increase.

Mrs. Green was being treated like custy royalty while spending less than an employee.

I guess that's what happens when you get a permanent discount from Satan! Smart rat!

Flo had The Big Fancy of Burbank right where she wanted it. Feeding her bargains.

There was no stopping the Queen of the Discount Rats.

★

I used to be annoyed by aggressively rude custys seeking discounts, but things had gotten so terrible and, well, frankly desperate at The Big Fancy, my views had changed regarding these pesky sale hunters I have come to call Discount Rats.

They had become my number one income on the sales floor.

Sad, isn't it?

I once had an irritating rat custy named Patty who was from somewhere on the other side of the world, and she used to drive me insane wanting to get everything on sale, constantly saying, "Is deescount?" over and over. "You give to Patty deescount? How 'bout twenty percentages? You give Patty best deescount!"

How about I give you a smack on the head and send you to bed with no dinner?

Although I was happy I didn't have Patty's pitchy voice following me around every day, whenever I heard the phrase, "Is deescount?" I now said: "Yes, Patty! Is 20 percent deescount just for you."

Patty would have fainted from shock. Or gone broke from too many deescounts.

I was just as hungry for the Discount Rats' sales as they were to save a few bucks. A $250 sale with a small discount still added up to a sale of more than $200. Things had become so bad in the Handbag Jungle because of our awful merchandise and meager selection that on some days the only decent sale I'd get would be from a scratched Ferragamo that found a new home with a 15 percent helper.

We salespeople were fighting for our lives trying to not get fired and trying to sell the expensive dust-collecting trash in front of us, so the Discount Rats were our best source of custy food.

Getting to a $2,000 day, which was considered a decent amount, wasn't easy anymore. Our store had become a place where custys stopped in to make returns after shopping in Pasadena, Venice, Sherman Oaks, or Hollywood, not to buy hot new fashion—because we didn't have it! So we were all taking advantage of loopholes in The Big F's markdown system. The new registers gave up number codes to enter for markdowns, so it was easy to hand out discounts to the rats and still be Big Fancy compliant. We could mark down products because the season had changed or for scratches, shopworn merchandise, damage, or competitor pricing—the most popular.

Between Maude, Cammie, Sharky Sherry, and me, the D Rats of The Big Fancy were being well fed. I rarely said no.

Except when Mrs. Green caught me off guard.

I knew she'd complained to Corporate about Cammie and her attitude over the Kate Spade bag, but I didn't know she had magical discount powers. Flo had waltzed into Handbags one afternoon when I was working alone and decided she wanted a price adjustment for a $500 *brand-new* Coach patchwork satchel that she had purchased from Dok the day before. Mrs. Green claimed the bag was on sale at Bloomingdales and she wanted 50 percent off. However, I knew something was up right away. The Coach company doesn't allow sales on merchandise, let alone 50 percent. I knew the custy was lying.

Now, even though we salespeople need to take advantage of Discount Rats, Maude didn't like giving the store away, and she usually forbade us to discount anything brand-new.

The problem for me when I waited on Mrs. Green that fateful afternoon was that I had no idea who the horrid nasty rat on a power trip was. I just thought it was unreasonable she wanted a huge discount on a bag that was so hot women were fighting over it on eBay. I had no idea she had cast some sort of discount spell over The Big Fancy.

And I certainly didn't think she could get *any* discount she wanted. With my experience I should have known better.

Freeman, you dumbass! You were a manager! How many times did you cave and give a crazy 25 percent off just to get rid of them? You picked the wrong rat to say no to.

I should have just given in to her, but when I found out a few days later that the Coach bag she saw at Bloomingdales was a completely different bag from what we carried, and it was an old bag from *last year*, I thought this D Rat was trying to turn water into wine.

Sorry, Flo! No Merlot for you tonight!

I gave Mrs. Green the bad news over the phone and she went into such a rage that I was glad for the phone line. If she'd been standing in front of me, I would have disintegrated on the spot.

"This is not The Big Fancy way!" Flo wailed in my ear. "I don't know where you are getting *your* information, but you don't know what you are talking about! They need to retrain you! I will not take no for an answer! You leave me no further recourse but to report your horrible customer service skills and attitude to Suzy."

It would have ended fast if Suzy had been there; she'd have caved before Mrs. Green finished the words "Coach handbag on sale." But Satan was at a corporate meeting and the new manager of Women's Clothing who'd been left in charge agreed with me. The incensed Queen of the Discount Rats just moved on up The Big Fancy managerial ladder and went to President Mark for her discount approval.

"Yes, we've taken care of it, let me get it for you," I purred to Flo in my most fake slick-salesman voice, reaching for the department drawer where we kept the scary documents—like discount decrees from on high.

"I hope from now on, Freeman, you will never again question me when I tell you something is on sale," sniffed the Queen of the Discount Rats.

Aside from wanting to grab her big nose and twist it till it turned blue, I held steadfast to The Big Fancy's customer service standards and flashed the brightest shit-eating douchey salesman smile I could muster up. "It's my pleasure to help you, Mrs. Green, and I will absolutely remember."

To run as fast as I can into the stockroom when I see your discount ass coming down the aisle!

"Have a wonderful afternoon," I added, dripping sarcasm.

"I always get the best price," Flo said with a wink before walking off to terrorize Women's Shoes.

I replayed the giraffe-bag-beating fantasy in my head.

Only this time I added honey and fire ants.

Discount Rat bitch!

★

A few days later I was opening. An overly happy Maude greeted me at the Corral.

"I got you a latte! It's going to be a great day," she said, buzzing. "The Isabella Fiore markdowns just came through and are they ever juicy! Call Lorraine! And it's just you and I working! No Sharky today."

I imagined the Discount Rats, employees, and my Shoposaurus all fighting over Fiore bags with Maude and me manning the registers and ringing them all up. My heart warmed and raced.

"And the best news of all?" Maude said, "Dina in Customer Service told me Mrs. Green forgot the mall doors were glass and walked straight into one, smacking her face! Mall security had to call paramedics. She needed stitches and was bruised pretty bad."

Hallelujah! Cue birds singing, rainbows, and rays of sunshine! I couldn't wait to call Cammie!

"OMG, that makes me feel warm and fuzzy inside! You think mall security got it on camera?"

The image of Mrs. Green smacking into the door played over and over in my mind. Flo's Door Dive was one movie I wanted to see more than once. With popcorn.

"That's not even the best part!" Maude continued, "She wanted The Big Fancy to pay for it! Bitch hits the mall door like a pigeon on a suicide mission and expects us to write the check! She can go to hell. I'm not paying for her black eye! It was her own stupidity. Well, I guess Suzy said no, and Mark told her firmly that it was the company's position because the mall's property was involved. Can you believe this woman?"

Oh I could believe her, all right. But nothing made me happier to hear about D Rat Flo getting refused. It *was* going to be a great day at The Big Fancy. I guess sometimes an entitled Queen does get what's coming to her.

Lazy, Whiny, and Bitchy

Sunday was the day off everyone wanted at The Big Fancy.

I didn't mind working Sundays, although they were unpredictable, sales-wise; you could have a killer sunshine kind of day with $2,500 in sales or go home with a blood-draining, pathetic $500. I'd been known to call them Swap Meet Sundays because custys did a lot more exchanging on Sunday than any other day. Perhaps it's the weekend garage sale and flea market mentality that gave custys the gall to think it was okay to walk up to the handbag counter and say, "I've been wearing this Dooney I bought here for a few months now and I still have the receipt, but it's just not performing the way I'd like it to. This Coach looks like a much sturdier bag. Can't I just exchange?"

As long as 441064 isn't on that receipt, you can exchange your entire closet, for all I care. But today you just won yourself a new Coach bag! Happy Swap Meet Sunday!

At Broken-Down Burbank, exchanging a dirty old bag without a receipt could end up garnering you a sale if it was bought at another Big Fancy or if it was sold by someone like Sharky who didn't play by the rules, so why should *I* play by the rules when it came to saving a sale of *hers*? At The Big Fancy we were required only to save the original salesperson's sale if the custy was exchanging for color and the service time was not over ten minutes. The ten minutes part was the sale-stealing loophole, so many of us used it. If it was Maude or Cammie, I saved their sale without a second thought, and they did the same for me. The rest of the bitches on the handbag crew I wouldn't trust to walk my grandmother across the street. Life as a salesperson was brutal and bloody on The Big Fancy sales floor.

Normally a Sunday started off hushed in the store because there were few managers around and no horrible rallies if we weren't in sale or holiday mode. That's why I liked working Sundays. Before The Big Fancy opened it was a sleepy, darkened, well-dressed dinosaur and I loved the library-like quiet it had to offer. Even when I was a manager I worked many Sundays; we didn't open till 11 A.M., so I always got a lot of department work done.

Why can't that be our opening time every day?

But my serene Sunday morning plans of doing some department cleaning and enjoying a bagel and latte went to hell fast after I passed Suzy sitting in her office, trying not to be seen.

Moments later, Satan was nailing me to The Big Fancy Decrease Cross over the PA. In a screechy bellow that echoed across the nearly empty store, the droid screamed: "*Free-man*! Handbags dropped three grand yesterday! What's going on down there? I hope you have a plan today. I'll be stopping by. You have to make it up today! *No exceptions!*"

This was not how I wanted to start my serene Sunday at The Big Fancy.

No problem, Suzy! As soon as the mall doors open I'll run out and rob Bank of America, I'm sure they've got enough to carry us for a few days.

A girl named Brenda in Customer Service rolled her eyes as she handed me the department's money bags. "Oh, God, I didn't know she was here today."

"Neither did I. Maybe we should go home sick."

Suzy was normally off on Sundays like so many managers, but every now and then she would show up to make sure we weren't relaxing too much with our fashion magazines and coffee.

Like me, Maude also loved working Sundays, but she and Cammie had taken this one off to go see the Salvatore Ferragamo vintage shoe exhibit at the Los Angeles County Museum.

I realized that without them, I'd be alone with my least favorite coworkers. I wished I was spending the day gazing at gorgeous empty heels rather than hawking handbags with three pairs of cheap pumps that were going to walk all over me and leave holes.

As in most places of employment, you don't get to choose your coworkers. If I could have, I would have ordered up Oprah Winfrey, Julia Roberts, and Tom Hanks—all ethical, sweet, and lots of laughs. I bet not one of them would try to steal a sale.

Instead, my Big Fancy Sunday lineup consisted of Lazy, Whiny, and Bitchy.

Lazy = Sherry

Whiny = Dok

Bitchy = Linda Sue (no surprise)

In fairness, they all three had bitchy qualities, but Linda Sue took the biggest-bitch prize. The minute Cammie and I arrived back at The Big Fancy, there was no love lost between us and Linda Sue. She knew we were friends of Maude and that we'd both worked here before her. She felt threatened and often acted like everyone was out to get her and we were using her. I had taken to calling Linda Sue LSD behind her back. Bitchy was one nauseating acid trip.

And that Sunday it was no different.

Bitchy rolled in fifteen minutes late, all frazzled because of something that happened with parking and mall security. (I didn't care and didn't ask—it was always something with her.) Looking like she had just rolled out of bed, makeup-free and with scrunchy-bound unwashed hair, Linda Sue started right in with the bitching when she checked out sales from Saturday.

"Oh, I see Maude had a three-thousand-dollar day," she said dripping with bitchitude. "Great way to set an example for your team as a manager, selling like a shark while some people are going home negative."

Yeah, you just go on, Bitchy. We all know you won't be able to reach those numbers looking like you're doing laundry.

I hesitated to see if Bitchy would add something more, like "She's a huge shark," but Linda Sue knew better than to say anything negative about Maude around me. Maude did sell a lot because managers are graded on selling. She was aggressive and always watching the floor (which is why we managers are good salespeople, we've been trained to notice the exact moment a custy steps on the carpet). But truth be told, Maude was also a much better salesperson than Linda Sue.

I ignored Bitchy's jealous comment because another Big Fancy bitch was headed for the counter. The place was crawling with them.

"And a happy Sunday good morning to you, Freeman!" sing-songed Suzy Davis-Johnson, sounding as if she was enjoying her ride on the Sunday Woohoo Train.

Look who's in a better mood now that she's done castrating the troops!

"Hey, Suzy, so you're actually workin' a Sunday?" I said, playfully.

"When the ship is sinking the captain needs to be on the boat to get those holes plugged! We're not going down on my watch!"

I didn't realize the Titanic *had a choice.*

Big Fancy execs love to use crazy analogies when they talk about store business. Suzy was the queen of ridiculous analogies at The Big Fancy.

"So, Freeman, did you figure out how you're going to make up that three grand today?" she pestered.

Luckily, I was used to Satan's asking me a question I had no answer for. But on Sundays we didn't have aggressive selling plans. We relaxed into the day with the custys, took care of their Swap Meet needs, and tried to have some fun.

My idea of Sundays wasn't a match for Satan's, so I pulled something from my managerial ass for her like I'd done so many times before when the store was hitting icebergs.

"Oh, yes," I said in a fake excited voice, "we just got in new pink Coach Signature bags yesterday and they will be the item of the day. We're going to recommend one to every customer, show them to as many people as possible, and talk about how hot they are."

"Good boy," Suzy praised me like I was her Best in Show, but alas, no treats were tossed my way.

The minute she walked off Bitchy started in: "I don't want to recommend pink Coach to every customer!" said Bitchy. "Why did you say that? People get upset with me when I show them bags they aren't interested in. Couldn't you have just told her we were calling custys or something?"

Oh that's brilliant, LSD! Then Satan would want to see call lists and receipts from the custys we told her we were calling. It's Sunday! I want to drink my coffee and eat my bagel.

I thought about telling Linda Sue that I'd only said that to Satan to get her off my back, and I wasn't really planning on all of us pushing the ugly new pink Coach bags. But Linda Sue pissed me off. So I said nothing and walked away.

Let her think she has to push the Coach to every custy. Maybe I'll even remind Bitchy, "By the way, you were having an LSD moment and forgot to tell the custy about the new Coach. Don't let it happen again."

My Sunday morning hell with Bitchy continued just after the store doors opened. A woman was looking at a gold satchel in the Marc Jacobs shop. Linda Sue pulled a sharky move on me and cut me off as I headed toward the customer. It turned out the custy didn't want an expensive Marc Jacobs; she had a repair on an old one, and she wanted it fixed by Marc Jacobs. Whatever Linda Sue told the custy caused her to become uncomfortable and ask for a manager.

Thanks a lot, you conniving shark whore!

I hadn't been back at The Big Fancy after my screenwriting break for very long when Linda Sue, Dok, and Sherry found out I'd been a manager in the old days. They all found ways to take advantage and push custys who weren't buying on to me when Maude wasn't there.

And of course, while I was handling the repair, Bitchy would net herself a Kenneth Cole, LeSportsac, and Kate Spade from a custy I'd been about to help before she called me over.

Okay, LSD, if that's the way you want to play, my fin is up!

I suddenly knew what kind of day this was going to be.

★

"I don't know why I'm working today," I heard Bitchy whine to her husband over the phone while ringing up a return. "I always get Sundays off. She knows this!"

That's right, Maude did know this, and it was one of the many reasons why I hated Linda Sue so much. When it came to scheduling requested days off or special shifts, Maude was the fairest manager I'd known, and she almost always gave Linda Sue Sundays off.

Being fair and flexible with employee day-off requests wasn't a requirement by Big Fancy managers. If the manager wasn't a controlling douche bag, she would give a day-off request with no problem. But there were others who were corporate droids and they didn't care about your personal life or what days off you wanted.

"I'll see what I can do, but there are no guarantees it will happen," they would say. Or they would only give the day off if they needed something from you. "Okay, you can have it off, but I need you to work three closing shifts next week."

Bitchy didn't know how good she had it at The Big Fancy.

The morning was so slow you could have fired a missile down the main aisle and not even hit a returner. But that didn't stop LSD bitching about custys, Maude, and returns. Finally noon arrived with the appearance of Whiny and Lazy, ready to do damage for their closing shifts.

"Why do we have to push Coach?" Whiny Flower immediately started nagging at me after Linda Sue told her what I had told Suzy. "That so stupid, nobody want. I'm not doing it. They ugly."

Deal with it, Dok. Not everyone or everything is as pretty a flower as you.

I decided not to tell her it was a ploy. Let it ruin Whiny's day. I just didn't care at that point.

Of course Linda Sue also bitched it up to Sherry. But Lazy could care less. She did whatever the fuck she wanted. Lazy just stared at LSD and muttered, "Okay," before walking off. Sharky Sherry would only do whatever served her selling needs.

Now, working on Sunday meant one thing in Maude's Handbag Jungle: You had to clean all the glass shelves, fixtures, and countertops. Sunday was cleaning day—another reason why Maude liked Sundays. "I used to love ironing when I was a housewife," she admitted to me once when we were cleaning the glass shelves on the back wall. "It relaxes me. That's why I like working on Sundays."

Cleaning and ironing never relaxed me, but I got what Maude was saying.

So if you worked on a Sunday, the rule was the cleaning had to be divided up among the crew. And working with Lazy, Whiny, and Bitchy couldn't have gotten any worse when I initiated cleaning duties. My three ogre-like coworkers were less than an ideal cleaning dream team. While Lazy pretended to be engaged with a custy, following her around, Whiny joined Bitchy and me at the back wall, armed with glass-cleaner bottles and cloth rags. The dust-eradicating party was just about to begin when Whiny had to drop the bomb that pretty much obliterated all remaining goodwill from a Sunday that had already made me want to run screaming for the doors.

"So I guess Cammie went with Maude to the Ferragamo show today," said Dok, making me gulp. I knew Bitchy would not be happy about having to work a Sunday because of Cammie's request.

And sure enough, Linda Sue freaked the fuck out. She turned red and completely unhinged, screaming "Are you fucking *kidding* me?" in such a loud voice I was sure Lazy's custy must have heard.

"Shhhh, Linda Sue, customers can hear you!" I tried to quiet her.

"Well, it's fucking bullshit! I always ask for Sundays off and today was Tommy's baseball game. I am so sick of this place. I should not have to be working today!"

That's because you are an entitled Sunday-Off bitch! You're lucky Maude hasn't fired you!

Bitchy continued ranting about Maude, Cammie, the schedule, and how the department was run, turning redder and more jittery as she cleaned. LSD was not only cleaning with a rag, she had turned into one.

"I'm going to lunch," she announced. Normally the polite thing to do when working with someone who came in earlier is to ask rather than announce. But I didn't care. I was glad to get rid of her.

Moments after the psychedelic freak-out, Dok said she was going to the bathroom, but I knew where she headed: to do her Sunday shopping around the store before it got busy in the afternoon. Pretty Flower would magically show up on the floor when it got busy.

Sherry ended up waiting on three people at once while opening a new account. I tried to offer help while her phone call was on hold, but of course she waved me off.

That's when I noticed that the Bally shop was a mess. Bags were knocked over and stuffing was strewn everywhere. Maude hated it when we didn't clean up from our last custy. The mess belonged to Sharky—I'd seen her selling a Bally only minutes before her big windfall at the register.

Lazy sharking bitch.

Suddenly a return custy sidled up to the counter.

I'd had enough.

"Sherry will be right with you," I told the woman, who didn't look happy at having to wait.

I left for lunch like I was being chased by a pack of bloodsucking Discount Rats.

★

When I came back for the last part of my sucky Sunday with Lazy, Whiny, and Bitchy, things went from bad to worse with more returns and exchanges making us sink faster into negative waters. We were now down $300. I just knew at any second Satan would be calling, "*Free-man*! What is going on down here? Did you guys close up the department?"

Yes, Suzy, we shut her down and put up a Gone Fishin' sign! It's Sunday and the sharks are hungry. There's no food here in Broken-Down Burbank.

That wasn't all—a pissed-off custy called wanting to know why Bitchy hadn't called her back about a Bally the custy wanted repaired, so I needed to call her back, but I sure as hell wasn't going to take that mess over; Bitchy answered the phone, and Bitchy needed to face her own Big Fancy nightmares. And apparently several nuclear sharking bombs had exploded during the hour I was away because Bitchy was pissed at Lazy for putting a bag on hold for a woman who was one of her own personal custys. "I will be talking to Maude about this," complained Bitchy. And Lazy responded the way she always did: "She didn't tell me she was your custy, and you never approached her, so I helped her. It's not my fault." Whiny complained that Lazy and Bitchy weren't doing any cleaning, only selling, so therefore she had stopped in protest and whined that she was not going to clean. At least sales for the day had improved. Lazy had over two grand in, Bitchy was at $1,400, and Whiny cried and moaned about the measly $200 she was up for the day (though I should note, Whiny would get some help at the last minute, pushing her to $1,700. Whiny needed to shut her trap). And Bitchy was still angry that she didn't get one of her $5,000 Sundays off. I heard her snapping on the phone about it—*again*—to her husband: "She plays favorites, that's why I didn't get today off."

You get just about every Sunday off, you ungrateful bitch!

I bit my tongue so hard I felt blood.

My Swap Meet Sunday ended with mediocre sales of $789.45, and that was only because I did a $350 Fendi exchange. A nice custy really only wanted the zipper repaired. We had a new one in stock, so I did the bag swap! Custy was beyond elated and I had a sale.

Finally, a decent easy Swap Meet Sunday sale for Freeman!

Unfortunately my loophole sale wasn't enough to salvage the ugly Big Fancy mood I'd been cast into. The antics of Lazy, Whiny, and Bitchy caused me to yearn for a beer, a hammock, and a long Sunday afternoon nap. I hoped Maude and Cammie enjoyed their nice relaxing Sunday gazing at the exquisite array of heels by artisan Salvatore Ferragamo.

I felt like I'd just been run over by six pairs of exquisite Ferragamo masterpieces.

The Custys Nobody Wanted

There were many custys of The Big Fancy that salespeople like Sharky and Pretty Flower would run away from. Dok ignored anyone who wasn't part of the beautiful-people crowd, and Sherry would pretend to be busy if she saw someone who didn't look like they had a hefty limit on their credit card.

I, on the other hand, am riddled with Boy Scout DNA, which has allowed my humanity to get me in trouble quite at bit at The Big Fancy. I sometimes unconsciously let crazy custys drain me to the point of becoming comatose.

Come on, ladies, commence the bloodsucking! Talk my ear off, buy nothing! I'm all yours!

So when Boy Scout met an older lady named Bee Cook and her thirty-something daughter, Darlene, it was a match made in handbag hell. They were two custys who had been haunting the department for a while, yet no one seemed to want anything to do with them. They didn't have a personal salesperson, and not one shark wanted to try and sell to them.

I quickly found out why.

Bee Cook never spent more than $100 at The Big Fancy.

In fact, she often wanted her sales below $75, and that would include any purchases her daughter Darlene might be adding (which wasn't a lot).

Longtime Burbank residents Bee and Darlene were both petite women, below five feet tall. Bee always dressed to the nines, as if she were headed to a Presidential Inauguration. Bee's makeup and hair were done to perfection, and even though her husband wasn't rich and worked for the power company, she loved to dress classy, like a lunching lady. With many custys, this would end up being a recipe for entitled bitchiness, but Bee was always nothing but sweet to me; often she'd bring me a See's candy bar or a mocha latte. She wasn't wealthy or one of the Big Spenders. In fact, Bee was just what Satan wanted least: a Big Fancy custy on a budget.

Now with Bee looking like she's heading a charity auction, it was noticeable that her daughter Darlene wasn't cut from the same fashion-maven cloth as her mommy. Darlene's look featured greasy black hair and a makeup-free face sprinkled with zits. She wore the same thing every time I saw her: a hideous long navy nylon quilted coat and a pair of big black sunglasses she would never remove. How could she have such a gorgeous mommy yet look like such a midlife waif?

The other thing that sent many Big Fancy salespeople running was the fact that Bee always put things on hold before she bought them.

"Can you hold this cute little DKNY?" she told me, handing me a black clutch the first time we met. It was on sale for $31, and I knew it wasn't going to help me beat Sherry at Super Seller stardom, but who was I to say no to such a sweet little old lady dressed like she was going to have tea with the Queen?

Apparently the hold deal was the other reason Cammie, Maude, and others ran from Bee and Darlene Cook as well.

The two sweet custys were notorious for putting things on hold all over the store. For hungry sharks like Sherry, a $50 bag on hold wasn't worth walking up to the register for if someone else was nearby. She would wait for something better, always on the lookout. Dok wouldn't wait on Bee because she thought Darlene was homely: "Who let her daughter look like that, when she dress so nice?" Bee was sometimes known as Linda Sue's custy because she had held things for Bee before. But LSD had no love for them and would either sell Bee's hold and tell her it expired or she would pretend not to know Bee and Darlene. Lucky for them I ended up sparking a friendship with Bee and Darlene. It was less lucky for my shrinking commission.

Maude was on the fence about my keeping Bee and Darlene as personals, because when we held merchandise for custys, it was kept in the back, not out on the floor where it could be sold. Maude let me extend Bee's holds only because the things she was putting on layaway, so to speak, were cheap, and not the only model of a Ferragamo or Isabella Fiore that we had in stock.

"How long have you been holding that LeSportsac for her?" Maude asked me when we were cleaning hold for inventory.

"Two weeks, but she said she'd buy it soon," I replied.

"That's what they all say," Maude answered, shaking her head.

But Bee kept her word, as always, and did buy the LeSportsac. She had bought everything I ever held for her. Even if it sat on the shelf for months.

Super Seller 31 percent discount, here I come!

Besides the small benefit of their sales, the thing I loved most about Bee and Darlene was the fact that they knew all the juicy gossip of The Big Fancy.

Yes, Bee was a custy who knew more about the personal goings-on of the salespeople and management than we did ourselves. She was so sweet and personable, it was no surprise this woman was Big Fancy's yenta. She knew details about people in every department of the store.

"You know Deborah over in Jewelry is going to have her gall bladder removed," she whispered to me, looking around to make sure no one saw her.

"I guess she'll be out for a while," I replied.

"She's single with two kids, and Tammy in HR is giving her grief about the dates," Bee said, looking glum.

I'm not surprised. Two-Tone thrives on giving grief.

Darlene nodded, which she always did when Bee spilled the gossip. She never added anything and rarely spoke when Bee was delivering the goods.

"And you know that new girl Sara in Men's Shoes?"

"Can't say I do," I responded.

"Well, the reason you don't know her is that the second day she was here, they caught her stealing right out of the register—fake returns or something. They took her out in handcuffs!"

Damn! I'm sorry I missed that!

If you screwed The Big Fancy over, they made sure you were embarrassed in front of your coworkers. "After only two days? That's unbelievable!"

"And that's not the best thing I have to tell you," said Bee, Big Fancy's TMZ, as she leaned in, whispering, "Did you hear about the Ventura store manager Dan Williams getting transferred back east?"

"Oh yeah, he's hot." I remembered noticing his good looks at a managers' meeting. Bee knew I was gay and was totally cool with it.

"Well he's not so hot now," Bee crooned. "Apparently the reason he got transferred was that he was screwing the Cosmetics manager in a fitting room early one morning, and Housekeeping caught him!"

I had not heard that one! Maude would be thrilled. She said that Dan may have been good looking but he was a walking prick.

"Now how in the hell did you get that info, Bee?" I wondered how she could know so much about a store manager at another Big Fancy.

"I'm friends with Alena in Housekeeping, and her mother also works at Ventura. She was the one who saw them going at it."

Bee Cook: Big Fancy's Hedda Hopper. Well dressed and well informed. She's got the scoop! You'll hear it from her first!

We finished talking about less-interesting troublemakers in The Restaurant and indulged in a gripe session about Suzy—Bee was well aware how psycho Satan was—and, my sweet gossipy custy wrapped things up by placing a little pink Coach key-chain zip clutch on the counter: $48.

"I'd like to get this one, but there's a mark on it. Do you have another?" asked Bee.

Although Bee and Darlene were not Big Fancy Spenders and were definitely not D Rats looking for bargains, I was thrilled to take advantage of The Big Fancy markdown loophole.

"How about if I take 10 percent off? Would that work?"

Bee lit up like I had given her a free trip to Hawaii!

We all have a little Discount Rat inside of us!

"That would be wonderful! Thank you, my dear," said Bee. "You are so kind and such a great salesman. Would you hold for me until next Thursday?"

"No problem, Bee! Next Thursday it is," I replied, knowing that it would probably be the Thursday after that when she actually came in to buy it, even though I'd have seen her many times before then and put other low-priced items on hold. I would hold anything for my gossipy Bee.

It was well worth it to get The Big Fancy Booty Call Report.

It's Getting Hot in Here

I had a feeling Rabbit Girl would not survive The Big Fancy.

Satan wanted *more* salespeople selling in the Handbag Jungle, and the freaky newbie Maude had just hired was in over her head. Every time she failed to do a project or did it incorrectly and someone called her on it, she would drift over to the wall like a firefly seeking light and start straightening handbags.

Even if they had already been straightened a million times.

By her.

"If she does that one more time," Maude whispered to me, "I'm going to strangle her with a Dooney and Bourke!"

You and me both! I'll use Coach!

We had suspected our twenty-something, somewhat shy new girl was missing a few screws. If any of us called her out on her newbie mistakes or tried to help her, rather than let us talk it out gently with the patience of the adoring grandmother of a slow-to-learn toddler, Rabbit Girl would shut down and silently float over to the back wall to commence Operation Straightening. Once there she would methodically rearrange and perfect the viewing of every bag.

As far as I knew Rabbit Girl did not have OCD or anything. In fact, she didn't seem obsessive or neurotic about anything except walking away from us to straighten. If she thought this was dedication that The Big Fancy approved of, she was wrong. Avoiding custys was costing her sales, and no sales at The Big F meant one thing: a death sentence.

If you'd like to clean up after my sales before you get canned, it's quite all right by me, Rabbit Girl!

Rabbit Girl's real name was Annie, and you're probably thinking I called her Rabbit Girl because she looked like one, or had a rabbit tattoo . . . or perhaps made rabbit noises and hopped around like a bunny. Nope. The reason I called Annie Rabbit Girl was pretty simple. The first time I worked with her she told me she had sixteen rabbits for pets.

"You have sixteen rabbits!" I said, thinking of my sister's own two bunnies. "Wow! That's *a lot* of bunnies! You must have several cages and a big yard for that many rabbits."

"Oh, we don't have a yard," replied Rabbit Girl. "We live in an apartment here in Burbank."

Sixteen rabbits in an apartment? Holy shit!

I imagined Rabbit Girl knee deep in bunnies and their pellets. Certainly she doesn't let them run all over?

"Oh, uh . . . er . . . that must be tough, you have cages for them inside then?" I said, not sure of *what* to say.

"I'm against caging rabbits. I think it's inhumane!" Rabbit Girl snapped, followed by a lengthy rant of how wonderful rabbits are and how people abuse them. It was the greatest number of words I'd ever heard Rabbit Girl utter all at once. "People are so cruel to rabbits. They should not be locked up," she tied up her sermon.

Oh, excuse the rabbit shit out of me. You have sixteen rabbits running all over your apartment and probably in your hair and up your ass while you're sleeping! That's just not right.

"One day I want to build a place where all the abandoned bunnies of the world can go to, like a sanctuary for them all," Rabbit Girl said dreamily.

Hate to crush your dreams, but I think the world already has that. It's called the Playboy Mansion.

My last day with Rabbit Girl started like the few others I had shared with her. She had closed the night before and I was off. We were both working the opening shift, and so was Maude, who had a managers' meeting. While Rabbit and I unwrapped new Maxx handbags, Maude noticed a Kate Spade dog carrier behind the counter that had been sitting there for days. She had asked Rabbit to make a ticket, but our new little Bunny had either forgotten or didn't want to do it.

"*Annie!* Why haven't you made a ticket for this?" Maude semi-yelled in her pissed-off-manager voice. "I need you to get it done *now*. We could be selling this; it's costing us sales."

Maude was right. Why couldn't Rabbit Girl do a simple task? How could she forget about it for days when the carrier was in plain view where she'd walk past it all day long?

Rabbit said nothing and headed over to the wall to straighten.

The look on Maude's frustrated face could have blown up an armored tank. "I'm going to my meeting," she sighed. Maude didn't like firing people she'd just hired, but I had a feeling Rabbit Girl's days in the Handbag Jungle were numbered.

And so did she.

That afternoon, Rabbit Girl went to lunch and never came back.

I had a killer day selling almost four grand. No rabbits were harmed.

Thanks for not coming back, Rabbit Girl! My Super Seller 31 percent thanks you also! If I have any money left from shopping, I will definitely donate a fiver to your bunny island when you build it.

★

"I want another Freeman," Satan told Maude after getting the news of Rabbit Girl's sudden runaway from The Big Fancy.

Maude did not relish the thought of interviewing people. She claimed her new hires always turned out to be new nightmares. So she asked me if I could find a guy for the department.

Handbag-selling men were now a hot commodity to crews in many stores. Having a man in Handbags was no longer the little old lady shocker it was when I started, when I felt like the only dude in a women's leather world. And now women were selling suits, guns, and tractors. The old days of gender bias and strict rules about who could sell what to custys were pretty much gone (unless you lived somewhere crazy, like Dubai, where men sell lingerie because women aren't allowed to work in sales).

Within The Big Fancy chain, there were now more men working in the women's areas besides *moi*. There were also women working in the Men's area. Big Fancy High had gone co-ed! Some regions had even started allowing men to work in Women's Designer, which is very advanced for a conservative company like The Big Fancy. However, Mr. Lou was never one to look away from successful trends. The designer boutiques and high-end stores of Beverly Hills were seeing sales increases with men selling in the women's areas.

After interviewing several guys for Maude, I ended up giving my stamp of approval to someone who was already working for the store: Jeremy from Cosmetics. In his late twenties, Jeremy looked a lot like the French actor Jean Dujardin from *The Artist*, with dark hair and suave, heroic good looks. Jeremy's warm, funny personality made him a favorite with women at the Chanel counter in Cosmetics. Give him some time and he could charm you to the moon. The women loved him, but his managers? Not so much. They weren't happy with his overall performance, and he blamed it on overstaffing and poor counter management. The Cosmetics manager, Jasmine, was a two-faced psycho, and even Maude hated her. Jasmine wanted Jeremy gone and we were happy to take him. We thought his fashion sense and sensibilities waiting on women would make him the second Freeman that Satan was looking for.

And the awesome thing about Jeremy's coming from Cosmetics was that we wouldn't have to train him on the registers or Big Fancy procedures. "Thank God for that," said Maude.

The not-so-awesome thing about Jeremy arriving in the Handbag Jungle was that he didn't know shit about handbags or wallets. Like my own first foray into the bag world, Jeremy could not stop saying the word "purse" to save his life. In the designer world Gucci and Fendi don't make purse collections, they make handbags. Although women casually use the word "purse" often, when you're a salesperson selling them, saying the P word is a huge no-no. For Maude it wasn't such a big deal, the way it was when I first started and General Judy jumped on me constantly until I learned. Maude just told Jeremy to make sure he never said the word *purse* around the buyer.

"She'll fire you on the spot," she warned.

Jeremy's eyes grew big and scared.

"I'm joking with you, Jeremy," Maude said. "She won't fire you, but she may eat your balls."

"I think I'd rather be fired," Jeremy replied uneasily.

I bonded instantly with Jeremy. We were two dudes surrounded by women all day, with some of them being as moody and nasty as they could be. I was so glad to have another male in the department to balance out the noise Lazy, Whiny, and Bitchy made. We also had a lot in common, discovering our mutual adoration for horror movies, alternative rock, and sci-fi.

When we were hanging out after work or at lunch, we had such a good time being pals that often people thought he was my boyfriend. Because Jer was the embodiment of a metrosexual, he was often gossiped about in the store. People couldn't figure out which team he wanted to play on. Even Bee told me she was most certain he was gay, though she had no facts to support her hunch. She had no facts because he isn't gay. Although there was wide speculation at first, the more I got to know him and his taste for women, the more I knew he was not the gay handbag salesman everyone wanted him to be. The boy loved pussy!

And like Cammie and me, Jeremy had his lifelong dreams outside The Big Fancy. He wanted to be the next Rick Baker and do special-effects makeup in Hollywood, not wedding makeovers at The Big Fancy.

Jeremy's first days in the Handbag Jungle were spent shadowing me.

And boy were they rough. They were way worse than my first days being surrounded by dead animal hides.

The problem was Jeremy's memory. No matter how hard he tried to learn all the handbag names and materials, he could not get them right or remember them.

"What kind of leather is this?" asked one custy he was helping with a Ferragamo.

"Umm . . . some kind of cow, I think," said Jeremy, getting a cross look from the custy, "but I'm sure it was a gorgeous cow!" Or a custy would want to see Kate Spade and he would head over to the Coach wall. "Other way, Jeremy," Maude would say through gritted teeth. Her patience often wore thin with him, but she was glad he didn't adore rabbits.

★

One morning a week or so later I was opening with him and looking at the previous day's sales totals. Jeremy had only sold $700 while Sherry had sold a whopping $5,796.

"What the hell happened to you yesterday, Jeremy?" I said.

"I was her bag bitch," he replied with a frustrated sigh, "answering phones, doing the returns. And she made me help this one lady who wanted to know the price of a sale Longchamp and I couldn't find it anywhere. I had to call a bunch of stores. It took forever."

At times we've all been Sherry's bitch.

"Jeremy, you are no longer allowed to let Sharky boss you around," I told him. "You have to stand up to her. She is a greedy ass. All she cares about is gobbling up sales. You've worked at this store longer than Sherry!"

"Well she knows so much more than I do," he said, defeated. "I can't remember the bag names or what they're made out of. I'm gonna get canned if I don't start selling more."

I suddenly thought of some good advice I'd forgotten to give him. I used it when I was a newbie who couldn't remember anything, and I still use it to this day. So I told him: "Just make shit up, Jeremy."

"Won't they get pissed?"

"Before I knew the difference between lambskin and pebble-grain leather, I was just like you and the only way I got sales was by taking creative liberties with handbag facts."

"Yeah, but if I'm making shit up, I'll look like a fool and probably end up with complaints. Maude will have my balls on a platter."

"I'm not talking about the names and skins and shit," I told him. "You know how to charm women. Tell them stuff like this: 'That bag looks amazing on you,' 'It's our number one best seller,' 'It's a brand-new arrival,' 'The color looks stunning with your hair,' 'It's the bag of the season,' or whatever floats your handbag-selling boat. Women also love to hear how popular a bag is. Say it's *hot!*"

"Hot?"

"Yeah, like Paris Hilton," I said, "only don't sound like that blond whore—just use the idea of hotness to sell handbags. I do it all the time."

"But what if the bag isn't hot?" he said nervously.

"Only you will know that," I explained. "Your job is to make *everything* in the Handbag Jungle the hottest merchandise on the planet! You don't need to know anything about the bag. You've been waiting on women for years. You know what they like to hear. Compliment them and the bag! Make shit up! I do it all the time!"

"You do?" Jeremy replied, his eyes growing big.

"I don't lie about what they're made out of or the style name, I simply focus on what the custy likes and expound on how gorgeous and hot the handbag is that she's considering. You can find nice things to say about any bag—the color, size, shape, pockets, or how popular it is. Here's one of my favorite lines I like to use on a custy while convincing her the bag is hot:'I wouldn't think on it, you might come back and find it gone. It's our last one!'"

"That's a great idea," Jeremy replied.

"It's so easy and fun at the same time," I continued. "I told a lady last night that the Bottega Veneta bag she was looking at was all over the magazines because Jennifer Aniston was photographed carrying it, and they were so hot they were selling on eBay for thousands. We were lucky and just had one transferred in from a store in Alaska that wasn't selling them because they didn't know what they had."

"Wow," said Jeremy, "what did she do?"

"Well, she bought the fuckin' handbag, Jeremy, what do you think she did?"

"Man, you are the handbag dude," he said with a smile that I hoped had a light bulb moment behind it.

An hour later I saw my Bag Boy in action.

"That's one hot bag," he said to a little old lady looking at a navy LeSportsac.

I didn't have the heart to tell Bag Boy that LeSportsac wasn't exactly on the hot list with most women, but much to my surprise, my handbag guru knowledge was immediately proven wrong when the custy replied, "I know, I have a closet full of them!"

"Well, let's add another one then!" said Jeremy, the Handbag Jungle's newest salesman.

A Big Fancy Parade of Crazy Custys

The Big Fancy crazy custy parade never ends. It keeps on rolling by.

Day and night.

By aisle. By carpet. By escalator. By phone.

They come to drive us crazy.

Ring. Ring. Ring.

Me: "Good morning. Handbags, this is Freeman. How may I help you?"

Caller: "Hi, I have a handbag fashion question. Can you help me?"

Yes, but if it gets too intense, we might lose the connection.

Me: "Sure, no problem."

Caller: "I want to know if it's okay to wear my cream shoes with a cream-colored bag that is slightly a different shade of cream."

Only if you want to end up as a Don't on Fashion Police.

Me: "I would probably suggest a different color altogethe—"

Caller (interrupting): "They don't look horrible together! And I kind of like it when colors don't match. And cream is so versatile. I was going to wear them with navy, but I may just change outfits completely and wear a green dress with a purple bag and black shoes. What do you think about that?"

I think I'm done.

Click.

"What is wrong with this store? There's nothing classic anymore," said Elvira, Mistress of Buy Nothing.

"I'm sorry," I replied.

Saying sorry to custys was starting to become a regular thing. We just didn't have what they were asking for. Then again, we never had what Elvira was asking for. Only she knew what that was.

Nearly every Saturday, she would wander into the Jungle hunting for her dream handbag and wallet. Her noticeable boobage and big black hair piled on her head earned her the name Elvira throughout The Big Fancy. The crazy custy was also the spitting image of cult horror movie star Cassandra Peterson's Elvira—except that Big Fancy Elvira was five feet tall, had a wonky nose, smelled like an ashtray, and looked like a poor version of Snooki pushing fifty.

Maude and Linda Sue had warned me about Elvira the bloodsucker before I met her, and I saw her as a challenge. Just about everyone in the department had put things on hold for Elvira and even though that may sound like a minor offense, the smelly zombie would sometimes keep merchandise on hold for weeks with different salespeople.

She claimed to be a real estate agent and would complain constantly about how all the merchandise was too young, small, or ugly. She was weighed down with an oversized satchel the size of a suitcase and a bulging wallet that looked like a football, and she whined constantly about downsizing.

I always tried in vain to help Elvira, knowing in the back of my mind that she was one custy who would probably never be happy and find what she needed. Elvira hated everything. But what she did love was having me help her move all of the crap from her bag and wallet to whatever she was thinking of purchasing. She would go through the bags and wallets in slow motion, picking through them more thoroughly than a TSA inspector, and it was always the same—a feeble attempt to cram her size 14 shit into a size 6 handbag. Then the tiny zombie with huge eyes would look at me silently, as if she were trying to decide to eat me or not.

"I'm not really happy with this Monsac bag and wallet," she'd say, gazing at them like they were a crystal ball, "but you can put them on hold for me a week."

I live to put shit on hold for you, Elvira, you stinky wacked-out little elf!
As always, she left my brain fried and my sales anemic.
Bloodsucking Elvira wasn't buyin' anytime soon.
There was no need: My blood was free.

★

Ring. Ring. Ring.

"Good morning. Handbags, this is Freeman. How may I help you?"

Young Woman's Voice: "I'm looking for the bags by Las Vegas?"

Las Vegas bags? Maybe she should try the airport. They sound horrible.

Me: "No, I'm sorry. We don't carry them."

Young Woman: "Are you sure?"

Yep, I just asked my ass, and I'm sure!

Me: "I'm the assistant manager. Yes, I'm sure."

Young Woman: "Is there a woman who can help me? You obviously don't know anything about handbags."

Well, I know you're not worth my time, and I'm done.

My finger hovers over the disconnect button.

Young Woman: "You are so blind. How can you not know what I'm talking about? Las Vegas bags are everywhere! Jessica Simpson has one! They're dark brown with gold LV initials all over them! They come in colors!"

I had to cover the phone to stop from guffawing right into the dumb bitch's ear. Oh how I love it when a horrible custy makes an ass out of themselves, young or old. Time to play.

Me: "I believe you're thinking of Luis Vuitton."

Caller: "Tone-*what*? I've never heard of that. I'm talking about Las Vegas bags. They come from Las Vegas! You should really know your purses if you are going to work here!"

I know Luis Vuitton is not a purse! It's a designer handbag, you dumb skank whore!

Me: "I assure you, ma'am, I know a lot about *handbags*. Perhaps you should try going to Jessica Simpson's website. I'm sure she'll have them for you."

Young Bitch: "I'm sure she knows more about them than you!"

Click.

I'm sure she does!

I couldn't help telling everyone who was standing nearby, custys included. We laughed our asses off.

Viva Las Vegas!

★

"Are you sure he's not gay?" Creepy Dr. Dolores was interrogating me about Jeremy. "He looks gay to me. Want me to ask him? Maybe you should go out on a date with him."

"He's not my type, Dr. D. We're just good friends," I replied.

Dr. Dolores Silverman liked for us to call her Dr. D.

She was full-on crazy.

Ever since I met her she'd been trying to set me up with one of her gay friends. Now that she had spotted fresh meat in the Handbag Jungle, her matchmaking hormones were raging out of control. But it wasn't the husband hunting on my behalf that made Dr. Dolores crazy in my eyes.

She was a crazy Nasty-Ass Thief.

We all knew this about her, but we could never catch the fat weasel. Dr. Dolores was a white middle-aged blobby woman with freeze-dried blond hair. She often waddled with a limp, always wore sunglasses like she was a celebrity in hiding, and was a total space invader, followed by the kind of touchiness that would get me thrown in prison.

Dr. D was high maintenance, entitled, and overly demanding. When she was upset about some drama that she created, she'd grow combative. But that was when she was usually up to shenanigans, stealing things or doing complicated weird exchanges with credit cards. She claimed to be a child psychiatrist. I always found it disconcerting that someone as unstable and seedy as she was gave advice to children. But I don't even know if that was true because she also liked to ramble about becoming a shrink for pets. "I'm going to start counseling animals because I love them so much," she said, moving close enough to me that I could smell her corn-chip breath, "and I want to counsel people over the loss of their pets or help them with behavioral problems. Do you have any pets, Freeman?"

No, and if I did, you sure as hell wouldn't be talking to them, you crazy NAT!

Dr. Dolores always complained about everything—the merchandise, the service, the people, and how the store was declining. "This is not The Big Fancy way," she was known to scream at Customer Service, like a hysterical mantra. My belief about all these problems and drama she sprayed all over the store was that she was secretly screwing The Big Fancy.

When I was a manager and I had to be in charge of the store one night, I was called to Fine Jewelry by Dane, the manager. When I walked in, there she was, dirty snowball Dr. D with bags all over the place and expensive jewelry all over the counter. There was another salesperson there as well. Dr. D was like a tornado, with nonstop talking and subject changing. I cleared up a minor complaint about bad service from another employee and made a beeline back to Handbags. After D left, Dane told me she stole a $2,000 necklace! Her trick was to cause chaos by talking and laughing and bitching about bad salespeople, and while that was happening he was sure she must have pushed the pricy necklace into her shopping bag.

I knew she was up to no good, but once again Dr. D got away with it. And to top it all off, she had the gall to call me later that night and complain some more before turning sweet on me and wanting to become my best friend.

"You know, I'm a fag hag," Dr. Dolores said for the millionth time.

"That's wonderful," I replied for the millionth. "Good for you!"

What else do you say? "You're also a fuckin' thief?!"

★

★Ring. Ring. Ring.★

Me: "Good afternoon. Handbags, this is Freeman. How may I help you?"

Caller: "I'm looking for the perfect wallet!"

Me: "Aren't we all!"

Caller: "I was hoping you could describe them all over the phone and I could pick?"

You hoped wrong. Hell to the NO!

Me: "I will get Dok to help you, Ma'am."

Caller: "You have a wallet doctor?"

I smacked the phone against my head. I hope she heard it.

Me: "Sure! You bet. I'll get the wallet doctor."

★

Ermalita was the crazy custy thorn in Maude's side.

She was in her late fifties, a sticky woman who looked like a red-headed sickly church mouse. Ermalita had shopped at The Big Fancy for years. When she was younger, Maude Legend had it, she was a bit of a slut, dating married men with money and living quite luxuriously. Now that years had passed and her looks had faded, she no longer had the money to shop, but she still came into The Big Fancy often.

And whenever she came in, it was not without drama.

Or tears.

You see, Ermalita had a habit of walking around The Big Fancy and crying all over the place.

Wearing her emotions on her face where everyone could see them, Ermalita wandered around the store like a storm cloud, tears streaming down her mottled pink face.

Often she'd end up at our counter to do a handbag repair or to chat with Maude. Ermalita would be fine one minute, and then two minutes later, Maude would be handing her tissues.

Custys would notice too: "Did you know a woman was up in Customer Service crying just now?" said a lady I was helping. "I felt so bad for her!"

"Oh that's just Ermalita!" I replied. "She's always crying! She cries all over the store."

I don't think there is one place in The Big Fancy where Ermalita has not cried.

Oh wait, the employee break room! Don't let her in there!

I never knew what to say to Ermalita. It was sad to see her cry, but it was also . . . annoying. I could understand her crying once if she had problems in her life. But to randomly start sobbing every time you go shopping at The Big Fancy, well that's just plain crazy.

So, I confess, I always wished I could have done a little Andrew Lloyd Webber on her ass:

"Don't cry for me, Ermalitaaaaaaa! The truth is you drive me crazeee! All through my hell days, Big Fancy existence, I've kept my jo-ob, just keep your distance . . . "

But one day Maude couldn't take it anymore and turned into her mother: "Buck it up, woman! Stop crying, you blithering baby! You're in a department store, for God's sake. It's an embarrassment!"

★

★Ring. Ring. Ring.★

Caller: "Do you sell pet food?"

Me: "You betcha, it's on the fifth floor next to Lingerie."

Ring. Ring. Ring.

Caller: "Do you have the phone number to the Olive Garden?"

Me: "Hold on. I'll get that for you."

Presses hold button for eternity.

Ring. Ring. Ring.

Caller: "What kind of bag do you think a blond would like?"

Me: "I would suggest something easy to operate. Too many pockets and zippers might confuse a blond."

Ring. Ring. Ring.

Caller: "Hi, I was wondering if you could call all the other Big Fancys and find a bag just like the one I got on sale there last year."

Me: "I'm so sorry, I'm with a customer. Let me get you Linda Sue."

Ring. Ring. Ring.

Caller: "I gots a Gucci purse and two wallets that I needs to return and don't have no receipts. I want my cash. Can you authorize that before I come in? I don't want no problems."

Me (in my best Suze Orman voice): "Are you kidding me? *Denied.*"

Click.

Ring. Ring. Ring.

Caller: "Are you open twenty-four hours?"

Me: "Only in my nightmares."

★

There were shopping bags all over the counter.

Twelve, to be exact.

And the crazy returner was causing quite a stir on the hard aisle, the main store aisle.

She was a mean-looking older woman with short red man hair, brandishing a cane as if she were being attacked by imaginary creatures. "Stay *away* from me! Don't come near me! It scares me!" she repeated, even though the closest person to her was me, behind the counter. I had no plans to do any space invading.

Crazy Returner was hard not to notice.

Why?

Because besides the twelve shopping bags she dragged down the hard aisle, she was wearing a black T-shirt with a white Playboy logo, floral Day-Glo leggings, and bright green rain boots.

It wasn't raining outside, and I wasn't sure whether she was trying to be a cutting-edge fashionista or a poster child for the FAIL Blog.

Psycho Bunny had come to Burbank to return twelve handbags in twelve shopping bags that she had purchased at the Hollywood store.

Broken-Down Burbank's worst nightmare.

I was glad Maude had the day off because a return like this might not ruin just one day, it could damage several, including the month end! Maude would have fainted. Or cried.

Or tried to kill Psycho Bunny.

As I started to do her returns, she freaked out.

"You are going too fast! Slow down! You are making me *nervous*."

How about I go to lunch and come back? Is that slow enough for you, Psycho Bunny?

I s-l-o-w-l-y began doing the returns. She wanted them on separate credit slips.

WTF? Why the hell would she want each bag in its own shopping bag? That's just OCD Big Fancy crazy.

As people walked by, Psycho Bunny raged on. "Make sure you do the returns right. I don't want to come back to this hideous store."

Finally, something positive. That would be a dream come true for all of us at Burbank.

"Be careful," cried Psycho Bunny, "you're making me nervous. There's too much going on around here. I'm disabled, it all makes me nervous! *Stop it!* You are going too fast!"

★

★Ring. Ring. Ring.★

Me: "Good afternoon. Handbags, this is Freeman. How may I help you?"

Caller: "Hi there! I'm calling to find out if I can bring back a Michael Kors bag for my boyfriend's mother. It blew her back out and she can't use it anymore."

Me: "Sure, just ask for Sherry. She'll be happy to be of service!"

★Click.★

★

Imagine my surprise and momentary fright when I turned to see a skinny tall woman standing in front of me with a weathered oblong face, blond mullet, and too much brightly colored makeup.

Frankencusty.

In the flesh.

Part Frankenstein. Part redneck trailer trash. Part custy.

And the crazy didn't end there either. It was only getting started.

With her was a female little person who looked like a combination of Linda Hunt and Mini Me. Were they girlfriends? Maybe. I did get the lesbian vibe. But I couldn't tell for sure. I just know they looked odd.

"I am *very* upset about the way I was treated in your Ventura store," announced Frankencusty.

I hate to tell you this, but you are at the wrong store.

Although Frankencusty seemed extremely upset, I didn't feel like she was going to murder me or anything, so Boy Scout DNA went to work.

Apparently my fragile little trailer queen and her girlfriend were treated badly at our Sherman Oaks Big Fancy, where the salespeople had *apparently* dropped the ball on helping Frankencusty replace a defective $48 Big Fancy–brand nylon backpack.

I know Sharky wouldn't even pick up the phone for $48.

"I know it's because of the way we look. They's prejudice!" said Frankencusty.

"Well, here we aren't," I reassured her. "Let me see your backpack."

Franky pulled out her cheap nylon backpack. A smile slid across my face. Lucky for her I knew we had one more in the back. For some strange reason I remembered seeing it in the stockroom.

It's Franky's lucky day!

"It just so happens I have one in the back. I saw it earlier," I told her.

I thought Frankencusty was going to kiss me. Even her Linda Mini Me cracked a smile.

"Really?! You have one?" cooed Franky. "Sherman Oaks said everybody sold out! They're such liars. I'm never going there again. . . . I will always come to you at this store . . . but wait, I don't have my receipt . . . is that going to be a problem? Because my dumbass drug-dealing boyfriend took my truck last night *without* my permission, and the receipt is inside. I'm going to cut his fucking balls off. Especially if I find out he was with that *whore* Francine again; last week he got us all crabs . . . "

TMI! TMI! You can stop now, Franky! You have a boyfriend? My head is going to explode. . . .

"No problem at all! I can do the exchange without a receipt! In fact it's better!"

Even if it is only $48. This sharky salesman will take whatever he can devour. Thank you, Frankencusty and Linda Mini Me.

★

Ring. Ring. Ring. ★

Me: "Hello, this is Freeman in Handbags."

Caller: "Uhhh . . . is this . . . the purse department?"

Me (wincing): "Yes . . . "

Caller: "You're having a sale, right?"

Me: "It's a clearance sale."

Caller: "What's on sale?"

I rattled off the standard short list of markdowns we'd just done.

Caller: "Is Coach on sale?"

Me: "No, Coach isn't on sale."

Caller: "Why not?"

Me: "Because Coach doesn't want to be on sale."

Caller: "Don't get smartass with me."

Don't ask me smartass questions.

Me: "I don't know why Coach isn't on sale. Sorry."

Caller: "What do you have on sale that looks like Coach?"

I bet your mama looks a lot like Coach.

Me: "We don't have anything on sale that looks like a Coach."

Caller: "Well why not?"

Me: "I don't know."

Caller: "Well, you should. What else is on sale? Is Marc Jacobs on sale?"

Me: "No, it's not."

Caller: "Why not?"

Me: "Because he doesn't want to be."

★

I approached a crazed pregnant woman digging through a Burberry tote.

"Those Burberry bags are new," I said in my friendliest salesman way, "We just got them in."

Preggers looked up at me with maniacal eyes.

"I feel like I'm going to pop," she muttered, becoming more frantic as she dug deeper in the bag. "There's only one small zipper pocket! One pocket! What the fuck??? Why is there only *one* pocket! There should be more fucking pockets!"

My mouth fell to the floor in a million pieces. Preggers had gone to crazyland.

Time to bow out. Run away, Freeman, run away! Angry pregnant lady on the loose, and she will take the department scissors and try to cut your dick off.

"I'm so sorry," I tried to calm her. "I'm sure I can find you a nice tote with more pockets."

"I know why it doesn't have pockets," Preggers sighed as she tossed the empty lifeless bag on the display, leaving stuffing all over the floor. "It's because *men* design all the handbags! They design the shoes and clothes. They design *everything*. It's *all* about the men!!"

For me, yes, it's all about the men. But I understand, Preggers, I really do.

Okay, I get it. She's done with pregnancy. I'm a man and I have no idea how hard it is to give birth. But over the years I have witnessed the births of many children of my friends and relatives. I do know that when a woman is hours away from a due date, her legs and feet are swollen, she is tired and cranky, and she wants the baby *out of her belly*. I don't blame her. After all those months of a life growing inside my body, I'd want it out too, but let me just tell you that shopping is not going to make everything better.

"We have lots of bags designed by women. There's Kate Spade, DKNY, and Isabella Fiore, and they have tons of pockets!" I tried to cheer her up with an upbeat voice.

But Preggers didn't want to hear anything I had to say.

I was a man. And it looked like my gay card was no good. She gazed at me dismissively, ignoring my comment.

"That's because women have to do everything. Men have it so easy. They just sit back and relax. I'd like to see a man try and give birth to twins from the tiny hole in his dick."

She had a point.

Touché, mama to be. Touché.

What could I say? "I'll be nearby if you need me, miss."

Then I ran to lunch. There were plenty of women around to help Preggers. Today I knew she needed that feminine touch.

★

Ring. Ring. Ring. ★

Caller: "Hello, do you carry Dooney and Bourke?"

Me: "Yes, we do."

Caller: "Do you know the tag on the inside with the serial number?"

I hope she doesn't want to try and return one!

Me: "Yes, Ma'am, I know them."

Caller: "We are trying to find one with an eight. Do you have eights? They are lucky."

Me: "I'm sorry, Burbank doesn't have lucky Dooneys; all of ours have sixes."

★

At closing time a hurried Puerto Rican woman with big blond hair parted down the middle and feathered back, 1980s style, came in, followed by a trendy hot, gay chick who didn't say much.

Blondie was in a flurry. "I need bags for my vacation months in St. Tropez. Show me what you have! I need a lot of bags. I'm in a hurry, I don't have much time, and you're closing!"

A custy concerned about us closing? That's a switch!

She then flashed me her Black American Express card and began bragging about how she was one of the store's high rollers who bought thousands with Cindy in Designers.

I've hit the jackpot—it's a huge sale and a boat sale all in one!

Blondie had me pulling out one bag after another. She was all over the department collecting and lining up bags on the countertops. The place was a disaster, but I hoped the woman would be a good sale for me.

After a sweaty jaunt around the Jungle destroying dozens of carefully arranged bag displays, Blondie had decided on six or seven bags for St. Tropez.

"Okay, I just need the card," I said, eagerly adding up the bags in my head to a total of nearly three grand.

Sweet Super Seller noise to my ears! Ka-ching! Ka-ching!

But Blondie was on the move with her posse, heading for the door. "Oh, you can get the number from Michelle upstairs in Designers. She has it on file. We can't wait and you're closing. You can get the number from her and ring them up. She has my info and I'll be back to pick them up. We've got a plane to catch to Miami! Bye!"

Okay, several things were wrong with what she had told me, but I was under the Black American Express spell. I couldn't wait to get that card number.

And like that, Blondie was gone, leaving me with an awesome sale, and a huge mess that took over an hour to clean up. I was working with Linda Sue and since it wasn't her sale, she started bitching, so I told her she could go home and I'd clean up after my custy.

The next morning I called Michelle to get her information, and instead got this piece of news: "That big-hair bitch is crazy. It's not *her* Black Amex. She's a prostitute to the rich and famous. She doesn't buy anything. We call her Lion King."

Fuuuuuuck.

That Tone of Voice

"I don't like her tone of voice," Linda Sue had told Two-Tone Tammy behind closed Human Resources doors.

The Big Fancy HR manager knew a thing or two about tones; she was the proud owner of both the sickly sweet and the fire-breathing-dragon models.

In a store where the employees are mostly women, *that tone of voice* can become a huge matter of contention when the bitch meter spins to red.

And all hell had broken loose in the Handbag Jungle over the way Maude was perceived to be speaking to some of her crew members. Linda Sue had reached a boiling point with Maude and stormed up to HR, dragging Dok with her, to make yet another formal complaint in the hopes of getting Maude fired.

Once she had Two-Tone's undivided attention, she proceeded to unload a bunch of complaints about Maude's leadership and the way she spoke to her employees. LSD blamed Rabbit Girl's abrupt, mysterious departure on Maude's nagging and mean-natured ways.

Mean-natured ways? Rabbit Girl was a slug! Maude is anything but mean!

She went on to bitch about Cammie's getting a Sunday off because of favoritism, when she had already requested it.

What? Because the fifty Sundays you had off weren't enough?

Then Linda Sue crucified *me* by saying I was watching her every move and then reporting lies to Maude.

WTF? Sorry LSD, I am not a mole. But I will be happy to tell the world that I'd love to kick your butt.

Leaving no stone unturned, LSD even brought Bag Boy into the fray, claiming he was also out to get her because he told Maude she was shopping when she went to the bathroom. (The truth here is that Linda Sue *was* shopping! She told Jeremy she was going to go exchange something, Maude came in and asked where she was when it got busy, and without thinking, Jeremy replied that Linda Sue was shopping. LSD never said anything about a bathroom, according to Jeremy.)

The final straw that broke Linda Sue was when Maude came in for a mid-shift, working 11 to 8. It was no secret LSD didn't like to do stock; she was a pro at complaining about her back or her legs. It was also no secret she was almost always fifteen minutes late in the morning. That fateful morning a shipment had come in, and the latecomer failed to check the stockroom even though openers were required to look for new merchandise and get it out on the floor. Lazy LSD needed her social coffee fix first.

How could she not check the stockroom! New stock is our paycheck!

The stacks of new boxes contained juicy Fendi sale bags we'd been waiting for. The buyer had bought up a bunch of discontinued styles, and since our business was so bad, Maude had begged her to send some our way. Now Linda Sue was slacking off. Maude became even angrier that there had been few sales and the department was negative. LSD claimed she was helping a custy on the phone (Big Fancy lets custys call when the store is closed) and didn't have time to look and see what had arrived, but we all knew that was bullshit.

But Maude uncovered the truth. Her good friend Kathy in Security didn't even blink twice when Maude asked to see video coverage of the handbag counter. Sure enough, Linda Sue was standing there drinking coffee and chatting it up with the girls from Shoes across the aisle.

Not even an hour later Maude had LSD in the stockroom for a confrontation that shook the building like an earthquake. You could hear the arguing all the way out into the Handbag Jungle.

"How dare you accuse me of being lazy!" screamed Linda Sue. "I was talking about a customer's order, I'll have you know! I'm sure it's against

the law to spy on me with the camera! I bet your friend Kathy was the one who showed you. And that's probably against the law too!"

"If you had gotten the Fendi even started, we wouldn't be having this conversation," Maude yelled back. "It's your duty as an opener to check for new merch!"

"You want me to do all the stock work so you can shark and sell more!" howled back Linda Sue. "You're supposed to be the manager!"

The Big Fancy Battle Royale continued for a good twenty minutes.

Then the stockroom door flew open and Linda Sue stormed out, marching up to HR. On the escalator she ran into Dok, who was approaching the department to begin her shift. At that moment of rage, LSD decided she needed all the ammo she could find, so she took Pretty Flower with her as backup to rattle off in halting English how she "also not like Maude's tone of voice."

I had just arrived for closing when Maude got the call to see HR and Suzy. She was pissed and shaking. "I've worked here for too many years. This is my *life*! I'm not going down without a fight. I'll rip every hair out of that fucking redneck bitch's nasty Clairol-dyed head! And then I'll make a handbag out of it and beat her to death with it."

It's not pretty to a see a woman in her sixties lose it and unload like she's on a battle front, but can you blame her?

Maude felt the complaints about her voice tone were happening because she was a woman manager. There's an old business adage: "If a man tells someone to do something with a slightly raised voice he's being assertive, if a woman does it, she's being a bitch." I had to agree with Maude.

In the drama-filled ugly-tone-of-voice end to all of this, after many meetings and discussions, Maude did not get written up. LSD did, however, for failing to do her job when the Fendis came in.

Suzy had a sit-down with Maude. "How you say things to employees can sometimes come out a little cranky. You just need to monitor that tone of voice. Add a little sugar and you'll be fine."

Satan is one to talk.

★

Man or woman, when you work at The Big Fancy, it's usually not long before you get in trouble for your tone of voice—either with a coworker or a custy.

Sweet Cammie went down in flames one day when she had a group of custys carrying Kate Spades. Kate Spade was one of our most popular vendors at the time. The three women were checking out a cute new plaid group we had just gotten in. Suddenly they all started commenting on how they were sure it wasn't a real Kate; it looked like a fake to them.

As the critical buzzing continued, Cammie noticed that one of the women *was* carrying a fake, so she said, "We don't sell fakes; we are an authorized Kate Spade dealer. I can tell the difference easily. Like the one she's wearing isn't real. Kate Spade has never made a print like that."

You'd have thought Cammie had called all three women dirty whores by the way they went off about her in Customer Service.

After that incident Suzy forbade us from telling any custy that her bag was fake.

So does that mean we have to take the fake ones back with a smile, Satan?

I have also gotten in trouble many times for having a tone to my voice, both as a salesperson and a manager. Many custys have marched up the escalator to Customer Service and complained. "He took back my old bag, but I did not appreciate his tone of voice when he said, 'I guess we'll have to damage this,' and then threw it to the floor. I don't appreciate him throwing my bag on the floor!"

First of all, it's an old, dirty bag that isn't yours anymore. You returned it! And what did you expect me to say? "I love this! I think I'll clean it up and buy it back for my mother! Thank you so much for returning your old dirty bag"?

That tone of voice will get you in trouble every time.

★

As the drama built and the lackluster sales of the first quarter came to a close, The Big Fancy headed into spring with Suzy Satan screeching over the PA: "You are on the *Super Seller Highway*, Burbank! We are rolling out some juicy new technology and training during the second quarter! You won't want to miss it!"

Do I have a choice? If only I could quit. Kill me now.

I don't think any of the crew absorbed Suzy's enthusiasm. Like me, they would begrudgingly attend the mind-numbing training classes, learn the new technologies, and swallow all the bullshit The

Big Fancy could shove down their throats. But at the moment, Satan's ear-raping monologues over the PA were background chatter to all the personal dramas going on. Maude was barely speaking to Linda Sue—only when necessary. She was still incensed about LSD's formal complaint against her after giving Linda Sue nearly every Sunday or day off she ever asked for, not to mention all the times she let her go home early or did something nice for the crew, like buying everyone coffee or cupcakes. Linda Sue appreciated none of it. After the blow she had quieted down, keeping to herself, looking even worse than ever when she came to work. One day she walked in sporting her infamous just-got-up natural look with black slacks and a top covered in cat hair. She didn't care anymore. And neither did Maude. "If I say anything, she'll treat it as retaliation. Let Suzy say something about her hair-covered ass!"

Cammie and I were supporting Maude, of course, so we worked hard for her, doing whatever she needed with floor moves and markdowns. Cam decided she was done with acting and now wanted to be a handbag designer after being inspired at the Ferragamo show. "Maybe I can get The Big Fancy to buy my line," she fantasized. Dok's unhappiness with Maude and the whole drama kept her somewhat quiet, but she and Sherry continued their sharking ways, setting sail for that 31 percent. Jeremy became more comfortable with the bags and custys and was overheard to say, "This Marc Jacobs is the hottest bag of the season! Cameron Diaz wore it to her last movie premiere. It's our last one, too. I heard the company sold out, and they're going for a lot on eBay."

Way to go, Bag Boy! Good job!

And me? I was just trying to survive the sharks, bitching, crazy custys, and overall, never-ending Big Fancy shit storm. The writing bug hadn't bit me yet, but The Big Fancy had managed to take a nice piece out of my ass.

1st Quarter Sales Associate Rankings

Sales Associate	Year-to-Date Volume
Sherry	$50,325.24
Freeman	$49,175.16
Cammie	$49,003.28
Dok	$44,482.98
Linda Sue	$38,673,81
Jeremy	$12,472.93

The Big Fancy

Freeman Hall
Handbags
Burbank

Dear Freeman,

Only a quarter into the year and you are on
Sherry's heels. Look at you go! On target and over
by $2,543! You go, Handbag Power Ranger, knock
down that goal and kill it!

Sincerely,

Suzy Davis-Johnson

DANCING FOR THE BIG FANCY MAN:

Corporate Ridiculousness

The Visitors

Broken-Down Burbank was getting an early-morning makeover.

We were trying to make her look like an elegant swan, but she was heading more in the direction of a redneck princess. Gallons of glass cleaner were only polishing the grime, not removing it. The store was still decrepit and the merchandise shitty, looking like sad leftovers from a markdown event at Ross Dress for Less. The Big Fancy's current advertising slogan was "We are your one-stop fashion destination!" At Broken-Down Burbank we were actually the stopover on the way to a fashion destination; our neglected little store was shabby without the chic. The ugly duckling status hadn't changed, but the tarnish was dusted so perfectly Martha Stewart would have given us a thumbs-up. And then she would have tried to sell The Big Fancy some paint and products from her home line.

Martha, help us! Maybe you can give Mr. Lou a discount!

Visitors were coming.

That afternoon a corporate crew would be walking through our store, sans Mr. Lou. The only two suits I knew that would be making an appearance for sure were Leather Boy Mark and Vice President Don McCormick. But there were always last-minute surprises. Satan declared that it was mandatory that everyone work. She wanted the top people there during the first part of the day when they were expected to arrive. So Maude had Cammie and me open with her,

Sherry and Linda Sue on the midday shift, and Dok and Jeremy closers.

We'd be staffed full for a Tuesday.

Sharking would be at an all-time high with so few custys and too many sales-mouths to feed. The department's goal was only $3,600, but we had not been meeting our days' goals. You can do the math. A few people wouldn't even be close to their Super Seller goals.

It's a good thing we're having Visitors! I hope you execs buy something with your 31 percent discounts!

It was an hour or so before store opening and I was down on my hands and knees trying to scrub a brass handbag tree. This was an eight-foot pole with three rows of arms with hooks mounted onto a platform with wheels. The fixture was probably twenty years old and covered with scratches, stains, and marks from God knows where. The harder I scrubbed, the more it looked the same.

I decided I'd had enough useless cleaning and just when Suzy Davis-Johnson's voice roared across the store:

"Department managers and salespeople! You *must* know your Super Seller goals for the Visitors!" she screamed, sounding pissed. "I am in Cosmetics and Pam at the MAC counter told me she didn't know she had a goal! *Come on, people*!!! Do you guys want to see me cry!?"

Actually, oh great Satan, yes! Yes, we do! I could sell tickets to that! Maybe you can pull up a chair at the Coffee Bar and do a bawling duet with Ermalita.

There was Satan crucifying over the PA again.

I tuned her out as she began to go over a heinous checklist for the corporate visit. There were more important things to do than listen attentively to Satan's to-do list. We had to make the Handbag Jungle sparkle.

As Satan continued to yammer about giving great service and not standing around when the suits arrived, I suddenly heard Cammie scream "Aaaagh!"

My girl had been cleaning one of the ancient handbag trees while Satan was delivering her lengthy diatribe. When she said "great service," she screamed "*great*" at such a glass-shattering level it made Cammie jump and ram her head into an old nasty tree limb.

"That fuckin' bitch and her voice!" Cammie said, touching her head. "Fuck, it hurts. I hit the piece of shit hard." She kicked the fixture in anger and it wobbled dangerously. "I feel kinda nauseous . . ."

Maude was on the scene in seconds and ushered Cammie up to HR, where Calindy gave her an instant cold compress. Cammie was not feeling well and wanted to go, but when Two-Tone picked up her pager to call in and approve the authorization, who was standing next to her? Satan. And Satan flipped the shit out, "Oh noooooo! Cammie is one our best! She can't go home!" And that was the end of that. Maude returned with Cammie and let her rest in the stockroom till the suits arrived, telling her that after they left, she could go to lunch, then go home and stay there.

As the morning wore on, Maude medicated with coffee after coffee. She allowed Cammie and me to take a much-needed break from the monotony of watching nothing happening on the sales floor. Later she treated us to mocha lattes and bagels with cream cheese. "Screw the no-food-in-the-stockroom rule," she said. "The suits won't be coming in here, and you two deserve it. Just hide everything."

Satan forbade food and drinks in the stockroom, claiming we'd have rats, which was BS; the only rats at The Big Fancy Burbank were the ones I was giving discounts to! But Suzy and her Gestapo *always* had their morning drinks, and their afternoon drinks, and their evening drinks as well! Not to mention the countless times she ordered lunch in from the restaurant. And I can't tell you how many drink accidents I saw happen in there as a manager.

Maude always said that Suzy Davis-Johnson's MO was "Do as I say, not as I do."

You got that right! Cheers, Satan! Let's clink coffee cups!

We had done everything Satan demanded. Now all we could do was wait. Broken-Down Burbank looked as pretty as she could: an old whore wearing Gucci. It was now in the hands of the Visitors.

Not much later, Sherry swam in and immediately started circling a custy, and then Linda Sue arrived for mid-shift at least five minutes late trying to act all up and positive, commenting about how great the store looked.

And you didn't do shit to help, did you, bitch?

Maude didn't buy her a bagel, but she did say, "At least Linda Sue doesn't look like she's going camping today."

★

The day before the visit I had also come in at 7 A.M. to help Maude do a merchandising blitz and to get the bags and wallets of our leathery jungle looking gorgeous. It should have been a fun, creative morning because Maude and I could work while chatting about movies or Linda Sue or whatever, and we could still get our projects done. We worked and talked at the same time, a skill many Big Fancy salespeople lacked.

The reason it wasn't a fun morning?

Regional accessories director Rochelle Dupree.

If it wasn't bad enough to have Suzy, the buyers, and Display nagging us about the way we put out the merchandise *we* were selling, there had to be some droid with a three-part title right behind them.

Another fucking Big Fancy Chief that we Indians don't need!

Maude had taken to calling her Roach: "Don't be feeding the Discount Rats today, Roach is coming." Rochelle was on the buyers' side, and they would have come unglued if they knew we often used a discount as a selling tool.

I need to make sales, buyers! Get us something good! Five hundred black nylon totes that sell for $50 each are not going to get me to Super Sellerhood.

Merchandising the bags was one of the fun things about working in Handbags, and Roach took the good times right out of it. She was slow, confused, and overly critical of her own work and others', doing things like staring at six bags on a shelf for ten minutes and then rearranging them over and over like she had handbag OCD in slow motion. I got exhausted just watching her. And apparently Rochelle had been critical of Maude many times before I came back to The Big Fancy—which was another reason Maude was happy to have me. I'd won awards for merchandising handbags at The Big Fancy in the past.

Roach didn't care about my awards or abilities. She had her own ways. After Rochelle finished doing several cases, I caught Maude's wide eyes. Her frown showed she and I agreed. Roach's display didn't look attractive or inviting. The way the colors had been organized on the shelves inside the cases made them look as if she'd tossed them inside and shaken them all around, ready to pull one out and read a lottery number off it.

Sure, they were straight and tidy, but the order for color or design made no sense. *At all.* There would be a red bag on the top shelf and then one on the bottom. Normally we would group the same colors together on a shelf from left to right. That's the retail rule of thumb when it comes to colorizing: left to right.

For Roach it was up and down; she said her version was a "modified" way of colorizing. She called it color blocking. "I've always done it this way. I learned it from a successful buyer."

Who was the buyer? Helen Keller?

She might have called it color blocking, but Maude and I called it color blindness—a monkey's way of merchandising.

"I've never seen that colorizing technique," I said as Maude, Rochelle, and I looked at the way she'd done the Isabella Fiore, Ferragamo, and Marc Jacobs.

"Really? I'm implementing it in our region because the buyers love the idea," she said. "So you guys can just follow my lead."

We'll need to put bags over our heads first. Have the buyers gone blind too?

I wouldn't be surprised.

Maude and I shut our traps and followed the Roach.

While she was there.

The minute she left, we changed everything back. It took all afternoon while the store was open and it was a full-on retail-hell nightmare. It's always a bitch to be moving merchandise while custys need help and you need sales. It made more work for us—another gift from the crazy executives at The Big Fancy. At least the sharks weren't working, so we were fair about calling custys over for each other to wait on—something that never happens when working with the others.

And luckily Roach wasn't coming with the Visitors. We would just have to hear her bitch about our refusal to conform to her color blindness "creativity" the next time she flew in on her broom.

★

After a boring-ass morning, suddenly there was movement.

Three members of the Gestapo came running down the escalator. Brandi, Richie, and Stephanie held walkie-talkies and raced across the main floor like the CIA.

Within minutes Radio Gestapo was upon us, inspecting and checking out the floor.

I think there's a bomb in that Coach bag, Stephanie! Don't go near it!

"How are you, Maude?" asked Richie. "You need anything? Coverage, cleaning?"

"No, we're fine. I just want them here already," said Maude.

"Green Leader, this is Red Leader," said Richie into his radio. "Where are they now?"

Is the fucking president coming? I thought it was just Leather Boy and his masters?

A man's voice crackled over the radio—Jose, the Receiving Dock manager: "I see Suzy and Tammy over by the Restaurant, Mark and Don must be close by."

The Gestapo was having Jose follow the Visitors.

I'm sure he was lovin' that!

I knew for a fact Jose hated all of them, especially Two-Tone. Jose was a cool older manager like Maude, and he'd been there forever. When I was a manager he used to bitch about how Tammy would cut his hours and he'd have to do the work of three people while the whole store complained about how long it took him to get trucks unloaded. And the number one complainer was Satan herself!

"Thanks, Green Leader," said Richie before his ever-annoying, "This is Red Leader. Over."

"So, they're up by the restaurant?" Maude asked.

"Looks to be that way," replied Richie. "You guys are good, they should be here soon."

"This is Blue Leader; Hosiery and Handbags are clean!" yelled Brandi with her pitchy voice.

Okay, just stop the Star Wars playtime already!

As the Gestapo moved on to Shoes, within minutes I heard Jose's voice yell out of Richie's radio, "Oh my God! Get up here now! Nine-one-one!" All three of the Gestapo took off in a sprint for the up escalator.

I turned to Maude: "What the hell was *that*?"

Moments later my question was answered.

Jeremy and Dok arrived, breathless and animated, for their closing shifts.

"Oh my God! You guys!" Jeremy panted. "You won't believe what just happened in Juniors while the suits were going up the escalators! Two sharks got into a fistfight! It was awesome! They wouldn't stop, and the tiny little tween manager was trying to pull them apart, and the one bigger girl just tossed her aside like she was throwing a T-shirt across the room. The two bitches tore at each other . . . hair pulling, name calling . . . better than a UFC Championship fight! I wanted to get me some popcorn!"

"It disgusting," added Pretty Flower. "They ugly girls. Act like trash at work."

"I don't know, I thought it was kind of *hot!*" Now that he mentioned it, Jeremy did look a little flushed.

Maude was about to comment when her attention was suddenly diverted.

The big moment had arrived.

The Visitors appeared on the hard aisle.

"Everyone spread out and look busy!" Maude whispered, breaking up the crew. "Linda Sue, get Cammie out of the stockroom. The Visitors have arrived."

The only thing missing from the anticipated arrival of the Visitors was smoke and a lighted platform dropping from the ceiling.

Hey, suits! Your theatrics are lacking! You really should hire a pyrotechnician! We'd like to see fire and explosions when you hit The Big Fancy hard aisle!

Even though there was no light show or backup dancers, I always find it hilarious that the custys notice all the action. "What's going on?" they say, "Is someone famous here?"

Oh yes, Madonna! And Cher was spotted in Lingerie!

It's also funny that the suits appear to be oblivious to the fact that the regular custys know they're executives who are here to give us crap.

"Well, here come the good ole boys!" Virginia had just walked in from the mall. "They look like hit men!"

Quickly Maude ushered me away from her, saying, "Virginia, Freeman has work to do—you can chat with him later." She added under her breath, "If that old bloodsucker isn't buying, stay away from her. I need you."

The suits headed down the aisle toward Handbags, but stopped in Hosiery, where the girls there were running around like scared deer, and department manager Bonnie was more out of her mind than Maude.

I knew all the Visitors, a curse that comes from having been a department manager.

There was Leather Boy Mark leading the pack. With him was Vice President Don McCormick, a tall skinny nothing of a man with an emotionless face. I shook his hand once and it was like shaking a spoiled banana. He never said much to me as a manager and I doubt he'd talked with Maude much either. Also along for the corporate joyride today was Sandra Cartlidge, president of Human Resources. She was one unfriendly bitch, Maude had told me. When Sandy was an HR manager, she was notorious for spewing lies at unemployment hearings, while trying to get benefits of fired salespeople denied so The Big Fancy didn't have to pay taxes. HR evilness at its worst. I did not know the four other suits, but they were a mix of assistants clutching day planners and taking notes. I would imagine that today the suits would arrive for visits with iPads and Blackberrys.

If you've never worked in retail and survived a walk-through, it's an odd experience. Although I knew most of the suits in this group and I had no problem walking up and saying hello, under normal circumstances they just stand on the hard aisle.

And stare.

And stare.

And stare.

In a typical walk-through, there will be whispers, and you, the sales associate standing in your department, may be helping a custy, or you may not, but one thing is for sure.

You'll feel like a caged animal in The Big Fancy Zoo.

Please throw me some peanuts! I'm hungry. Would you like a discount on a scratched Ferragamo?

When the Visitors arrived in front of the Handbag Jungle almost seconds later, Linda Sue was pacing around like a nervous chicken, Cammie had a well-known returner at the counter, and Jeremy got scared and ran to the bathroom. Dok and Sherry were still circling with their fins out.

The Visitors stayed on the outskirts of the hard aisle. Even after Cammie finished her return. The suits have always loved Cammie—she is Suzy's personal shopper with Kate Spade, Fendi, and Ferragamo—and they still didn't enter the department. They stayed on the hard aisle.

And stared.

Well, they did at least acknowledge me.

All The Big Fancy execs remembered me upon my return. They weren't overly friendly or anything, but they always shook my hand and said hello. Suzy and Tammy followed them like emotionless droids, their power buttons completely turned off. We'd seen a million visitors over the holidays, so as Maude rushed to greet them this time around, all Mark, Don, and Sandy did was smile and give me a wave.

Of course, that could have been because I was helping Virginia.

"Don't you go anywhere!" I whispered to her. "I'm going to show you all the new Ferragamo."

"I'd like to see those four on the bottom, please," she said with a wink.

Minutes later, Maude was finally jettisoned from the pack of suits, and I could see relief on her tired face.

"Thank God that's over," she sighed. "They make me sweat! But at least they said everything looked beautiful and they were happy to see that I was building a new crew. And thank God they didn't say anything about the shitty business."

Next week they'll just want you to hire fifteen Sherrys!

On cue LSD walked up in true bad-apple form and started bitching. "Sherry is waiting on two people at once and with the suits here, it's not looking good for you."

I was dying to tell Linda Sue, "Maybe you should liven things up and give Sherry your best left hook."

But I didn't. Maude looked like she was about to use hers on Linda Sue.

★

As Maude refereed between LSD and Sharky, and the Visitors ascended the second-floor escalator to view more sales-animals in their cages, Maude let me go to lunch. I just had to get out of The Big Fancy. I wasn't hungry—just beat from being there so early and the stressful memories of it all, even though it fell on Maude's managerial shoulders and not mine.

So I did what I've done many times before and took a temporary holiday from The Big F by walking to my car in the employee section of the parking structure. I could rest my achy eyes and throbbing head from all the morning's activities and try to rejuvenate enough to make it through the rest of the afternoon.

Once I'd curled up inside my beat-up Nissan Altima, all comfy with my suit jacket protecting me like a blanket, I nodded off quickly.

An echoing piano plays . . .

Followed by whistling . . .

Letters begin forming words in Courier font . . .

While the piano and whistling continue, a title appears . . .

THE BF FILES

An original screenplay by Agent Freeman

Down at the bottom on the left corner:

Revised: TOP SECRET.
Represented by: TOP SECRET.
Produced by: TOP SECRET.

Then those famous screenplay words appear.

FADE IN:

Followed by a script writing itself on my lunch hour.

If only that were really possible!

EXT. NIGHTCLUB—EVENING

A huge crowd of Big Fancy salespeople are lined up in front of a club called **Super Seller 31**. It's a riot scene, with salespeople fighting each other to get in. Madonna's song "VOGUE" plays LOUDLY and the inside walls vibrate. "STRIKE A POSE" can be heard repeating over and over. Fat-ass Security guy STEVE is holding everyone back. Among the throngs of salespeople is LINDA SUE. She's a maniac, yelling, pushing, and pulling hair to try to get in.

Agents MULDER MAUDE and FOXY FREE are watching the salespeople fight to get into the club.

> MULDER MAUDE
> This is the place.

> FOXY FREE
> The place where Jeremy disappeared. Cammie said he told her he was coming here with Dok, and neither one of them ever came home.

> MULDER MAUDE
> What's in there that they want so badly?

> FOXY FREE
> I don't know—Madonna? But we need to find out and find Jeremy.

> MULDER MAUDE
> The POWERFUL THREE are meeting us in the back to help us gain entry and take out the Gestapo.

CUT TO:

EXT. BACK OF NIGHTCLUB

Mulder Maude and Foxy Free stand before the POWERFUL THREE: CHER, HARRY POTTER, and CAPTAIN JACK JOHNNY DEPP. One of the green dumpsters starts to shake. The lid blows off. Out of it rises up a giant, slimy, froglike blob MONSTER that has Mr. Lou's face with a bushy afro.

> CAPTAIN JACK JOHNNY
> Aargh, I got this tired ol' sea hag, mateys! I think Louise needs a haircut!

Captain Jack Johnny pulls out his sword and scales the raging creature, laughing.

Harry points his wand at the secured back entrance and blows a hole in it. He runs inside, and the others follow.

INT. NIGHTCLUB BASEMENT

Maude, Free, Cher, and Harry travel down darkened wide hallways. Big Fancy slogans such as "The Customer Is King" and "Service Rules" litter the walls. The pulsating "STRIKE A POSE" voice is heard over and over, shaking the building. From out of the darkness SATAN and THE GESTAPO appear, ready to battle.

                    CHER
     Go, Maude, I got these Gestapo Bitches.

Cher flies through the air with magical martial arts moves, kicking and punching while singing "Gypsies, Tramps and Thieves." Her foot slams right into Two-Tone's face as she spins, and then Cher's fist takes out Brandi. Cher takes Suzy by the hair and twirls her like a toy she doesn't want anymore. Terrified of Cher, Richie runs off.

Harry, Mulder, and Foxy continue down the dark hallway. They find a side stairwell, and they creep up it until they come to a dance floor. They peer out at the dance floor.

INT. NIGHTCLUB DANCE FLOOR

It's not your typical dance floor. Salespeople are in line-dancing positions, just barely moving, with vacant looks on their faces. They sway back and forth to "STRIKE A POSE" as though they've been put into a trance by Madonna's voice. Among the line-zombies are the TWO SHARK BITCHES from Juniors. (They aren't fighting anymore.)

Suddenly DON, SANDY, and MARK enter, escorting LINDA SUE, who is no longer acting like a wild animal. She

has been tamed like the rest of the sales-zombies.
They add her to a line that leads to a door marked
PROCESSING ROOM.

                    MULDER MAUDE AND FOXY FREEMAN
          Processing Room?

Don and Mark see them, pulling out scan guns.

They begin FIRING green lasers at Foxy and Mulder, who
immediately pull out their own scan guns and fire back
with blue lasers. It's a battle on the dance floor,
but Harry steps out and does wonders with his wand,
transfiguring Sandy into a purple featherless duck and
turning Mark into a drag queen holding lipstick instead
of a gun. Harry throws the awesome Cruciatus curse at
Don, making him fall to the floor in pain and cry like
a girl.

                    HARRY
          I've got them! *Go!*

Foxy and Mulder run through a series of DOORS and
HALLWAYS trying to lose The Big Fancy execs. Mulder and
Foxy see a room labeled SHIPPING DEPARTMENT.

INT. SHIPPING DEPARTMENT

There are thousands of large cardboard boxes, all the
same size.

                    FOXY FREEMAN
          What are they up to?

                    MULDER MAUDE
          Let's find out, shall we?

Mulder pulls out a pair of broken scissors from the
Handbag department and slices open a box to reveal
tightly packed snack bars in gold foil.

BIG FANCY POWER BARS

A DELICACY FOR EXECUTIVES ONLY

They reach in and each grab a bar in spite of the
warning label.

                         FOXY
    I've never heard of these bars before.

                        MULDER
    Well, it says they're for executives only.

Maude turns hers over to look at the ingredients. Foxy
leans in to read with her. Both of their eyes grow wide
and scared.

CLOSE ON BAR'S LABEL INGREDIENTS

Highlighting the second ingredient, after corn syrup:

Salespeople's Brains.

Mulder Maude SCREAMS.

                         FOXY
    Poor Jeremy!

Nooooooooooooo! I will never let The Big Fancy eat my brain!

I jumped out of the nightmare to find my sport coat in the back
seat and my head pounding worse than before my catnap.

*The executives of The Big Fancy are noshing on our brains? Yeah, that's
about right.*

Only in real life they didn't need to eat our brains. The Big F got
what it wanted by washing them.

I stumbled out of the car, my head fuzzy and my body like Jell-O.

I sure could use one of those energy bars.

How May I Help You Not Open
a Big Fancy Credit Card?

Like most people who work in retail, I loathed opening up new accounts, and like most stores, The Big Fancy had been known to fire people for not opening enough new store credit cards for their custys. I had lost the Credit Super Bowl, and now my sentencing had arrived.

In the form of Asshat Richie.

At the handbag counter on the hard aisle.

Ten minutes before the store was opening with my co-opener, Jeremy.

"So strange to see just men in the Handbag department," said Richie.

Like I said. Asshat.

I hated when people said that to us, and unfortunately, in the short time that Jeremy had been there, we'd heard it a lot—from custys as well as coworkers. "Wow, the men are taking over Handbags, look at you!" said the nasty Cosmetics manager, Alexis.

That's right, bitch, now buy something or leave.

Richie wasn't done harassing us. "So you guys know why I'm here, because you both only opened two accounts last week, and that is unacceptable. So Suzy's minimal expectation is ten per salesperson so that we can try to beat Ventura next month in the Credit Super Bowl. So I want to test you first on how you're approaching customers on new accounts. So Jeremy, why don't you go first!"

Jeremy looked like a Hosiery deer in the headlights, and after a long pause he said the cleverest Big Fancy credit-card application opening line ever: "Ummmm . . . would you like to open a Big Fancy credit card?"

I thought Asshat was going to shit Big Fancy credit cards. He looked like he'd just gotten off the phone with Mrs. Green, who calls regularly to drill him about her account and see what she can get for free.

"Jeremy, that's not funny," he said.

Dude, I don't think Jeremy's joking!

I intervened before Asshat discovered the truth and sentenced Jeremy to credit-card training prison. The poor pup had no idea of the brain melting hell that would cause him.

So before Asshat could take out my metro bag boy, I had to feed him the corporate bullshit he so wanted to hear. I had heard it all before. I'd been to ten new account classes. Asshat could go fuck himself with some Big Fancy plastic.

I grabbed a beat-up Marc Jacobs that had been bought and returned at least four times, probably involving a few Big Fancy credit cards. I held it up and said, "Would you like to save 5 percent and put this on your Big Fancy Rewards Savings Card?"

Of course, Asshat took the bait, because I said *exactly* what he wanted to hear.

He then replied, "Five percent! Wow! I don't have one. What is that?"

I proceeded to go into great detail about the discount for opening it, the rewards program itself, the great events we had in Handbags that were connected to it, blah, fuckin', blah. I dazzled Asshat with all the right answers. And that didn't stop his annoying test; next he asked me about the interest rates. I pulled out a credit-card application, opened it up and said all the bullshit I'd been trained to say when custys wanted to know more details.

Bite me, Asshat Richie.

He was obviously thrilled that I knew my credit role-play and flashed me a big creepy grin.

Suddenly we were saved by Satan as she yelled across the PA: "It's a goooooorgeous spring day, Burbank! I hope you are all dressing in spring fashion *bought from our store*! I don't want to see any Mervyn's shopping bags coming down my office hallway. You all get a discount!

And we need the volume! The store dumped sixty grand yesterday! What are you going to do to make it up!??? We're sinking, you guys."

As she continued her tirade, Richie said, "I better go. Hosiery is next. So Freeman, maybe you can do some shadowing with Jeremy and teach him what you know?"

You fucking Asshat. That's your *job!*

"Sure, Richie, you bet. My pleasure." I dazzled him with my own fake smile.

You actually think I'm going to bitch out for you?

As soon as Asshat was gone, I turned to Jeremy and said, "Dude, I can't help you get more new accounts, but I can help you get more sales by *not* opening them and having your blood drained by staying on the phone forever while Sharky rings up half of Burbank."

"Oh my God, that happened yesterday . . . and the account was denied!"

I love how companies like The Big Fancy castrated and fired people for not opening enough accounts when the truth of the matter is *plenty* of credit-card accounts were getting opened. They were just getting denied. The Big Fancy didn't care that we were giving at least 100 percent in attempting to drain the last bloody dollar out of every customer.

"You just stop asking people. That's all," I said.

"Dude, that's not my problem," he replied. "The bitches ask *me* to open them at the counter! I'm like a freakin' magnet for failed new accounts!"

"Okay, Jeremy," I said, "since Richie asked me to shadow you, I will."

So we waited.

Not even an hour later this teenage girl with designer dreams sashayed up to the counter fondling a Big Fancy credit-card application. "Can I open an account?" she asked sweetly.

"Sure, do you have other credit cards?"

"No, is that a problem?" she answered in a hushed voice.

"Well, to get approved quickly for a credit card at The Big Fancy you have to have a certain credit score," I told her. "Do you know yours?"

"Oh no," said the girl.

"Do you have any credit cards?" I asked.

"No, but I opened, or I tried to open an account at Macy's, then at Mervyn's . . . they said no. Let me see . . . umm . . . oh, I tried Target also."

"Yep, Big Fancy and everyone is going to deny you now because you tried too many times," and then I added, just to seal the deal, "and it could totally ruin any chance of you *ever* getting a Big Fancy card. I would suggest coming back in a few years. They will definitely approve you then!"

"Oh really? Oh my God. That's awesome. Thanks so much for telling me," and one of Big Fancy's next generation of custys was off and running down the aisle.

"Dude, you rock," said Jeremy reaching for a high five. "I'm gonna make Sherry my bitch!"

Glad to be of service.

FISH! Sucks

"I hate these fuckin' stairs," Cammie wheezed, hanging on to the rail like we were on the *Titanic* and it was a life preserver.

Broken-Down Burbank was definitely sinking; we could get sucked under at any second.

Cammie rarely climbed Mount Fancy, opting to sneak in through the mall doors with half the Cosmetics department. I had done that a few times myself because Handbags was next to those doors and Security always opened the gate early so the Coffee Bar could reel in employee business. All that was keeping custys out was a curtain.

A curtain that many of us were parting to avoid Mount Fancy.

But this morning I was dragging Cam up the steel monster because we were both opening.

And late.

The dreaded rally had already started—I was sure of it—so we shouldn't sneak in past the curtain. We'd get busted. And we still needed to get the register money bags.

We were going to have to sprint up Mount Fancy.

"Are you fucking kidding me?" Cammie exclaimed as our hoofing began.

I thought her remark was about having to run up the mountain, but Cammie was objecting to Mount Fancy's newest bullshit theme: "Ascend to Service."

At a national planning meeting with store managers, Mr. Lou unveiled "Ascend to Service" as a company-wide mountain-climbing theme to inspire everyone to work harder.

And climb those stairs!

Which Cammie and I were sprinting up, breathing heavily and sweating.

Large posters of Mount Everest with the words "Ascend to Service" sat on easels. Suzy spared no expense with the "Ascend to Service" theme (though Tammy was cutting Jose's receiving dock crew hours). All the walls and rails in the stairwell were painted glossy white. There were flakes of fake snow dumped all over the steps and on the level platforms. (Housekeeping would have a hell of a time cleaning up this snowy ascension—Consuela was not going to be happy.) Mountain-climbing gear was mounted all over, along with climbing phrases that had been Big Fancy–tweaked, such as, "Scale Your Way to Super Seller!" There were also photos of famous mountains everywhere, from Mount Fuji to Kilimanjaro. Display had even painted a giant mural that looked suspiciously like Disneyland's Matterhorn.

Do we really need to look at other mountains when we're climbing our own?

As we passed the Matterhorn ride, there were two well-dressed mannequins in parkas deciding on whether to take a ride and look for the snow monster.

"What the hell is this?" Cammie huffed. "A mountain-climbing fashion show?"

"Terror at forty thousand feet! Ralph Lauren's new fall line," I gasped.

At the top of Mount Fancy, Suzy had an inspirational surprise waiting for us.

A giant banner over the door to enter read: "YOU MADE IT TO THE TOP!!! NOW SHOW OUR CUSTOMERS WHAT YOU'VE GOT! ASCEND WITH SERVICE!"

Every time I read that after hauling my worn-out retail body up those heinous stairs, all I could think was, *I don't have anything left!*

But the morning we were late, Cam and I ran through the door, down the hallway past Satan's office, and into Customer Service like Olympic athletes. We grabbed the register money bags and darted for the elevator so no one would see us. We could slip in to the rally from the back.

When the elevator doors opened, it was oddly quiet for a normal rally. Suzy must have blown through all the ten salespeople and departments with an increase (which did not include Handbags).

Maybe it's over and they all went home? Maybe a wormhole opened up and swallowed the rally!

Oh, how I wished.

But we quickly saw that the rally was still going on. Satan had been giving one of her soft talks, a rare happening. As Cammie and I sneaked up to the edge of the rally crowd, I tuned in Suzy Davis-Johnson and heard her muttering something about needing to be inspired.

And when I heard her say the word, I nearly screamed like a girl and ran for the Coffee Bar curtain.

"I think we all need to try a positive pick-me-up!" she said. "So to give us a leg up with that, we are going to watch the *FISH!* video!"

OMG Nooooo!! Not the FISH! *video! I'd rather be forced to eat live octopus! Anything but the fuckin'* FISH! *video.*

Suzy Davis-Johnson had found a way to punish us all for missing yesterday's figures.

"They still show that stupid-ass thing?" said Cammie, looking worried.

I thought about dropping to my knees in front of Satan and everyone at the rally and pleading for mercy from the fish.

Pleeeeeeez, I can't bear the FISH! *video again. I'll do anything. I will clap and shout nonstop for the next ten minutes! I will sell handbags out of the trunk of my car to make increases. I will clean your office and bring you lattes. I will do anything so long as I don't have to watch the fucking* FISH! *video again!*

I've seen the *FISH!* video more times than I've seen *The Rocky Horror Picture Show* and the original Star Wars movies combined. I've seen it so many times I've lost count. It's shown at all the meetings and training classes at The Big Fancy.

Over and over and over.

For Satan, it's the ultimate inspiration. She likes to alternate it with other annoying video classics, such as *Sexual Harassment and You*,

Customer Service Makes Your Paycheck Bigger, It's a Fact Take It Back, and *What Happens to Employees Who Steal.*

Occasionally we are also forced to endure other visual propaganda at the rallies, straight from the board of directors. If they're having a corporate contest or trying to drive home a theme, like *Take It Back,* they'll smile real big and deliver Oscar-caliber speeches about how we make a difference and it's our company—*yeah right!* Or they'll dress up in wigs and lip-sync to "Girls Just Want to Have Fun." It's not pretty watching Mr. Lou mouthing the words to a Cyndi Lauper song when I haven't even had coffee yet.

FISH! is about the success of Seattle's Pike Place Fish Market, and at the time it was made it was one of the latest motivational training tools to circulate throughout corporate America. It began as a video, but over the years it evolved into several books. The *FISH!* video depicts how the people (all of whom were male from what I could tell) working at Pike Place Fish Market in Seattle absolutely love their smelly fish jobs because they stay positive and have fun with what they do all day long. They play catch with the fish, joke around with customers, and sing songs while they work.

They make the most of their filthy fishy jobs by changing their attitudes about it.

Well goody fuckin' good for them! You wouldn't be singing that tune at The Big Fancy.

I wished life at Big Fancy could be as fishy fun and carefree, but it wasn't. The guys at Pike's don't have to worry about half the things we were faced with every second of a retail-hell day. They're not fighting with custys returning fish after it's been cooked and half eaten. They don't have to pay back money out of their pockets for those returned fish. They don't have to call custys and beg them to come in and buy fish. They're not pressured to sell multiple fishes in multiple sizes, and I bet they have no daily fish-selling quotas to meet. They aren't forced to sell fish that don't look all that great, they don't have to worry about fish getting stolen, and their store closes at 5 P.M. most nights. No late nights for the guys at Pike's! All they have to do is show up, cut fish, wrap fish, and throw fish.

No wonder they love their jobs! It's the complete opposite of The Big F!

FISH! pissed me off every time I saw it. The dudes in that video wouldn't last five minutes under the track lighting of The Big Fancy. There are no fish to throw, we are under constant pressure to sell, and if we were ever caught laughing too hard or playing like that, it would end in a corrective coaching conversation.

On the other hand, I must confess, I wouldn't last five minutes at Pike's either. I cannot stand the smell of fish and I certainly don't want to cut it or catch it. Just thinking about it makes me want to puke.

After trying to plug my ears and sleep with my eyes open while the guys at Pikes tossed fish and sang, the nasty piece of corporate propaganda finally ended with Suzy's ending rally remark: "I want everyone to have fun in the store today! Remember, be happy that you're here! You have one of the most fabulous jobs in the world. We dress people!"

And they bring it all back!

As we entered the Jungle to open, Cammie had an idea. "Let's have some fun! Suzy authorized playtime, and I'm going to take full advantage!"

"We don't have fish to throw," I said.

"What about handbags?"

"Handbags?"

"Fuck yeah, let's play football with the handbags!"

Cammie's idea was brilliant. Suzy had already given us permission to "have fun." What could she say? The *FISH!* video was so completely up her ass, she would have no grounds to stand on if we were told to stop. She'd have to support our throwing handbags in the name of *FISH!*

"Hell yeah!" I responded. "Let's throw handbags!"

We both scanned the room for a fish replacement. While I wanted to toss a LeSportsac because they were light, Cammie had her heart set on a new group of Big Fancy–brand faux fur handbags from France in various fall colors, priced around $200.

"We could throw these!" she said, excited. "They look like hairy fish!"

She had me at "hairy fish." I was sold. "You be the quarterback and I'll go for the touchdown over by the Burberry."

Cammie pawed the fur handbags, looking for the perfect one to throw, until her hands fell on a tall north/south tote bag that had two short handles and an open top.

"Cammie," I yelled from the Coach shop, "that one's too big!"

She peered inside it. "Hey, this is kinda roomy. And the lining is silk. It would make a beautiful hat!"

Before I could utter a word, Cammie plopped the tall furry handbag on her head. It fit perfectly. The look was Buckingham Palace guard meets sexy Russian spy.

A very sexy Russian Spy Guard.

James Bond would have been all over her. She was hot. Good thing Jeremy wasn't working!

"Oh, yeeeess," she crooned, "I should be on the Jean Paul Gautier runway in Paris."

She struck several mean model poses.

I quickly left my Coach touchdown zone. Seconds later a fake black bearskin handbag-hat sat on my head. "I feel like Dr. Zhivago."

"I vant to be spy, sexy plus deadly," Cam said in a bad Russian accent, making menacing faces in a mirror. "You try dis also, darlink."

She handed me a luscious sable-colored brown fur bag, which I exchanged.

"Free, you look like a Russian Kiefer Sutherland! Sex-ee!" she said, before deciding, "Let's be Boris and Natasha!"

Minutes later we were at "play," "having fun," and just "being" in our big ol' fur handbag-hats at The Big Fancy Department Store. We pretended we didn't speak English, we changed our names, and we made up stories about our lives and why were wearing handbags on our heads. Some of the customers were greatly amused, while others were shocked and bewildered.

One customer actually thought the fur handbags doubled as hats and we caught her trying a smaller satchel on her head. We didn't stop her.

Salespeople from other departments stared at us in disbelief, wondering how much coffee we had consumed. A few department managers walked by with raised eyebrows, but what could they say? Our handbag fur hats were *FISH!* inspired, and they knew it. Suzy had instructed us to have fun, and that's exactly what we were doing. *Having fun!*

Unfortunately for us, the fun Cammie and I created wasn't quite as successful as what was portrayed in the *FISH!* video. I should have known that if any situation was going to put a halt to our *FISH!* playtime, it would be one involving a return.

A dumpy-looking middle-aged woman came up to the counter with a Kate Spade that was three years old and so dirty it looked like she had used it as a garbage can. The insides looked like the bottom of a birdcage. Disgusting.

Disgusting Returner looked very unhappy. My handbag-hat did nothing to brighten her day.

"I want to return this," she said with a poker face. "It was poorly made."

Cammie and I had gotten really loopy from playing our Russian Boris and Natasha, and here was this abusive returner ruining it all. But still, I felt powerful and intimidating in my big fur handbag-hat, so I decided to fight her.

"No, Madame. I'm zefraid not. Tis impossible. We cannot take dis back. Dis has been used," I said.

Then Cammie looked inside the crumpled Kate Spade and said, "Dis bag no good. Dis bag is very, very dirty! Ewwwww! Dis no good."

We probably shouldn't have made the comments we did, but hey! We were having fun and being playful the *FISH!* way. It was what the video said to do.

"You can drop the ridiculous accents," Disgusting Returner said. "I don't appreciate either one of you mocking my situation. In fact, it's rude, and I should report both of you."

"I'm sorry," I said.

I have an excuse. I drank the FISH! Kool-Aid today.

"Do you have a receipt?" I asked formally in newscaster English.

"Of course I have a receipt," she scowled. "I save all of my receipts."

Within seconds Disgusting Returner produced her receipt *and* a tag from three years earlier.

To my complete horror it was *my* employee number, 441064.

I never should have asked her for that fucking receipt! What was I thinking? Not only has the Mean Returner ruined my fishy playtime, but the filthy piggy was going to make my commission from three years ago disappear! Boy, this sure is fun, working at Big Fancy. One big party! Woohoo!

"If you give me any kind of problem over this, you'll regret it," Disgusting Returner threatened. "This bag has not worn well. I have my receipts, and I want to return it. If you don't let me, then I'm going to the store manager. I know *she'll* do it!"

I knew she would, too. Suzy would cave and give the return whore her money back. Then I'd be admonished for not providing the customer with unconditional service involving a return. I'd lost.

Time to take it up my Big Fancy ass! Broken-Burbank style!

"Okay, Ma'am. No problem. I'll return it for you," I said, trying to control my tone of voice.

"And by the way," Disgusting said, "You look like an idiot wearing that fur handbag on your head. I hope you don't have some kind of hair lice or disease. What kind of place is this? I thought this was a respectable department store. I wonder what the Health Department will say about this."

I didn't give her the satisfaction of watching me take my handbag-hat off.

Once she was gone, both Cammie and I removed our fur handbag-hats, and that was the end of *FISH!* play as we knew it in the Handbag Jungle.

FISH! inspired it, The Big Fancy killed it.

I Will Never Be an A Student
at The Big Fancy

With a face overcome with doom and hands gripping two large coffees, Maude marched toward the stockroom door like she was going into battle with the Dark Lord of Sauron to save Middle Earth.

The only other time I'd seen her look so solemn, and getting ready to consume two coffees, was when they forced her to crunch yearly numbers and plan promotions for a buyer's visit. Today's caffeine two-fister meant there was an ugly tedious project keeping her in the stockroom.

"Okay, mister, one of these is yours," she said. "Follow me. Team review hell time."

Ah no. Fuck. But wait! What do I care! I don't have to do them! I'm not a manager anymore. Yay!

For managers all over the store it was that dreaded time of the year when they had to write up reviews of all their salespeople. While the managers stressed over what to write, the salespeople had a what-the-fuck attitude.

Why?

Because there was no monetary reward backing up how well you performed. Like so many other corporations, The Big Fancy did not give raises—only Super Seller discounts.

Two-Tone Tammy loved to tell newbies in training that the sky was the limit. You could make as much money as you wanted to. It just depended on how much you sold.

And that's why The Big Fancy thought it wasn't necessary to give raises. Many times Satan had been known to say, "We offer the best benefits in the world and the best discount! If you work hard, you can have a raise every month!"

Such bullshit.

So even though The Big Fancy passed on the idea of giving raises to its employees, it wasn't about to stop evaluating who should be kept on and who was short-circuiting and should be deemed a wrong fit and spit out. To do all that, they had Team Reviews.

When I was a manager I had written plenty of Team Reviews, and they were never fun. If you had a Linda Sue in your department, there were bound to be fireworks when you checked the line that said "needs improvement." The old Team Reviews were two pages that you filled out with a pen. The first page was the review and the second page was for manager and employee comments—very clean and simple. It focused on Customer Service, Teamwork, and Productivity. That was it.

The Big Fancy's new Team Review form was a manager's nightmare to behold.

It was ten pages long.

There were six different sections with over 200 questions regarding everything from hair style to how well the salesperson kept the register area clean. There were short-answer boxes requiring managers to write lengthy summaries about their employees. It looked like the SAT.

When Maude showed me the templates weeks earlier after her two-day training from hell, I was stunned and very glad I was no longer a manager.

"How long does it take to fill out one?" I asked.

"They say a couple of hours because at the end of every section and at the end of the review you have to write summaries! Just thinking about it gives me an ulcer. Not to mention it's all on the computer."

"And then how long does it take to give a review?"

"They say about an hour," she replied, "unless you're Linda Sue! Double that."

Again I thanked my lucky stars.

"It doesn't end there," said Maude. "You won't believe what the bitch said in the manager's meeting last week. There are to be no As issued to anyone. What the hell? Why have an A?"

Are they fucking serious? I'd have hated to have her for second grade. And I thought Mrs. Flyke was mean! What's with all this letter-grading ridiculousness?

Now, I've heard of many companies not handing out As or whatever the highest grade is in their grading system. But usually when that happened and a store didn't want to give an employee a top grade, it was because they didn't want to hand out a raise.

But The Big Fancy doesn't give raises.

WTF?

"I want everyone to run a little faster and jump a little higher," said Suzy Davis-Johnson, explaining in a managers' meeting why there were to be no Team Review As. "Even if you are exceeding expectations, there's always room for improvement."

Always room for improvement.

There it is. The reason no one will ever be an A student at The Big Fancy.

So this year's Team Reviews were even more distressing to Maude because of the amount of time she'd be spending at the computer. Technology was not her strong point. She was afraid that she'd delete something or fail to save a file correctly.

"So, are you ready?" Maude said.

"Yeah," I replied, taking a sip of latte.

"Okay, have a seat at the computer."

"Isn't that where you're supposed to sit?" I asked.

"No, because you're going to fill out your own review," she replied with a smile and a chuckle, sitting in the extra folding chair. "I'll tell you what to say, and you can agree or not, or change it. I don't really fucking care, Freeman, because you know I think you're great, and you always give 100 percent of your blood, and I appreciate it! So let's go."

We both had a good chuckle and a hug, and then she said, "And I'm taking you to lunch, too!"

"Wow, thanks, Maude!"

"That's bribery because after you're done with your review, I'm going to have you help me with everyone else's. Suzy wants synopses of everyone's. You're the writer, not me," she said with an evil smile.

"California Pizza Kitchen, and you got yourself a deal!"

I couldn't wait to write a novel about Linda Sue.

I was giving her a D.

My Expensive Noncompliant Circle

When I saw half the Gestapo, Brandi and Richie, walking toward the Corral clutching piles of papers and folders, I quickly looked around for a nightmare custy to glom on to.

Shit!

No nightmares to be found. No Elvira or Dr. Dolores waiting to slurp my blood. Even Virginia didn't seem to be haunting the main aisle that afternoon. Why weren't the crazies around when you needed them?

I was screwed.

The Big Fancy Compliance Gestapo pulled up to the counter eyeing me like I was one of the usual suspects in need of questioning.

"Hey, Freeman," said Officer Richie, "are you with a customer? Quick chat?"

Quick chat? Shall we start with the weather, or how about what bar I'll be hitting after you give me your happy news?

"Sure," I said, watching Officer Brandi dig through a folder and bring out several sheets of paper with custy checks stapled to them.

"We have noncompliance we need to go over with you," Officer Richie stated formally.

"Alrighteeeeeeee, let's see what we have here for Mr. Freeman," said Officer Brandi in her annoying parental voice. "Freeman Hall . . . 441064 . . . chargeback for a returned check taken on January sixteen for four hundred eighty-seven dollars and sixteen cents. No circled phone number."

Oh yay! Lucky me! No circled phone number! Sound the horns, release the doves! I just got fucked over by a check-writing NAT!

Dark clouds formed over the Corral. Thunder and lightning. Hurricane-force winds.

I knew what was coming next, and it was not going to be pretty.

After doing some quick math in my head, I concluded that my subsequent failure to circle the custy's phone number on the check was going to cost me $35.

Aw, damn. There's so much I could have bought with that $35. Like a cool Green Day T-shirt I saw in the mall, or paying my gas bill, which was a month late.

Whenever noncompliance occurred with a check or credit card, the salesperson's commission was taken away. Just like a bank or credit-card company collecting fees for custy missteps with their balances, The Big Fancy's chargeback rule took commissions back from salespeople—salespeople who themselves were victims of thievery. When the item purchased with the bad check was returned at some Big Fancy three states away, the commission would come out *again*, thus creating a double payout for The Big Fancy.

So in total, my noncompliant circle would end up costing me around $70.

The inhumanity! Missing circles at The Big Fancy are expensive! At that price I could have gone to a strip club and had a lap dance!

"You know how a chargeback works, right, Freeman," Richie confirmed. I kept thinking about all the things I could have bought with seventy bucks.

Two cases of Rockstar from Costco. New haircut and color. A Ben Sherman sale shirt.

"Your commission is deducted," added Brandi, who felt the need to answer for me.

Tickets to RENT. Madonna's Sex book. A Madonna concert ticket!

"Yes, I know." I held back the urge to smack her in the face with the lid from the Customer Comments box.

Of course I know my commission is deducted, you moron. It's not like this hasn't happened a trillion zillion times. It's total Big Fancy corporate bullshit!

Brandi thrust the check in my face.

It might as well have been written in Greek on a piece of bark from a dead tree in New Zealand.

"Maybe you can help Security out," said Richie, trying to redirect in a positive way. "Maybe they can identify the person or recover the merchandise if you remember any details . . ."

"Like what the customer looked like? Or what bag it was?" said Brandi, chiming in.

Oh yes, Brandi! I remember it like it was yesterday. The custy looked just like your mama, and she was buying Richie's ass! A sale to remember, for sure! WTF?! I can barely remember birthdays in my family and you want me to give you details on a random custy from a month ago? Go watch some more CSI *repeats, annoying cow.*

My mind was flooded with rage over the whole incident and the fact that they could care less how unfair chargebacks were to salespeople who were thrust into a situation with a thief and no protection. But I knew my anger would get me nowhere. Time to defuse it with humor.

"I have an idea!" I said, sounding like I was going to give them something good. "How about if I give the info to my Uncle Tony Soprano! He'll make the bitch pay up!"

No laughs. Not even a smile. Officers Brandi and Richie did not like my mobster joke.

"That's not funny, Free-man," a frowning Officer Brandi said. "This is serious stuff. The company loses millions of dollars a day because of bad checks and lazy salespeople not following procedures."

The company loses millions because salespeople are not circling phone numbers? How stupid do you think I look? They gain millions by making salespeople pay with their commissions!

This was just another notch in the pegboard of corporate ridiculousness running amok at The Big Fancy. How can they say that the company would have saved millions of dollars if those salespeople had circled phone numbers on a check that was destined to be stamped NSF—Non-Sufficient Funds? The truth is they wouldn't have saved a dime. The check-approval company—there really is a separate company that does nothing but approve checks—is the one not catching the bad checks, but The Big Fancy needed to find a way for someone else to absorb the selling cost. And I guess taking back salespeople's pay for forgetting to circle a phone number was the perfect way to do it.

"I'm not lazy, Brandi," I said, starting to get pissed and resorting to my lengthy Big Fancy history as a way of chastising her. "I've been a manager before and know all about procedures. I must have been busy and not circled, but you can clearly see that the check *does* have a phone number. It also has all the other requirements in the T-bar. Everything was correct."

"Except you didn't circle the phone number," replied Officer Brandi with a smirk.

Now I was annoyed.

"And so I'm supposed to pay The Big Fancy thirty-five dollars because the check-approval system couldn't catch it when it went through the register?"

Richie jumped in before Brandi and I got into it. "Just let us know if you remember anything about the customer."

"I don't remember what she looked like," I said, spotting a custy over at Coach. "I'd better approach that lady. If I think of anything, I'll let you know."

Along with my lawyer, TMZ, and Congress. Seriously, why didn't any of us hit The Big F with a Big L?

"Well, let's hope it's your last mistake," Brandi felt the need to preach as she followed Richie to Hosiery. "I'm sure you learned a valuable lesson."

I had indeed learned a valuable lesson from the Compliance Gestapo—an expensive lesson.

I learned that working at The Big Fancy can cost you actual money out of your own pocket if you're not on your game every second.

How to Date Your Custy

The Big Fancy's Client Capture rollout was underway.

And Satan was so high with happiness you could have docked her at the space station.

"This is the greatest tool we could ever give you," said Suzy Davis-Johnson, turned down three volume levels lower than normal. But I was smart enough to know it wouldn't last. "It will change the way you do business with customers, and I'm expecting great things from you, Burbank! So go out there and capture those clients! And let's have a *huuuuuuge* increase this month! *Woohooooo!*"

God help the animals at The Big Fancy Zoo. I think they just hanged themselves in their cages!

Client Capture was a hot new high-tech computer program built into the registers that maintained our custys' contact information and purchase history. If you're thinking Big Brother in your closet, you are thinking right!

The Big Fancy knows what color underwear you're wearing right at this moment.

Just by entering codes into the computer, Client Capture would let us have digital access to our custys' info. While this futuristic move was inevitable, the transition to accepting it was tougher than grocery store custys giving up their plastic bags.

Client Capture was created to make our selling lives easier, but many believed The Big Fancy was trying to control personal customer lists. (In the past it was well known that if a salesperson was fired, managers were supposed to get a hold of the soon-to-be-ex-employee's client book before the firing because the salesperson might take off with valuable customer information.) Technically, the custys of Big Fancy are just that, The Big Fancy's custys; but since salespeople created their own lists, many felt protective of their custy information.

It was also easier for most of us to jot notes or draw pictures in a book than to navigate through several screens on the register.

Will this be just like trying to use the stapler while Linda Sue complains and takes forever to use it?

Although Client Capture did amazing things, the one thing it would not do was hold credit-card numbers. This was a bone of contention with many salespeople. The old books were nothing more than oversized address books made from the kind of plastic binders you'd find in any high school, and we could jot down credit info for our more demanding custys. I'd looked up and written down Lorraine's Big Fancy credit number so many times I had it memorized. I also had a few other personal custys who loved just being able to tell me, "Send it to me when you find it!" But this wasn't always a great customer service perk; there were Nasty-Ass Thieving Salespeople running amok with credit info, and they would sell or steal those numbers.

After my last paycheck, I can definitely see why a million-dollar suit shark would be tempted into selling off custy credit info to the highest bidder!

Most of us were excited that the register client books were coming to our ratty little store. Cam said, "I hope we can make notes about all the crazies and the bad returners."

"That would be so awesome!" I said, thinking of what I would write about Mrs. Green.

Sun-bleached Discount Rat with black eye!

When the Client Capture rollout started, there wasn't a soul in the store who didn't know about it; even the Discount Rats sensed change coming. Mount Fancy had taken on a horrible pirate theme to promote it. There were Client Capture flags everywhere and more cheap party store crap, and yes, they dressed up the mannequins as wenches who wanted to be captured by salespeople. Suzy did lame pirate skits at rallies and lame pirate voices over the PA, "*Arrrrrgh*, Burbank mateys! How many clients did you capture today?! Will it get you to Super Seller?" We were herded into a short training class showing us the wonders of Client Capture, how easy it was to keep information stored, and how everything the customer purchased would show up on their profile. Client Capture was going to make us develop great relationships with our custys and bring in more sales!

The day after the rollout, the real hell started for Maude.

The Client Capture Report Card was born.

It was just another report that no manager needed. Or wanted. But because The Big Fancy had spent a trillion dollars on Client Capture, they were wanting and needing to make sure the salespeople were using it.

The salespeople of Burbank Big Fancy were not. Oh, we were playing around with Client Capture like it was a toy we were about to lose interest in, but apparently our tinkering with the program for the custys we really loved wasn't enough for the hungry dreams of Satan and The Big Fancy. In their minds we should be capturing *every* custy. Client Capture, though cool, was sometimes a huge pain in the retail ass. Although it was amazing to see all of a custy's purchases throughout the store, when you needed to look up quick information, like a phone number, it could take forever. I can remember forgetting to call back many custys simply because it was busy and there wasn't a register free long enough to look up the number. Old-schoolers believed opening up a nearby book was much easier than tapping a bunch of times on a screen that may or may not be available.

When the news came down and Richie went to each department and collected all the client binders, some of which were over ten years old, the cries of Super Sellers could be heard all the way out into the employee parking structure, which is a very long way indeed.

The salespeople of Broken-Down Burbank did not want to have their paper taken away. Sadly for us, the future had arrived at The Big Fancy, and we had no choice.

There was more drama than ever during the Client Capture transition. Old-time salespeople like Maude and Linda Sue had had their books for many years, and they didn't want to let go of them. The old plastic binders were custy safety blankets. And some of the biggest sharks and salespeople in the store did *not* want to let go of them. However, Client Capture was not giving Satan the store-increase dreams she felt entitled to, so she decided to take things into her own hands to improve business. The company could spend $50 billion on Client Capture, and she could shave a little off the budget to do some personal training and bestow advice to her troops.

Time for some good old-fashioned desperate selling advice.

"*Gooooooooood morning, Burbank!!* And do I ever have exciting news for you! I am pleased to announce a new selling module that all of you will be attending! I take this store very seriously, and even though it's going to wear me thin to do it, I want to spend time with each of you, inspiring you on how to be the best salespeople so you can all become Super Sellers! So the new module is called *How to Date Your Customer!* Yes, Burbank, I have *five! secret! tips!* To dating your customer! And to getting those sales that will make you a *Super Seller*! I will teach them all to you! For free, even! Class sign-up sheets on my office window!"

Oh. My. God. Are they fucking delusional? Has Suzy turned into a pimp, and we're her whores? Oh wait, it's always been that way!

When I heard Satan announce custy dating, I was on the floor of the Handbag Jungle doing Dooney and Bourke markdowns with Maude.

"I don't want to date any of my custys!" I shuddered.

"I don't want to date any of your custys either, Freeman," she replied. "You attract some real crazies!"

You got that right. Just look at Mrs. Green, Dr. Dolores, and Ermalita!

Whether we wanted to date a custy or not, it didn't matter; Suzy's date on dating was mandatory—every salesperson in the store was required to sign up for a time slot to receive Satan's five golden tips. Even the cashiers of The Restaurant had to do it, and they had no need to date their custys because they weren't on commission!

On the day I was subjected to Suzy's custy-dating seminar, she had a sold-out house of about thirty sales-zombies from all over the store. I knew a few of the people. I was lucky enough to go with Jeremy, who kept me entertained by doodling monster depictions of the BF Gestapo in his notebook. We were in The Big Fancy's training room, which was as ugly as the servants' quarters on the *Titanic*. There were no windows, just posters of Big Fancy selling slogans and their ridiculous "Sun of Success" diagram that showed a child-drawn version of the sun and the word "YOU" inside. The sun's rays were the customers, buyers, family, Mr. Lou, and more bullshit like that. Every time I saw the poster, I wanted to tear it off the wall and light it on fire.

The opening act to Suzy Davis-Satan's big custy dating shit show was the Gestapo's own Brandi and Tammy. They had us trapped and took full advantage, locking the doors and banning bathroom passes, turning the session into a third-grade reading class, in which, to my horror, they went around the room and had us each read paragraphs aloud from The Big Fancy's code of ethics on scintillating subjects like misfire, noncompliance, selling ethics, stealing, and sexual harassment. (The last one was an odd choice, considering that we were being taught about custy dating.)

So this is how we pay the price for the two fighting bitch sharks in Juniors!

No one wanted to be there and we were all just about ready for our nappy time, when suddenly the door burst open and Satan crashed through with her earth-shattering voice.

"*Hellooooo*, you guys! Are you ready to get my magical customer dating secrets?"

Not unless you're moving me to the Magical Men's Suits department!

Satan commanded our attention in a skin-tight midnight-blue silk designer dress, posing and twirling like a whore nobody wanted, waiting to be chosen at the bunny ranch. She then launched into a creepy speech about how important it was for us to get closer to our custys and connect with them better for more sales. "And so I have five magical tips on how you can date your custy! You guys are gonna love this."

"Oh yes I am!" said Jeremy as he prepared to take notes.

I don't think Suzy's tips are going to get you the kind of date you want, Jer!

Satan could very well have been nipping the gin—although she was always sort of drowsy and loose—but when she went over her five tips for dating a custy, all I wanted to do was run. I looked over, and Jeremy was writing notes like a horny college boy.

"Number one," she said, "compliment your customer. But go beyond what they're wearing! That's the trick here. You want to comment on their body—their eye color, their hair, their face . . ."

. . . the bulge in their pants? Their boobage? Does this work: "What a lovely pair of knockers you have, Mrs. Green"?

"Number two," said Satan breathlessly, "be flirtatious, smile, use what God gave you! For number three I think it's important that you write a thank-you note to your customer, but make it a little more special and don't just say 'thank you'! Let them know you care!"

With what? A haiku? I'm swallowing serious vomit right now.

"For number four," the custy matchmaker continued, "when calling your customers on the phone, you should use a voice that sounds like you're asking them out on a date!"

And end up in jail or with a lawsuit? No thanks, Sexy Satan!

"And finally," said Custy Dating Doctor Suzy, proud of herself and smiling maniacally, "Make sure you invite your custy on a date somewhere in the store! We want to get them in the store spending and keep them there! That's the whole point to dating your custy!"

Barf. That was a waste of two hours from my life. Can I have a refund?

Suzy continued chattering about her divine inspiration, and I noticed that Jeremy was still taking notes.

What the hell, dude? No!

"There are so many way you can date your customer!" Satan affirmed. "There are many ways to get their attention and keep them as your personals. I encourage you all to be creative!"

Shocking the hell out of me, Jeremy's hand shot into the air with a question. "Suzy, I'm reading a fantastic book right now called *The Art of Seduction*. Would that work with this?"

It took everything in me to swallow my laughter. *The Art of Seduction* is a book for picking up women.

"I haven't heard of that," said Suzy checking the air in her head, "but it sounds amazing. I think selling is very seductive. I'm sure you'll get lots of customers giving it a try."

I know what he's gonna get lots of.

Suzy was just ridiculous. But my hell was only getting started as Suzy suddenly screamed, "*Okaaaay everybody!* Now that I've shared with you my magical secrets to customer dating, guess what time it is? *It's role-play time!!*"

OMG! Noooooooo! I hate role-playing at The Big Fancy!

I swallowed my screams, and a big smile slid across Jeremy's face.

I would have a talk with him and set him straight when this was all over.

He wasn't dating any of his customers. This could only lead to Stalker Shoppers.

The Open Door to Nowhere

Like many companies, The Big Fancy pretended to care about what their employees had to say.

At meetings, in videos, and on posters and fliers, the execs were famous for stating, "The door is always open." In a world where sales associates were treated like dog biscuits—devoured one day, and shit out the next—we were led to believe the company wanted to listen to our ideas.

Even though their hearing was selective and they had ears mostly full of wax.

Maybe it's all those deafening rallies!

One day I decided to walk through the legendary open door and see if I could make a difference—even though I was intellectually aware that it would probably be slammed in my face.

During my lengthy tenure with The Big Fancy as a salesperson and manager, I'd never unleashed any kind of complaint or displeasure in a formal way. However, the current conditions were so bad in the store, I felt I had to speak up for my coworkers.

The place had never looked gloomier: It was a morgue of melancholy faces and overall depressing energy. Whispers of unhappiness floated across every department. If it wasn't NATs and renters emptying out their closets and car trunks, it was the lack of buying custys and new merchandise to seduce them with. Salespeople were struggling to get sales and being fired left and right. Some were newbies left over from the holidays, but a few had long histories at The Big Fancy. The lucky ones got sales with low returns and didn't misfire. That was how you survived at The Big Fancy during slow times.

For most, if you had three bad selling periods in a row and you didn't meet volume expectations, you were terminated, regardless of how long you'd worked at The Big Fancy. Poor Lisa in Hosiery got canned, and half the store employees and many custys were crying over her departure. Lisa was crying. Her manager was even crying—because she didn't want to do it. But there was one person not crying—The Big Fancy high priestess, Suzy Satan. It was well known throughout the store that she'd issued forth the firing with the attitude "let's make an example." Lisa was an amazing, personable salesperson with a great custy clientele, and she'd been a Super Seller and a Super Star in her Big Fancy past. But unfortunately for Lisa, she had three crappy selling periods in a row during a slow part of the year. And when you work on the sales floor at The Big Fancy, you are only as good as your last sale. Not your next one. The obstacles to success at The Big Fancy were insurmountable at the moment.

It was taking a toll all over the store. I could almost hear Suzy Davis-Satan screaming from her Mount Fancy lair: "If they misfire, they're horrible salespeople, and I don't want them here! Off with their incompetent heads!"

While salespeople were scared of losing their jobs, managers were also shaking in their dress shoes for fear of being fired if they didn't follow Satan's decrees and the corporate guidelines. Managers had to fire people even when they believed those people were doing a good job and were an asset to the company. It was full-on retail hell insanity—a storewide meltdown caused by a company too blind to see that February is always a shitty month and perhaps they should look for another way to evaluate their employees' selling performance for one of the slowest quarters of the year.

So after consuming half a bottle of Jack Daniels, I wrote my Open Door letter to The Big Fancy, saying all that I felt was wrong and laying out my ideas to help fix the problems. The final manifesto was a lengthy document that, at its core, focused on how a commission sales structure fuels bad customer service at The Big Fancy. When you have departments overflowing with salespeople trying to provide the best service while desperately trying to sell like starving wolves, human nature kicks in, greediness and fighting ensue, and discontent *always* trickles down to the custys. But that's the problem here; The Big Fancy wanted packs of hungry wolves and ponds full of sharks because they believed that if you have sharp teeth and you're starving, you'll get more sales.

They want 100 Sherrys on every floor. A shark-eat-shark selling world!

I also spent a good portion of the letter going over how salespeople have no recourse when it comes to paying back commissions for merchandise custys used and returned. It's very hard to see the fairness in The Big F's taking back $34.56 in commissions for a $600 Burberry I sold three years ago.

Explain that one! I've forked out some pennies to Uncle Sam for taxes on $34.56. Are you going to reimburse me for that?

After recovering from one hell of a hangover, the next day I hand-delivered the letter to Mr. Lou at a town hall–like meeting in Beverly Hills. Thankfully, he didn't open the letter right there, and Cammie was with me to keep me from throwing up the whiskey stomach.

Three days later I had the opening shift. I arrived a bit early, so I decided to do some countertop cleaning. The phone rang. I always hated the fact that The Big Fancy would put custys through even though the store was closed; so many bloodsuckers would find out and call just to ruin our mornings by chatting us up and putting us behind in stock and floor moves.

I delivered my greeting with trepidation. Luckily I had stayed true to Big Fancy phone expectations by answering quickly and correctly, because this was the response on the other end:

"Hello, Freeman, this is Mr. Lou up in Seattle, how are you this morning?"

I have to say, not only did I almost shit my pants, but I almost tinkled too.

I'd heard of Mr. Lou calling salespeople on the floor before, but this was a first for me. I also got the creeps a little—the Big Brother kind of creeps! How did Mr. Lou know I was here this early? Does he see me on camera? Maybe he could watch any department in the whole company.

I wouldn't put it past The Big Fancy to have that kind of watchful eye.

"Hi, Mr. Lou, thanks for calling me," I said nervously.

What else can I say? "Are you going to fire me for walking through the Open Door?"

"I wanted to thank you for your letter and give you a jingle," he said.

How kind of you. I am impressed you have opened the door.

"Your letter was really, really well written. Wow. What a great writer you are," he started.

And here comes the but . . .

He went on to say that I'd made some very interesting points, but overall he didn't agree with me on any of it. The Big Fancy was at the mercy of the return just as much as the salesperson was, and he felt the commission structure was what created great service and gave employees a chance to make more money than they normally would (unless you are a goldfish instead of shark).

On the subject of our having to eat our commissions from old sales, he said, "The whole point of a sale is making it stick. If something gets returned, you do have the opportunity to sell it again."

Unless it looks like it fell into the Bengal Tiger exhibit at the San Diego Zoo!

"Not if the bag is used," I replied. "You guys in Corporate can do plenty with it, including writing it off, but what is the recourse for us salespeople?"

"Well, you are wrong about that Freeman, The Big Fancy loses. We have to damage it out."

And use it as a write-off . . .

"Exactly!" I said getting frustrated. "What can I damage out to get my commission back or at least not pay taxes on it after you've already taken it back from me!" I pointed out that two big chain stores had stopped taking commissions back from employees on things older than a month.

"I find that hard to believe," said Mr. Lou. "You're sure?"

Yes, frogman, I'm sure!

"I verified those facts, Mr. Lou, with friends of mine who work there, and the information is correct," I replied, figuring it didn't really matter.

"That's interesting," he said. "I'll pass the information on to Sandra Cartlidge, the HR president."

Oh, I know the bitch. And I know what she'll do with it: press DELETE.

So there it was. Just as I thought. Nothing was going to happen. The buck was getting passed. The Big Fancy knew exactly what they were doing, and asking for employee feedback now seemed entirely like a PR ploy.

We care about you and want to hear what you have to say! Our door is always open!

The Big Fancy's Open Door was indeed open; it's just that it opened up to an empty broom closet.

Minutes later I heard Maude's name paged. I suddenly realized I'd better tell her about the letter, just in case it got back to her.

When I saw her coming down the aisle, my heart broke instantly. She looked so refreshed after two days off, with new hair, a gorgeous cream-colored suit, and a bright, relaxed smile.

And I was about to nuke it all with my news of Mr. Lou.

"Did you just love the Oscars last night?" she said, starting the register-opening process on the computer. "I thought Halle Berry was stunning! Gwyneth Paltrow? She looked like a trollop . . ."

I had completely forgotten about the Oscars. And I didn't have the heart to tell her that Mr. Lou and I had just had our own showdown, and it wasn't over designer gowns. Just as I was about to answer her about Gwyneth's horrid dress, the phone rang. Maude quickly picked up and delivered an upbeat greeting.

"And a good morning to you, Suzy," she replied, still looking happy and content.

Seconds later her blissful face crumbled like a fast-moving avalanche, and she shot me an Ice Queen look that could have turned me to Lucite.

Shit! Word travels fast at BFHS. You dumbass, Freeman. I guess you forgot that Big Fancy's Open Door does lead somewhere: ruining a stressed-out department manager's day.

With Maude's Oscar morning afterglow now completely gone, I only had one idea that would save my ass from the aftermath my letter to Mr. Lou would cause.

I ran to the Coffee Bar.

There was just enough balance left on my Big Fancy credit card to purchase a large black coffee and a muffin. I would need all the ammo I could dig up to ease the hell Maude would face when she took that trip through Suzy Davis-Johnson's open door to discuss why Freeman was so unhappy he was sending complaint letters to Mr. Lou.

I prayed they had her favorite, double chocolate chip.

★

The mind-numbing, brain-melting second quarter was finally over, and I was none too glad. I was so exhausted from the pressure in the store, I had no energy or motivation to write anything. The pages in my journal even remained empty. Inspiration seemed like a million miles away. When I wasn't on The Big Fancy *Titanic*, all I wanted to do was hibernate away, read, go to movies with friends, and sleep. Maude was in the same place. She took some much-needed time off with her dogs, and drove up the coast. Cammie was spending her break drawing bag designs and shopping for fabrics. "Do you think I can get The Big Fancy to buy them?" she asked, showing me one of her shapes that looked like a skull. "Are you sure you want to do that?" I replied. "You know, they return everything to the vendors that the custys return to us." Although there were enough meetings and training sessions to make my eyes bleed and ears fall off, we were all getting down time. But things in the department were heating up, and when Jeremy and I weren't there to add diplomacy and humor to the atmosphere, it turned into Bitch Fight Central. Sherry, Dok, and Linda Sue had all stolen custys or slacked off on duties, and Cammie, a well-seasoned salesperson, did not take shit from them. Apparently there had been a lot of screaming and crying going on in the stockroom.

And I know my girl Cam wasn't the one doing the crying!

The good news about the shark bitches was that Jeremy had stopped being Sherry's—he refused to open new accounts when she'd call him over; he even took to lying and pretending to have a phone custy!

Well done, Bag Boy! You're learning!

The sharks all survived the quarter with nice full bellies, while the boys had dropped to the bottom of The Big Fancy Sea, like snail food. We got trampled. And of course, we had to hear about it from Satan and the buyers. "Why are the men's sales so low?"

So the fuck what? Do I really want a 31 percent again? It scares me, actually.

There were no more Big Fancy visitors, thankfully, but when the store had its worst month in a year, Suzy's morning PA tirades were out of control: *"People will get terminated if they don't start making their goals! Misfire is at an all-time high!* Start calling those personals, reel them in off the aisle. Pressure turns a lump of coal into a diamond, you guys!"

Not in Broken-Down Burbank, Satan! We are still coal here.

One day Roach stopped by when Maude and I were off and apparently flipped out in every shade of color that Ferragamo makes. Immediately she made Sherry, Dok, and Linda Sue move the entire Handbag Jungle around to suit her liking. Cammie and Jeremy escaped the sweaty exhausting disaster because they were closers, but Cammie called Maude at home and told her what had happened. Maude called me next, and I said, "Hell, yeah, I'll go in early and change what the Roach did!" The next day all three of us went in and moved everything back.

Fuck you, Roach!

Her junkyard displays lasted less than twenty-four hours. The best part was that we went in early with lattes and bagels and listened to Cher on our own portable CD player while rearranging the cases. When you're dancing just as fast as you can at The Big Fancy, it helps to have fun people to do it with.

2nd Quarter Sales Associate Rankings

Sales Associate	Year-to-Date Volume
Sherry	$115,278.12
Dok	$103,467.90
Cammie	$100,982.67
Linda Sue	$97,450.73
Freeman	$96,382.82
Jeremy	$48,908.76

The Big Fancy

Freeman Hall
Handbags
Burbank

Dear Freeman,

What happened? Where is my Super Seller? You
dropped $25,000!!! Eeeks! You can still catch up
with the July sale. I'm sure Brandi can help you
get your selling mojo back. She's holding selling
intensives for those behind in Super Seller. Just
give her a jingle! I'm sure she can help you get
back on track.

Sincerely,

Suzy Davis-Johnson

SUPER SELLER

Blood on the Sales Floor

Harpooning a Shark in Heels

"Shit on a handbag cracker! What the fuck happened in here?!" My Shoposaurus custy, Lorraine Goldberg, was standing on the hard aisle clutching her Fendi satchel. "The place looks like the motherfucking Salvation Army!"

My disappointed Shoposaurus was right.

Our Summer Clearance Sale had turned into a Summer Crap Sale.

Everything we had to offer the ravenous Discount Rats looked like handbag turds.

Handbag turds on a cracker, as Lorraine would say. A stale, broken cracker.

The Handbag Jungle's sea of wooden sale tables were loaded with tired summer fare that everyone had seen before or already had something similar in their closet; it was repetitive, boring, microfiber shapes in every color and size you could imagine, tacky-looking straw bags that looked like they'd come from the dollar store, several tables of big canvas beach-like totes, a bunch of tables holding a few new markdowns of ugly stuff, and then more clearance that wasn't selling. The Handbag Jungle looked like a Labor Day garage sale.

In the front was our wallet sale table, and Lorraine did actually pick up four cute Isabella Fiore cosmetic bags, saying, "At least Terri has good taste! Not like those other cocksuckers!" Terri was our wallet buyer, who—unlike the handbag buyer—did care about us and tried to get us good merchandise and vendors we asked for. She got along famously with Maude, and it showed. We always did good business in wallets, even when we were tanking in handbags.

This year's Summer Clearance Sale was turning out to be the worst of Maude's career at The Big Fancy. Used to working in busy stores with lots of fabulous merchandise, she'd never had a sale bomb so badly on the first day—a 23 percent decrease, missing the day's goal by thousands.

Well what do you expect, Big Fancy? You have buyers with a hard-on for ugly straw that nobody wants! That ain't the road to Super Seller!

The store was on the same deadly path as the leather jungle, having hit similar merchandise icebergs in some of the big money-making departments like Women's and Men's Shoes. The morning after the first-day sale tragedy, Suzy Davis-Johnson had given an extra-long rally talk. Like all of us, she was clearly out of her mind with exhaustion and disappointment, but with Satan's anxiety, that was letting crazy out of the cage. She paced the rally floor ranting, "It's the Chi! I'm telling you right now. The Chi is not right in this store! It's why I yell so loud and have such a sour puss, you guys! Don't you want to see my sweet side? The Chi is not right, my friends, and we need to find a way to change it!"

It won't be with our crappy sale bags, Satan!

But Satan also knew our bags were horrible. She almost always bought something from Cammie, but she said the same thing a hundred other custys had said when they walked in that morning: "I don't need another canvas or straw bag."

"Exactly," Maude had replied to her. "How do I come up with fifty grand of volume sitting on straw nobody wants?"

"You'll find a way, Maude!" said Satan, trying to act positive in the face of disaster.

At The Big Fancy they always believed you were capable of turning water into wine.

And Lorraine wasn't the only custy to comment on the awful merchandise. Virginia said everything was so ugly she wouldn't have bought it even if she'd wanted to, Bee and Darlene couldn't find anything to put on hold, and even Mrs. Green walked past without stopping (which I was thankful for).

The Summer Clearance Event was turning out to be a disaster, not just for Maude, but for her salespeople as well. No one even cracked $8,000 on the first day. Sherry was first, of course, with $7,900; then Maude, with $7,300; and then me, with $7,000 (because of Lorraine). Cammie almost hit seven, and Linda Sue and Dok were right behind her in the sixes. Poor Jeremy didn't even crack four for his first clearance sale. The result was lots of fighting over custys and a pathetic kind of desperation that saw screaming and tears in the stockroom over cheap sale bags worth less than $100. The Big Fancy Summer Clearance Event was sinking, and the salespeople of Broken-Down Burbank were starving.

And with Suzy's Chi not quite right, it was no surprise we were having more blood on the floor than usual during a sale. We constantly stepped over each other and custys, snapping and bitching. "I was waiting on her," "She's *my* customer," or "Are you waiting on two people at once?" There was jealousy nearly every minute. Linda Sue complained about Maude being a shark: "She stands at the bay entrance scooping up all the customers!" I reminded LSD that Maude and I had both been trained as managers to be in the middle of the department or on the hard aisle watching custys so they could get help. Linda Sue's MO was to lean at the counter, socialize, and comment on cute babies; she wanted the sales to come to her.

Not such a smart plan when you work in a shark pond, LSD!

So with everyone running on empty and sales and moods down, the sharking was way more intense than usual. I reached my harpoon moment with Sherry on a Tuesday after the first weekend of the sale. It started with Sharky asking me to do her stock work that morning. New Coach had arrived, and it was her responsibility because Maude had assigned us each a vendor. Sherry claimed she had allergies and wasn't feeling well, so being the good Boy Scout that I am, and wanting to change the Chi in the store, I decided to have some human compassion and help Sharky.

I went into the stockroom and spent a good half hour unwrapping several boxes of new Coach. We needed to get them out for the sales. The manager in me was also in save-the-department mode while Maude wasn't there. Some juicy Coach sales were what we needed at that moment! But my road to good Chi ended quickly when I came out of the stockroom lugging the bags like a tired donkey with too much load.

Sherry was over at the main bay surrounded by three custys.

That sharking whore bitch!

The minute she saw me, she said, in her best ass-kissing voice, "Freeman! I have a customer for you!"

I dropped the bags in a pile near the Coach shop and approached. Of the three women at the counter, I recognized the one Sherry had been helping for some time; she was buying a sale Kenneth Cole satchel and wallet. The lady next to her didn't have anything that I could see, and the woman next to her didn't either. But this last lady looked like an unfriendly Meryl Streep character mash-up of *The Devil Wears Prada*'s Miranda meets *Iron Lady* Thatcher. Although I'm a huge fan of Meryl, this hellish hybrid of her was not someone I wanted to help right before lunch on an empty stomach! The snooty hag would probably send me to the hospital. I felt it in her stare.

Whatever was going on at the counter with Sherry was bad, I was sure of it, but the only thing on my mind at that moment was French fries at the Golden Arches, a nap in my car, and how I could get those two things as fast as possible.

I turned to the friendlier-looking woman and asked, "Were you next?"

"Oh yes, thank you, but she took my card. That's my bag over there," she said, pointing to a $400 Burberry practically hiding next to the register. "She said she would ring me up as soon as she was done. You can go ahead and help your other customer. I'm not in a hurry."

I could feel my face heating up. Not only was she a walk-up, but she was *nice*!

It may be a while, ma'am, because I'm going to murder my coworker!

Sharky Sherry had not only doubled up custys and snatched a walk-up for herself, but the snake was about to give me a scary-looking custy who should have been hers to begin with because Burberry Woman was next!

It's a good thing the stapler is at the other register bay, Sherry, because I'd be using it on your head right now, you fucking bitch!

"So you're waiting on this customer too?" I confirmed with intentional sarcasm.

"Yes," she said. "You were in the back."

It took everything in me not to stab the conniving shark with the pen she was holding.

I wanted to unleash all over her, but having been a manager with plenty of Big Fancy drama experience, I held my tongue. I knew I'd be in just as much trouble for causing a scene in front of custys. I did, however, decide right then and there it was going to be the last time I would ever be Sherry's bitch in the stockroom again. She wanted to play dirty at The Big Fancy, no problem. If that was how our shift was going down, so be it. The only way to beat a great white shark on the sales floor is to become one yourself.

Get ready, Sherry, because I'm out for blood and I'll harpoon your ass!

"Excuse me," said Evil Authoritarian Meryl Streep. "Are you going to assist me, or do I need to call for someone else?"

Her pinched, unhappy face told me Miranda Thatcher was not messing around. I presented her with my best shit-pleasing smile. "How may I help today, ma'am?"

I hope you brought your Black Amex, and you're planning to spend big!

Evil Meryl pulled out a shoebox from a Saks shopping bag and removed a crystal-studded evening heel from a silver cover. "Stuart Weitzman. I need an exquisite bag to go with it."

Hallelujah! Praise Suzy Davis-Satan and the Sale Gods! Evil Meryl has been shopping with the stars! And she sounds loaded. Sherry, you are about to be outsold. You can have that Burberry walk-up!

Before I could charm her with my free personality and years of knowledge, Evil Meryl got nasty, turning into Miranda Priestly. "The color has to be exact. I won't settle for something that is not a designer, is a tad off, or doesn't look right. Do you know your stock well enough? Or is it better for me to get one of the women to wait on me?"

Fuck me with an exquisite handbag! A Shark and a Sea Hag all in one morning.

"I'm pleased to help you, ma'am. I know the shoe well. I have a customer who has it in four colors, and it just so happens we have a Stuart Weitzman bag that matches. Let me show it to you."

Demeaning Sea Hag or not, I will find you the bag of your sewage-filled dreams.

Evil Meryl transformed right before my eyes—like the amazing actress does on screen—and quickly became Angelic Meryl. I caught a stunned and somewhat jealous look on Sharky's face. She knew the bag, too.

The price tag: $900.

Now at this point in my shark tale everything would appear to be turning in Freeman's favor for a big sale win! Here you have a snooty woman in designer clothes with a Saks shopping bag holding a $400 pair of shoes and wanting a matching bag that by some win of Broken-Down Burbank's Shitty Lottery, we actually have in our evening-bag case.

But looks can be deceiving.

And everything can go straight to retail hell in a matter of minutes.

Evil Meryl turned out to be Discount Rat Meryl. Upon closer inspection, the Saks shopping bag was old and tattered and from a holiday of years gone by, the box was from a designer discount store, and apparently so were the shoes—at the drop-dead bargain of $39.99.

When I revealed the price of the matching handbag, not only did she bellow out, "*Nine hundred dollars* for *that*? Is Stuart out of his mind?" but she had to run straight into the custy crazy zone by bitching, "I cannot begin to comprehend why you do not have this bag on sale, while I got the shoes at an outlet store! Surely this is a missed markdown. I do believe you need to call your manager!"

I tried to explain to her that the bag was brand-new and all the rest of the designer bullshit that confuses custys, but she just kept squawking about how it should be on sale. Finally I got her to see that even if it were on sale at a 50 percent discount she couldn't afford $450. She eventually gave in. "I guess you're right. I might consider it at 75 percent off, but I know the store doesn't go that low." My worst bloodsucking nightmare followed as she attached herself to me like so many sale-seeking D Rats have done when they want to thoroughly scour every nook and cranny of the Handbag Jungle in search of the lowest price.

I was doomed.

For the next forty-five minutes, my stomach growled while I dragged Cheap-Ass Meryl around the department trying to find her something affordable. I eventually got her into an Allure clutch for fifty bucks. It was a shade off and not a high-end designer. Discount

Rat Meryl would just have to fake it. During my bloodletting, Sherry nabbed several more sales and had time to remerchandise the Coach shop with the new styles. I was sure she'd get praised for it all, too—until I told Maude what really happened.

The Big Fancy was a shark's world; they rarely paid for the injustices they brought upon others.

As soon as Ratty Meryl was out of my sight, I checked our numbers. Sherry was over two grand and I was at the whopping total of $132, which included an exchange Sherry was forced to do correctly while I was in the stockroom.

I had to get the hell out of there before I turned into the Hulk of the Handbag Jungle and started pounding my fists and throwing things around in a rage. Sherry knew I was pissed, and of course she had to walk right up to me and confront the issue, acting nonchalant, like she'd done no wrong.

"Sorry about the Burberry. That lady had come back from earlier in the day. I didn't want to bother you in the stockroom until the older woman showed up."

I could have hit her with a nearby jar of leather lotion.

"Come back from earlier"? Are you fucking kidding me? "Until the older woman showed up"? Don't you mean to say, "Sorry, I was stealing a sale when the Sea Hag attacked"?

"I'm going to lunch," I said without looking at the greedy whore.

★

After an hour of attempting to recover my mood with French fries and bookstore wandering, I was on my way down to the department ready to sell like a day trader when I ran into a custy of mine I had helped many times. She'd been looking at a $400 Longchamp for a week now, and she'd promised to come and buy it from me. As luck would have it on this ass-biting day, Sherry helped her make the purchase while I was at lunch. The sweet custy said that she told Sherry I'd been helping her and she should make sure I got the credit, and she said to say hi! My custy said Sherry's response was, "Will do!"

I believed that about as much as I believe that gas prices will eventually go down.

Not going to happen!

That was it. If I could have roared like Hulk right then and there on the escalator and started tearing things apart piece by piece, I would have! Windows would be shattered and people would scream. My fantasy was short-lived because I kept the rage in my chest and marched fast into the Handbag Jungle.

Time to have it out with Sharky.

As I arrived at the counter I saw her helping Cammie's personal with one of the new Coach bags.

Fucking bitch! Now she's ringing up Cammie's custys. I bet she'll lie and say the woman didn't ask for Cammie, even though I know *she always does!*

The custy was leaving as I attacked Sherry, asking why she rang up a sale *my custy* wanted me to have! Just as I figured, douchey bitch said the custy never mentioned my name or that I'd been helping her. Then Sharky had the nerve to get angry with me. "You're just jealous because I've had a good morning and it was busy when you weren't around. You've been like that all morning. I don't need this attitude. Go get your own sales."

And with those grand exit words, Sherry stormed off to take her lunch.

For me it was war.

Although I seethed with shaking anger, my mind went to work looking for a way to get Sherry back. And it was not long before I found it.

While Sharky had been waiting on God and everyone—and I cut plastic tubing from the straps of Coach bags with broken scissors in the stockroom—she'd been asked by several custys to temporarily put DKNY bags on hold behind the counter. The problem was that she'd forgotten two important steps: to give the custys her name or a card and to write a proper hold tag.

You are about to be harpooned, Sharky! You lazy dumbass.

I dazzled the two custys with my charm and wit—right out of the ugly DKNY bags. They were delighted with the alternatives I suggested. Even though I was technically stealing Sherry's custys, I wasn't breaking any Big Fancy rule (just like Sherry wasn't by not calling me for the Burberry custy). Sharky hadn't even given them her name. I felt no guilt, only redemption. I had a great time with the women, netting $450 between the two of them, and it changed my mood and garnered me more custys as I crept past $1,000 in sales.

When Maude showed up after a managers' meeting and I told her the story, Maude went ballistic. Apparently, unbeknownst to me, maintenance needed to repair the shelving unit hosting the Coach bags in the stockroom. All the bags were supposed to have been moved to the basement stockroom. Maude had told Sherry this the week before, and she had agreed to do it, but like a true shark, it wasn't important to her. So she never got it done before the new shipment arrived. The problem went from bad to worse when I unknowingly added all the new Coach bags to the unit maintenance was fixing the next morning.

Sherry had retracted her fin when she came back from lunch.

"In the stockroom *now!*" Maude said with her "don't fuck with me" face.

I didn't see Sharky for the rest of the afternoon.

I rang up every sale I could.

★

As I trudged down Mount Fancy, nearly slipping in my worn-out dress shoes, I felt like a retail zombie—both emotionally and physically.

What a fucked-up sales war of a day! But aren't they all like that?

I hated working under conditions in an environment like that. Outside of The Big Fancy, I'm sure Sherry was basically an okay person. She had a daughter and a husband and I was guessing they weren't made-up people or aliens or something, *but you never know!* Sherry was money driven and heartless with her coworkers. The sad fact here was that The Big Fancy had created this selling environment that made people act horribly toward one another.

After the long hideous day, a six-pack and *South Park* were the cure I needed when I got home. I collapsed on the couch like a vampire without an appetite and did not move.

As my eyes grew weary, I fantasized about what Stan, Kyle, and Cartman would do if they were suddenly pitted against Sharky Sherry in the Handbag Jungle.

I fell into a deep dark sleep.

The sound of the ocean and seagulls surrounded me.

A blank white page. Followed by writing. My dreamland moviemaker is back.

A title appears.

JAWS 5: SHERRY ATTACKS

An original screenplay by Chief Freeman

The screenplay begins its magical writing without my lifting a finger . . . love those screenwriting elves!

FADE IN:

EXT. THE HANDBAG JUNGLE DURING SALE STORM—DAY

The SALE storm rages on at The Big Fancy, with the two handbag bays transformed into pirate ships surrounded by swirling bloody water. As lightning strikes and tattered sale banners blow in the wind, hundreds of Discount Rat custy fishes surround the sale tables and start digging.

SHERRY, DOK, AND LINDA SUE are in the bloody water swimming like real sharks circling the tables, waiting to eat, when a custy pulls away from her school. The sharks have huge black fins on their backs, and their mouths have been replaced by air-brushed shark mouths with razor teeth.

Also devouring custys are DONALD TRUMP, BANK OF AMERICA, and SUZY SATAN.

A custy enters the bloody river carrying a Kate Spade, and a SHARK FIGHT breaks out between Sherry, Dok, and Linda Sue.

They battle it out, snapping and snarling at each other, with Sherry overpowering the others.

Sherry then EATS Dok, Linda Sue, and the custy.

Suddenly ratty Mrs. Green lets go of the sale table, and Donald Trump and Suzy get into a nasty teeth-gnashing brawl over her cheap sale bag.

INT. HANDBAG BAY 2—DAY

FREEMAN and CAMMIE are dressed as Sale Pirates trying to reel in custys.

> CAMMIE
> That bitch better not swim over here! I'll bite her fat ass off!

> FREEMAN
> I don't know how much longer we can hold her back!

Just then CARTMAN, STAN, and KYLE from *South Park* appear on the handbag bay in miniature form.

> KYLE
> We got it! It was right where you said. In Two-Tone's office at the very bottom of the big file cabinet.

ANGLE—BOOK

THE BIG FANCY DEPARTMENT STORE EMPLOYEE MANUAL

> CARTMAN
> Let's harpoon that sharking whore.

> CAMMIE
> We don't have much time. They're eating everything, including each other!

> STAN
> Sherry is one fat-ass shark!

> FREEMAN
> So is Donald Trump!

Just then Trump EATS Mrs. Green and Suzy Satan at the same time. This is followed up by dessert at the wallet table, where Trump GOBBLES up at least sixty custys, including Virginia, who was just passing by and wasn't even buying anything.

Donald Trump's greedy feeding frenzy sends Sherry into a SHARK RAGE, and she ATTACKS him, scary jaws SNAPPING with jealousy.

Sherry EATS Donald Trump.

Suddenly Bank of America is in the bloody water
GOBBLING custys up like Pac Man right as LORRAINE swims
in, carrying a bunch of stuff from other departments
and calling out: "FRAAAAYMAN! I'm ready to shop!"

Bank of America heads straight for her, its blue and
white logo snapping hungrily!

                         CAMMIE
           Bank of Bastards is going after Lorraine!

Freeman takes the strap off a Dooney and Bourke and ties it
around an old broken brass handbag counter fixture holding
cheap evening bags. He hurls it at Bank of America like a
spear.

Bank of America devours the broken fixture and cheap evening
bags. It immediately starts to CHOKE before EXPLODING.

                         FREEMAN
           It's a good thing Bank of America can't handle
           eating worthless junk.

Freeman's momentary relief from saving Lorraine does
not last. Out of nowhere, Sharky is on Lorraine,
nibbling at her and the merchandise.

                         FREEMAN
           Sharky, I will kill you! *Noooooooooo*! Lorraaaaine!

Sherry EATS Lorraine. Smiles. Then BURPS.

                 KYLE (reading from the manual)
           I found it! The only way to harpoon and kill a
           Department Shark is to force it to eat the cheapest
           item the department sells. Once the shark has
           swallowed, it will gag because the item is not enough
           to sustain its greedy sharking appetite. It will then
           implode from the inside out!

                    STAN
    Dude, what's the cheapest thing you sell?

                    FREEMAN
    Coach leather cleaner? I think it's $5.95?

                    CAMMIE
    No, a plastic credit-card window [we called them
    windows] sleeve! They're only a buck!

                    KYLE
    That's it!

Freeman grabs one of the plastic window sleeves and
shoves it into a $3,000 Bottega Veneta designer bag.

                    FREEMAN
    This is one piece o' bag meat Sherry won't turn down.

JEREMY suddenly swims into the Jungle after his lunch
break. He doesn't even have a chance as Sherry attacks.

                    JEREMY
    Let go of me, shark bitch! I don't want to buy
    anything from you! *Aaaagh*!

Cammie freaks out, wanting to save Jeremy, and jumps
into the bloody water.

But it's too late. Sherry EATS Jeremy and grows even bigger.

Cammie swims over to Sharky, and they BATTLE it out
with shark jaws SNAPPING.

Sherry EATS Cammie.

                    STAN
    Oh my God, she just ate Cammie!

                    KYLE
    You fucking bitch, I mean *you bastard*!

                         CARTMAN
            That selling slut will wish she never did that.
            Suck my retail balls!

        CARTMAN THROWS the Bottega Veneta and Sharky's open
        snarling jaws catch it in one big hungry gulp.

        Suddenly Sherry stops, paralyzed. Confused. Her stomach
        RUMBLES.

                         FREEMAN
            Smile, you sharky son of a bitch!!!

        Sherry EXPLODES, and her blue blood rains down on
        Freeman and the *South Park* boys.

                         STAN
            Dude, this is pretty fucked up right here.

★

Even though I awoke craving a shower after being drenched in Sherry's blue blood, I felt relaxed and serene from the high seas monster fantasy with Cammie and my favorite boys.

What a good feeling to blow up that bitch!

★

When I returned to the war-torn Sale Jungle the next morning, Linda Sue had called in sick, which was the best news I'd had all week!

I'd rather work alone!

I had a quiet morning of unpacking a few new DKNY and Isabella Fiore bags and then taking care of some 50 percent markdowns that had just been released. Much to my delight, Suzy was off too, so there was no screaming over the PA about how horrible we were doing for this shitty sale. By the time the store opened I was in such a good mood that when the custy walked up to the counter to return something, I decided it wasn't going to ruin my day.

Little did I know it was going to *make* my day.

You see, the custy at the counter was Cammie's personal custy whom Sherry had decided to help by ringing up her Ferragamo.

Sharky, Sharky, Sharky, don't you know better than to steal sales from custys with personals? They will *always* return what you sold them because you are not their personal and they don't trust greedy sharking bitches like you!

"I decided to return it," the custy said. "Cammie knows my style best, and this just doesn't work for me."

That's what you get, bitch! Harpoon initiated!

I was thrilled to do this return on Sharky. And that wasn't even what made my day.

This was:

One thing Cammie's custy did like and collect was Isabella Fiore. She decided to take one from the new collection I'd just put out! Unlike Sherry, I did not ring it up for myself, because in the handbag sea we aren't all sharks, and that's how we cool fishies swim.

$500 sale for Cam!

Attack of the Monday Crustys

Working on Mondays at The Big Fancy was always horrible.

But today was extra horrible with a sale cherry on top because it was the day after the godforsaken Summer Clearance Sale. In the end, Broken-Down Burbank took a sale nosedive and burst into 10 percent decrease flames. A bunch of departments went belly-up, including the Handbag Jungle. After weeks of working such long exhausting hours, it was all over, and The Big Fancy had hit full-on bitch mode.

Everyone was cranky.

The minute I came off the escalator, cranky Satan took to the PA: "Oh my gaaaaawd! What happened, Burbank?? The sale was a disaster! The store dropped a hundred grand! I'm having a heart attack, you guys! We need to react! We are having an extended managers' meeting today! I want a plan from each of you managers on what you are doing to *recover.* Thank *gawd* our big sale is coming, but seriously, you guys! We *have* to have increases! No excuses!"

And that right there was what made Maude cranky.

"That fucking Suzy," she groaned. "Now I have to write a recovery plan? I haven't recovered! The stockroom is breeding microfiber and straw that nobody wants. Is that my fault? We all worked our asses off for the sale!" She clutched her manager's day book. "I better go dream up some bullshit thing to tell Suzy. I'll see ya later. Oh, and Linda Sue will be here for mid-shift."

And that right there will be what makes Freeman cranky.

But unfortunately it caught up to me way sooner, because the cranky virus had spread, and we now had a full outbreak at The Big Fancy.

The phone rang. It was one of the handbag buyer's assistants calling to spew crankiness all over Maude by telling her we had to send merchandise out because we were now overbought, and they were going to pull some Coach units from our store.

The hell you will! The only place our Coach is going is in shopping bags with our custys!

Coach was our bread and butter. Besides Kate Spade, it was the only vendor we had decent stock on. Now I was cranky.

I let her have it, unleashing a firestorm of crankiness right at her through the phone. "Are you kidding me? There's no way in hell you're getting any of our Coach! You've already bled us dry!" It would probably get back to Suzy that I got cranky with the buying office, but Satan would commend me for saving the Coach, that much I knew.

In the end I gave her one more shot of cranky by hanging up on her.

I'm a cranky goner now. There's no recovering from a buyer wanting to gut you.

Jose got on the PA next: "Will everyone please stop dumping trash in front of the bin! Throw it inside! How hard is that?!"

Jose's right, dumbasses! Help the dude out! He's by himself. Right there with you, buddy! Cranky as hell.

Across the aisle crankiness overflowed as the Women's Shoes manager admonished his team for missing the sale and sentenced them to bring out extra pairs of shoes for every custy they waited on.

Ouch! There will be a lot of cranky salespeople over there!

The phone rang again. It was Roach, and she wanted to talk to Maude—or should I say, spray crankiness all over, instantly spouting off to me, "We need to come up with a sale recovery plan. Tell her to send me an e-mail with her thoughts."

Her thoughts will be "fuck off," I can tell you that right now, Roach!

Then over the PA we were treated to crankiness from Alexis the Cosmetics manager: "Whoever is leaving fixtures in our stockroom aisles, stop it! We are getting in trouble for *your* laziness!"

Super cranky! Wow, Alexis. It's probably your stock girl! We poor departments aren't privileged like you. Many of us have to do stock work on our own!

Crankiness came at me from the hard aisle as Two-Tone Tammy waved me over at the counter on her way to the Coffee Bar. "Freeman, there are still a lot of Cosmetics girls sneaking in through the curtain. If you see any of them, make them use the stairs and tell me their names."

Dream on, Gestapo bitch!

"Sure, Tammy," I lied with a big shit-eating smile.

How cranky is she?!

Two-Tone was no sooner bellied up to the bar ordering her triple mocha when one of the Cosmetics girls I recognized pulled the very stunt that made Tammy cranky.

I waved her over.

"Be careful, Tammy almost saw you!"

At least one person had been spared the cranky virus. But she's so stupid, it will probably get her before the store opens.

The girl thanked me and scurried on to her department. This made me feel good, and for a few minutes I thought I might recover in spite of the Coach incident. But Cranky Monday at The Big Fancy was still in my face.

Richie in Customer Service joined the cranky PA lineup with: "I want to make it clear to all of you, you should not be sending customers to Customer Service. You are supposed to handle all problems in your department. That's why we give you the tools."

Hey Asshat, my chainsaw broke. Got a new one?

More live-action crankiness arrived along with Gestapo bitches Brandi and Stephanie. They had created a Compliance Blitz Squad and were hitting every department in the store, ruining the mornings of many by handing out chargebacks.

The Cranky Squad!

I started to sweat when I saw the Compliance Torpedo coming toward the Handbag Jungle, but thankfully, they left a chargeback for Linda Sue and not me.

She will be cranky over that, no doubt, when she shows up!

I felt relieved at ducking a compliance missile as they quickly left to bomb Women's Shoes with chargeback crankiness.

As Denise from Customer Service announced that we were open for the day (with no crankiness, I might add) and Fat Bastard Steve from Security pulled back the curtain, the first people through the doors were a handful of custys with sour faces clutching crinkled shopping bags full of things they no longer wanted.

An old lady came right up to my counter and said, "You opened late. Can't you people be on time?" and then she turned and continued into the store.

I looked at my watch. It was one minute past 10:00 A.M.

The custys were carrying the cranky virus! God help me!

Then another lady said, "Do you carry Luis Vuitton?"

Like nails down my cranky chalkboard.

"No, I'm sorry, ma'am, we don't," I replied, trying not to sound cranky.

"This store doesn't have anything. I don't know why I come here," said the custy, taking the bus straight into Crankytown.

Why do I even try to be nice?

Then the phone rang.

"I'd like to speak to Jenny," said an older voice.

"We don't have a Jenny," I replied.

"Yes you do! I just spoke to her three minutes ago—are you an idiot? Why are you answering the Handbags phone?"

After pulling the phone away from my ear, I said calmly, "What store were you calling?"

A big sigh on the other end was followed by "Pasadena, of course! Are all of you people morons?"

Apparently our cranky operators transferred her to the wrong store.

"Ma'am, this is Burbank."

∗Click.∗

Take that, you cranky custy bitch!

Cranky Monday with the custys had officially begun.

∗

It was no secret in the Handbag Jungle that weekday mornings belonged to the older custys.

Like the living dead, they are either out walking the mall for exercise or just up early looking for someone's blood to suck, like Virginia does on a daily basis. On days when the crankiness virus has taken over The Big Fancy, you can bet the custys coming through the door will be infected with it also!

And when you have cranky custys, you've got *crustys*!

My first crusty of the day was a petite old lady who was digging around the Dooney and Bourke bags. She appeared grandma sweet enough until I said, "Hello, how are you this morning! Those Dooneys are beautiful bags!"

"Can't you people just leave me alone and let me shop without stalking me!" screamed Crusty Grandma, almost causing me to wet myself in shock.

That's Satan's doing, not mine! She wants us to approach within thirty seconds and date you!

Crusty Grandma walked away, muttering, "Greedy salespeople in this store. . . . I should complain."

Please do! I'd much rather not have to talk to your crusty self at all!

Minutes later I got another crusty with a handbag repair.

If there is one obstacle besides a shark that can keep you from getting sales, it's having to help a custy with a repair. We do local repairs, where the custy pays (sometimes), and we do vendor repairs, where the products are sent back to the manufacturer. The reason bag repairs suck and we all want to avoid them is that more times than not they end up being horrible bloodsucking dramas that take away from selling. It takes time to write up a repair and discuss it, and then when the customer comes in to pick up the repaired product, she has to check it out and then sometimes pays—or not. It never fails. The minute a repair walks up, so does a sale that goes right into the mouth of Sharky!

Because you know it: That bitch never does repairs.

"I need to have my bag repaired, and I hope there is no charge!" said the crusty.

"Mostly likely not, Ma'am," I replied, taking out a repair slip as she plopped a crumpled heap of leather on the counter. When I unraveled it, the bag turned out to be an old Perlina.

"It really hasn't worn well considering I paid over two hundred dollars for it," the crusty whined. "I mean look at it . . . the hardware is tarnished, the lining is ripping. It should be sent back to the manufacturer."

I should send you back to your momma, you lyin' crusty!

The Perlina bag retailed for $49.99 at a clearance sale when I was at The Big Fancy the first time around. I recognized it from my handbag nightmares.

"Ma'am, this bag is years old and it wasn't two hundred dollars," I said, hopping on my very own cranky train. "I *remember* it. But I'm happy to repair it for you for free."

Crusty eyed me, ready for a cranky fight, and then said, "I suppose, as long as there is no charge!"

While I was writing up the crusty for the repair, another crusty walked up nearby. She wasn't there a minute before she said, "I've been waiting for ten minutes; isn't there anyone else that can do my exchange?"

Crusty bitch! You ain't been waiting ten minutes. You just walked up! Fuck you!

"Hosiery," I said, all cranky, not looking up from the repair form and perhaps writing a little bit more slowly.

As those crusty bitches left, a whole army of them followed right behind as I dealt with a tornado of cranky returns, questions, and phone calls.

"Why is the sale over?"

Because you're a whore.

"Are you sure you know what you're talking about?"

I'm sure I'm going to slap you.

"The scratch is really bad! Can't I have more than 15 percent off?"

NO! Because I'm in a cranky mood!

"Well, I've returned used stuff without a problem before."

And I'm sure you will do it again and again.

"Why is your hair so spiky?"

So I can stab hateful crustys.

"Sherry usually helps me, I'll come back for her."

I hope you'll return with her too.

"Your prices are too high."

Your eyebrows are too high.

And just as I was about to hang myself with that nasty broken Perlina bag from the top of a gold handbag tree, in walked Linda Sue spreading enough cranky cheer to close down the 405 freeway: "I told Maude I couldn't work on the sixteenth, and she has me scheduled. I wrote it in the book like she asks. I can't do anything right around here. She wants another fight, I'll give her one!"

"She's been working long hours because of the sale. I'm sure it was an oversight," I offered, trying to contain LSD's spewing crankiness.

"I doubt that," Bitchy spat over her shoulder as she walked away.

I didn't care what Linda Sue said. I realized at any second she was going to find the chargeback paper by the register with her name on it and freak the fuck out. With any luck she'd sail down the cranky river to Big Fancy hell all shift long.

The thought of it warmed my tired crusty-trampled heart.

Just another cranky Monday at The Big Fancy.

Now go away.

It's Raining Returns

Whether you were trying to make Super Seller or just pay the rent, on some days it just didn't pay to get out of bed—no matter how many times Two-Tone Tammy or Mr. Lou liked to say "The sky's your limit! Sell more! You can sell yourself to the raise you want!"

They just forgot to mention that on some days, The Big Fancy sky was definitely limited, and at times it could go completely dark with storm clouds and start raining returns.

Lots and lots of returns.

And like any bag forest being hit with torrential return downpours, the Burbank Handbag Jungle could completely float away.

Maybe it'll sink like the Titanic . . .

"I'd like to end the day with a dollar up if I could," said Maude, exasperated at the department figures on the register's monitor. We were going through one of the worst return storms ever on a Saturday at the end of June. Our normally strong weekend day sales went bust as a monsoon of returns caused negative waters to rise up, putting the department nearly $1,200 closer to flood level!

Have the band start playing! My heart doesn't want to go on.

"I'm going to get a latte. I feel like I've been drawn and quartered," announced Maude, after a custy returned a four-year-old Bally tote with a matching wallet because she never used them and got a divorce.

"Drawn and quartered? What does that mean?" I asked, unfamiliar with the term.

"It was a gruesome punishment in England," Maude explained as she walked toward the Coffee Bar. "I don't think you want to know the details, but it involves ripping out guts and chopping."

A daily occurrence here at The Big F!

I had a feeling it might involve some kind of torture, because that is what a rainy return day feels like. It never ends.

Seconds after Maude left for her fourth caffeine IV drip of the day, the phone rang. I answered appropriately in my best noncranky voice, even though we were *all* cranky.

My ear was instantly blasted: *"Free-man! What is going on in Handbags?"* It was Suzy Davis-Johnson. "You guys are down *huge* on the hour! The worst in the region. All the other stores in the region are on fire! Did we close the doors?"

No, Satan, we're still open, just giving the place away!

"Suzy, we've become return central, and a lot of it is coming from Hollywood and Pasadena!" I replied. Satan was having her usual effect on me, and I was losing my composure.

"Well, you need to sell more!" she whined. "*Push it, Freeman!* You've got to get sales moving!"

And how do you do that when it's raining returns? Kick out all the returners? Put on an Amex Gold dance party? Strip? I don't know, Satan, but I'm sure you'll tell me!

I was so glad Maude had left as I considered hanging up on Suzy's nagging ass. (I'd done it before.) All the executives of The Big Fancy acted like that when they saw rotten figures—they were spoiled little children throwing tantrums. They thought we were all standing around with our thumbs up our asses talking about movies and cute shoes.

I had sensed the approaching return storm and knew The Big Fancy sunshine was about to disappear for the day when I helped the first custy of the morning.

With a return, of course.

From ten years ago.

It was a shitty beaded evening bag for $36. Amazingly, the ticket was still attached, and the numbers on the back were handwritten and from my old manager General Judy. The short plain custy in her thirties also had an old $49.99 Perlina sale bag from a few years earlier, but it was the ten-year-old evening bag that set my entitlement balls on fire.

"But it's ten years old, ma'am, it's not even in our new system. Wouldn't you want to just donate it to a women's shelter or somewhere?"

"No, I want the cash," she said. "I cleaned out my dead aunt's closet and I know she would want me to get the money so I could pick out something nice for myself."

I had to pick my jaw up off the counter.

I spent the next few minutes trying to get her to see our side of things, but she would have none of it. She wanted her cash. So I returned it, using the ticket from a LeSportsac bag (because the price was close).

Thanks for stopping in, Returner of the Dead! We'll see you again soon, I'm sure, when you find another closet or dumpster to ransack.

After that return left us all scratching our heads, the deluge started, trapping Maude, Cammie, and me behind the bays doing one return after another.

There were a few minutes when we had at least four women lined up at the counter doing returns at the same time. And here's the shocker: They were all legit! No NATs or abusers, just indecisive people who had gone shopping at other Big Fancy stores in the region: Ventura, Sherman Oaks, Hollywood, San Diego, Brentwood, the list went on. Behind us on the bay's ledge near the register, we had to line up all the returned bags and wallets; they were being returned so fast, we couldn't put them away.

I was putting a ticket on a Coach return from earlier in the day as yet another woman approached the counter. I muttered to Maude, "What the fuck is going on today—we've become a dumping ground!"

"It's more like a landfill," she replied, grabbing several bags and wallets off the register ledge.

Then Cammie chimed in. "And if I get one more bitch telling me she only 'tried her shit in it once' I'm going to turn the bag inside out and beat her with it!"

"Amen to that," Maude agreed.

When I turned to help the new custy, to my quick horror, I realized I'd helped her recently and she was probably returning. I was a little put off because I remembered her and she'd taken forever to make up her mind. She was nice, though, and seemed to really like the black Longchamp backpack she'd ended up buying.

I guess she changed her mind.

Of course, even though I was frustrated that the return rains suddenly got personal, she had done nothing wrong, and her receipts and tickets were all intact.

And she hadn't used it. (This was unusual. She'd even kept it perfect in its cover!)

The custy apologized profusely and was really sweet, thanking me for the time I spent helping her. She also said she'd be back to get another bag and would for sure ask for me.

Wow, a nice custy! How warming on this rainy return day!

For several seconds my stormy-day blues dissipated. And then the Handbag Jungle was hit again. Cammie got a custy who wanted to return a Gucci she'd worn for several months. It wasn't in terrible shape, but when you're cranky from a Big Fancy return storm, you tend to get a little snippy. Cam told her, "We can't take this back. It's a designer, and it's been worn, and we can't resell it."

As expected, the Gucci bitch went postal, yelling back at Cammie, "You have no idea the drama this bag has caused me! It's ruined my life, and if you don't take it back I'll sue The Big Fancy!"

We normally laughed at custys who threatened to sue us like that, but Cammie said nothing. She just wanted the abusive bitch to leave. She finished the return and added it to the growing pile lined up on the counter.

Not all the handbags from our stormy Saturday were used or old. Some were perfectly regular, fair returns with receipts—with many coming from other stores. Returns from other stores could cause a Burbank manager to want to throw herself off the parking structure. They were deducted from your department's sales, no matter where they were purchased. In Burbank we were surrounded by Big Fancy stores filled with designers and styles we didn't have, so it made trying to dig out of the hole even more difficult. When a $900 Gucci got returned without our having one to sell in return, it was a long way to recovery.

As Linda Sue, Dok, and Sherry came in with sharking shovels ready to dig the Handbag Jungle out of the proverbial hole, the return rains continued to pour throughout the afternoon.

And so did the custys' excuses to get their money back:

"I want to return it because it hasn't worn well."

You mean like your face?

"It was a gift. My husband said he bought it here."

That's what they all say.

"I just fell out of love with it."

I hope you two found a good divorce lawyer.

"I bought it at one of your stores back East."

Then why the hell aren't you taking it back there?

"I'm tired of it."

I'm sure it's tired of you too!

"My husband didn't like it."

Well, don't let him use it!

"My daughter didn't like it."

Tell her to go to her room!

"My mom didn't like it."

Tell her to go to her room, too! Bad Mommy!

"I scratched it and I don't like how it looks now."

That's what plastic surgery is for!

"I need the cash."

Don't we all.

"I'm over my limit."

Aren't we all!

"I need vacation money."

And I need a lobotomy. Bon Voyage!

"I spent too much at the Hollywood store last night with my girlfriends."

That's what binge drinking will get you!

"I already have this one at home."

Please don't bring that one back too!

"I don't like how it's performing."

Well write a review and send it to the Burbank Press!

Yes, the returns poured and poured in the Handbag Jungle.

And even when it was merchandise that I knew wasn't from our store, the return custys didn't let up, begging just like the rats do. "Are you sure you don't carry it? I know it came from here! I've seen you guys return stuff you didn't carry before. You just put a ticket on it and sell it. Maybe that's what happened to me?"

Yeah, I'm sure that's what happened to you, you lying NAT!

I couldn't take the annoying chatter anymore, so I scanned another LeSportsac for $28 for the refund info and sent the little return snatch on her way.

The minute Jeremy walked in, a return custy caught him in her claws. She had a Furla bag with no ticket or receipt and a tirade about how the bag came from The Big Fancy's flagship store in Chicago. Barely conscious, Jeremy stumbled to the phone like a lost lamb holding the bag while calling another Big Fancy for a price check. He was trapped there for the next twenty minutes.

I saw it as an omen of how the rainy return night would play out.

So glad I'm leaving soon! I didn't bring my extra-tall rain boots or return slicker with hoodie!

Maude was showing signs of cracking all day long from the deluge of returns, but it was a nasty old cream-colored-turned-black Paloma Picasso bag from God knows where or when that sent her to walk the cranky plank with a custy.

"I'm not taking this back," she told the scummy returner. "You have no receipt, this must be ten years old, the gold is tarnished, and it's disgusting. We haven't carried this vendor in five years, and you could have picked this up at any garage sale!"

Well, Scummy Returner flipped her shit out and started screaming at Maude, "This is The Big Fancy! I can return whatever I want! I don't like your tone or accusations! I'm going to the store manager!"

And the whore did exactly that. Three minutes later, Suzy called and told Maude to take it back.

And the worst part?

Asshat Richie wouldn't do it in Customer Service, so Maude had to do the return at our counter with the nasty bitch standing over her saying snarky shit: "You really need an attitude adjustment. An older person should know better. And a manager at that!"

What we really need is some kind of ray gun that can disintegrate horrible nasty crustys like you! Hey Satan! Now you know what's going on! It's Bitch, Bring It Back Day at Burbank!

If I had any retail balls at The Big Fancy, I would have used them on that hag for sure, and told her to take her dumpster-diving ass outside before I folded her up and stuffed her in one.

We were all just beaten up from the day.

Our own personal numbers sucked for a Saturday. Maude had only rung up $476 (because she had been hit by returns and had to deal with them at the same time), I had $978, and Cammie had managed to push out $1,300—luckily the return downpour had not hit her number. Linda Sue had been swept away, getting slammed with $800 in returns; she was in negative numbers and acting just as bitchy as ever. Sharky and Dok had managed to ring only a few things and were circling nervously with their fins out.

By the time this drama cleared out, the department was still struggling and negative at −$2,200.

Our efforts to try to save the Jungle from decrease disaster totaled $4,598, which is a pretty amazing amount, considering 75 percent of the custys were returning items, but some of our sales had come from doing exchanges for things bought at other stores. On a day like this, it was one of the few tricks we had to make a commission at The Big Fancy.

But it wasn't enough. The Handbag Jungle's rainy Saturday from hell had us taking back almost $6,798 in returns.

If the night sharks could bring us up to zero before closing, it would be a miracle, but with the time approaching 5 P.M. and only four hours left till closing, there was little time for recovery. "I'm going to hide in the back and read my e-mails," sighed a frustrated Maude, "then slip out. I've had enough return hell for one day. You can go if you want."

I didn't have to be told twice. I ran to my personal drawer and grabbed the *Die Hard* DVD I had purchased on my lunch break for $4.99 at Tower Records. My return hell day was going to end with Bruce yelling, "Yippie-ki-yay, motherfucker" while I got trashed.

Just as I was slithering out of the Jungle near the back of the store by Hosiery, I heard a woman call out, "Wait a minute, sir, please don't leave!"

Damn. I can't even escape! I hope it's not another fucking return.

I was half right.

The woman calling after me was the Longchamp returner from earlier in the day.

Oh, fuck me! Please don't ask me to help you find a new bag—the return storm has literally kicked my ass, lady. I have nothing left. I need to go.

I was about to tell her this in a more professional way and use Suzy's strict rule regarding overtime, but what came out of her mouth was something unexpected.

"I'm so glad I caught you before you left," she said. "I just wanted to thank you again for helping me with that backpack. You spent a lot of time and I really appreciated your patience and I know The Big Fancy doesn't let you guys keep your commission on returns, so I wanted you to have this."

She then discreetly placed a folded $20 bill in my hand.

For probably the hundredth time that day, my mouth fell to the floor.

But for a different reason: it wasn't because of some vile, abusive, irresponsible returner. Here was someone who actually cared about the service we gave and the consequences we suffered personally when purchases were brought back.

The Big Fancy certainly didn't care; otherwise they would see value in the service we give and pay us for it rather than say, "Well, your commission has to get returned because the sale didn't stick." The truth was The Big F did not want to let us keep our commissions on returns probably because they wouldn't want to see us making more money. Greedy corporations never want to see their employees making a lot of money.

I almost cried.

In fact, I hugged the lady, which startled her at first, but then she hugged back. Every once in a while during a Big Fancy return downpour, a rainbow will present itself.

And here was mine.

When I got home, I thanked the retail gods once again while ordering Domino's pizza for my date with Bruce—my unbelievable reward from a custy who actually appreciated the service I'd given her.

I cheered Bruce on as he picked off the terrorists one by one.

Ten Minutes to Hell

The Big Fancy was trying to keep us from tearing each other's hair out and starting fistfights on the sales floor (except in Juniors). There was a selling regulation called the Ten-Minute Rule, which was supposed to protect salespeople from losing commissions on exchanges done at the hands of sharks.

Unless you worked with Sharky.

It was understood by all salespeople of The Big Fancy that if you weren't working when a custy came back in to exchange, it was almost certain you would lose your sale. There was no way to recover your loss, except to "Go sell something else!" as Two-Tone Tammy would say to anyone coming into her office to complain about working with a shark.

That's how it was at The Big Fancy.

It's a shark-eat-shark world!

Lucky for me, Maude didn't like to operate that way. In the old days, department managers were allowed to set up rules that required salespeople to save each other's sales when they weren't around, and it created a much more team-oriented environment. But over the years The Big F got greedier and produced more sharks. Managers were reined in and weren't allowed to implement department guidelines for saving sales. (Though Maude, Cammie, Jeremy, and I all agreed to save sales for each other. At least some of our hard-earned sales were being saved.) Mr. Lou's excuse for this policy was that saving sales caused too much employee theft.

It always mystified me how he could view our desire to keep a commission from turning into a return as "theft." Is this still America?

So The Big Fancy came out with the Ten-Minute Rule, which had more holes in it than SpongeBob. If a custy came in to exchange something that one of your coworkers sold her and she only wanted to trade color, shape, or size, so she didn't take more than ten minutes of your time assisting her, you were required by Big Fancy law to save your coworker's sale.

Yeah, there's always that ten-minute problem with this rule. There was no fair timekeeper to actually deliver a just decision on who got the sale. If there had been, I have no doubt many exchanges would have been saved at The Big Fancy.

But it was up to the word of the good salespeople themselves.

And for most sharks, thirty seconds = ten minutes.

Do you know how many lying salespeople an unmanageable rule like that creates?

Now, if that same custy had decided she needed you to hold her hand and give her a grand tour of the department, along with an hour of your fashion advice, the way Mr. Lou and The Big F saw it, you had every right to take that sale.

He sure as hell wasn't gonna let the original salesperson keep her commission.

"I had to take the sale, Linda Sue! The woman made me pull a bag out of the case! Sorry!"

"Sorry, Cammie, but she made me go back into the stockroom!"

"Jeremy, she return, so sorry. She no like what you sell. Take forever!"

"Sorry, Freeman, the customer bought something completely different from what you helped her with."

Yes, in the Handbag Jungle the Ten-Minute Rule got tweaked and abused pretty often, though I have to say none of the sharks would ever try anything with Lorraine. There were moments, but I'm sure they were shaking in their heels when I wasn't around to control my Shoposaurus.

But one day I was quite amused by a custy and her Kate Spade bag, and I had to chuckle at the Ten-Minute Rule.

She was wearing a sun hat and big sunglasses, so I didn't recognize her right away. She seemed pleasant enough, taking the Kate Spade bag from her shopping bag and explaining to me she had been having a terrible time deciding what color or fabric to keep.

You and half the women in Burbank. Don't feel bad!

It wasn't until she handed me the pile of receipts that I realized she was not kidding.

There were six receipts with five staples going through them.

Big Fancy salespeople workin' that Ten-Minute Rule!

As I lifted receipt after receipt my eyes went to the magical spot that held the employee number, and the rewrite merry-go-round went down like this:

Most recently Sherry had taken the Kate Spade from Dok.

A week before Dok had taken it from Jeremy.

And oddly enough, Jeremy had taken it from Dok a few days before that—she must have been pissed at Jeremy.

But Dok had taken it from Cammie.

And no big surprise here: Cammie had taken it from Linda Sue.

Then the moment of truth fell upon me as I lifted up the last receipt to see who Linda Sue had stolen it from and who the original salesperson was in all of this mess.

The number I saw was 441064.

Yours truly. Aww, fuck. I thought the bitch looked kinda familiar!

If you wait on enough exchangers at The Big Fancy, your sale comes back around to you!

At least for ten minutes.

Only this time I didn't want it.

And because Sherry was such a sharking bitch, I chose not to give it back to her either. I had to consider that it might stick. (Even though I was 99 percent sure it wouldn't.)

No, since Linda Sue had stolen from me in the first place and this exchange was within ten minutes, meeting Big Fancy guidelines, I decided the fair and honest thing to do was to give it back to LSD.

Don't say I never did anything nice for you, Linda Sue!

After the lady left, I made a copy of the receipt, drew a happy face, and put it in LSD's personal drawer.

I can be just as big a bitch as the rest of you!

All Phone Shoppers Should
Be Pepper-Sprayed

Avalanches of rent-a-bags, sharky bitches in heels, and bloodsucking crustys weren't the only obstacles I faced as a salesperson at The Big Fancy department store. One of the more heinous departmental expectations was something that anyone who works with the public knows all too well.

Dealing with the fucking phone.

Now, I'm not just being my usual emphatic self: *The fucking phone* is what we called it. The phone was so maddening to so many of us, when its shrieking wail went off like a broken record of an air-raid siren, what came out of our mouths when there weren't custys around were phrases like this:

"The fucking phone has not stopped ringing all morning!"

"I'm going to rip that fucking phone out of its socket!"

"Can you please get the fucking phone! I'm up to my ass in markdowns!" (That was Maude's favorite.)

"It's not my turn to get the fucking phone."

Yes, we never edited out our swear words when it came to bitching about the fucking phone. The time zapper would take us away from helping people in front of us who *actually* wanted to buy something. And it never failed to deliver a barrage of hair-pulling demands. If it wasn't another Big Fancy store wanting us to check on product availability for a customer, it was the buying office demanding some price be changed ASAP, or Suzy Davis-Johnson wanting to know why sales were lagging.

Very rarely did anyone actually win a big sale over the fucking phone. If that miracle happened, being the lucky recipient of an instant $2,000 Marc Jacobs phone charge was like winning the Super Seller Lottery (though it might end in disaster if that $2,000 Marc Jacobs turned out to be a charge fraud!).

When you work with a bunch of sharks in heels, the last thing you want to do is worry about answering that fucking phone. I totally get when someone needs to call the store with a legit question. But it's the shopping by phone that made me want to gargle with battery acid before I picked up a call. I'm not a help line. Not a catalog. Not QVC. And I'm sure as hell not clairvoyant.

"Good afternoon, Handbags. This is Freeman. Would you like to hear about our item of the day, the new Kate Spade pencil case, available in four different colors?"

"No, thanks," said a woman's voice.

"How can I give you outstanding service today?" I asked.

Suzy liked us to say that instead of "How may I help you?" She was setting us up for failure every time. *Thanks, Satan!* I've heard the phrase "Your service is far from outstanding" more times than I care to.

"Do you have a copy of the latest *Style* magazine?"

"Umm . . . no. Not on me," I replied.

"Well can you get one? There's a handbag I want to ask you about on page 347."

Ah hell. Why didn't I pretend not to hear the phone like Sharky Sherry always does?

A Phone Shopper was on the line.

"Hold on," I said, followed by a huge sigh.

Whenever I discovered a potential Phone Shopper on the line, I instantly initiated my Super Seller Fucking Phone Escape Plan. Over the years I developed several secret techniques: Hang up on the Phone Shopper by accident and then run away fast, so when they call back, I'm not standing there to answer. Or simply tell them, "I'm sorry, I can't help you right now—we are swamped with customers, and there's a line down the aisle, so why don't you come in, have a nice day, goodbye."

Unfortunately, my Fucking Phone Escape Plan does not always work, because when you have Boy Scout DNA pulsating through your veins, you are unexplainably drawn to help people, no matter how crazy.

"Do we have the current issue of *Style* magazine?" I asked Sharky.

"Right here," she replied, pulling the magazine out of a drawer and handing it to me. I opened to page three forty-seven and saw a full-page ad for a bottle of Poseidon perfume.

"Ma'am, there is no handbag on page three forty-seven."

"There has to be, I'm looking right at it."

"Well, I don't know what to tell you. I'm looking at Poseidon perfume."

"I *know* what I'm seeing. It's a *handbag* on page three forty-seven of *Style* magazine for March. Are you even on the right page?"

The Tele-Idiot was becoming testy.

A hunch told me to check out the date on our magazine.

April.

"Are you looking at the March issue?" I said.

"Yes! The current issue!" she howled.

"I have April. March isn't the current issue."

Dumbass Bitch. I love how the really dumb ones always get really angry.

"Well it's current to me. I don't have the April issue yet."

"We don't have the March issue," I said without bothering to ask around.

And if we did, I'd pretend not to see it!

"Then I'll just describe it to you," she replied.

Oh God, no!

My finger hovered over the disconnect button.

Screw the Boy Scout DNA. This is too much. I'll just lose the nutball. But she'll probably call back. And Sherry already knows she's my problem. Shit.

"It's a Coach bag. Do you carry Coach?" said Tele-Idiot.

"Yes, we do."

"The one in the picture is kinda medium size, hard to tell. Could be on the larger size. It's a tan-ish, golden brownish color, sort of bronze-ish, I can't really tell from the picture. There's some silver-ish studs all around."

I wanted to grab the used Michael Kors bag that was returned an hour-ish earlier and strangle myself with it. Thank God for the studs. At least I knew what collection the bag was from. "Sounds like something from his Bermuda collection. What's the shape? Is it a hobo?"

"What's a hobo?" said Tele-Idiot.

It looks just like your fat ass.

"It's a sack-like shape."

"Well, it's not really a sack, maybe a pouch. I can't tell if there is one strap or two and, oh, there's a buckle hook thingy on the front."

Time for a different approach. Or I'm going to beat my head with the phone.

"Is there a price listed?"

"Yes, it says three hundred ninety-eight dollars, but I don't want to spend that much."

Okay, now she's not making sense.

"Ma'am, if the price is three ninety-eight, then I'm sure that's what our price would be."

"I *realize that*," she said, getting testy again. "I want you to find me a less expensive Michael Kors that looks just like it or another brand that looks just like it."

Seriously? You want me to find you a Michael Kors bag that costs less than and looks like the Michael Kors bag pictured in a magazine that I can't see? Lady, are you bat-shit crazy, or is it temporary insanity? Why don't you call up the Dollar Store and harass them? I've had it.

"Please hold for a sec while I ask someone."

I put the phone fiend on hold. Sharky Sherry was busy helping real shoppers, probably devouring thousands, while I dealt with Tele-idiot. Oddly enough, I spotted a customer trying on the very bag I had a hunch Bat Shit was looking for: the Michael Kors Bermuda satchel.

I took this as a sign from the universe.

Ditch the phone bitch and make the switch. Before she bleeds you dry and your brain explodes like that dude's head in the 80s horror movie Scanners.

"I'm sorry, Ma'am, but I just asked my manager and she said those bags sold out nationwide last month. Must be because of *Style*. Sorry

I couldn't help you. Come in and check out the Michael Kors bags we have! Have a nice day! Bye!"

Before she could say "But wait, I . . ." my hand slammed the phone down and I ran off to wait on a live-and-in-person honest-to-god customer in the flesh.

★

Besides being bloodsucking pains in the ass, Phone Shoppers also loved to call up and ask, "Do you have the Coach patchwork satchel bag?"

"Yes, we do."

"Great, my name is Emily. I'm a few blocks away. I'll be there in fifteen minutes. Don't let that bag out of your sight."

The next day, the bag was still in my sight. Phone Shoppers constantly make promises over the phone they never keep.

Then there are the ones who are information hungry.

"Do you have the new Kate Spade diaper bag in pink and brown plaid?"

"Yes, we do. Just got them in! Would you like me to hold one for you?"

"Not yet."

Not yet? Oh no, there's more. Let the bloodsucking begin.

"I'd like to ask you a few questions first. Can you get a measuring tape?"

Measuring tape? Kill me now. Here it comes. Interrogation time.

"I want to know how tall it is and how long."

"Umm . . . okay. I'll be right back."

I retrieved the measuring tape and the Spade baby bag, and then measured it.

"Ten inches high and nineteen inches long," I told her.

"What about the sides?"

I measured them.

"Six inches."

"The straps?"

I measured them.

"About twenty-nine inches."

"The changing pad?"

I measured it.

"Twelve by seventeen."

"The inside zipper pocket?"

"You want me to measure the inside zipper pocket?"

"Yes. And the depth. I also want to know the full measurements on the bottle pockets, both the inside ones and the outside ones."

Why don't I just give Kate a buzz and have her fax you the fucking handbag pattern?!

I measured everything she wanted, which also included giving her the dimensions of the outside zipper pocket, the zipper closure on top, and the pom-poms dangling from the strap. But it didn't end there.

"Put the bag on your shoulder and tell me where it hits."

"I think it's going to hang differently because of my size."

"I know that, I just want an idea. Does the top go right under your shoulder or just below it?"

"Just below it," I said through gritted teeth.

After that, Phone Shopper wanted me to tell her everything I knew about the Spade baby bag. What collection was it from? What fabric was it made of? What did Kate name the bag? Was the inside lining cleanable? Was the plaid fabric cleanable? What should she use to clean it?

What the hell are we doing? Playing Cash Cab—The Handbag Department Edition*? No Cab, but plenty of custys with questions. Can I have my twenty bucks now, please?*

Finally I found an opening to close the deal.

"Would you like me to charge it to you or put it on hold?"

"No thanks," Phone Shopper said, "I just needed the information. I'm buying one on eBay for thirty dollars less than what you're selling it for."

Aaaaaaaaaaagh! I felt my face turn red and my chest rise. Next stop: my skin turning green and me ripping apart this baby bag like tissue paper!

It took everything in me not to call her names her unborn baby shouldn't hear.

★

There's no doubt that information-hungry Phone Shoppers are annoying, but the ones who want a Phone Shopping Tour of the Handbag Jungle can become truly mind numbing. They call up asking general questions, like they're deep-sea fishing and hoping to catch a swordfish in a pond full of crappies.

"I need a really beautiful dark handbag. It must be average size."

"Do you have something really gorgeous in stock?"

"Hi, I'm looking for a bag I can wear every day. What do you carry?"

"I'm looking for a purse with lots of pockets but not too many zippers. What might you have?"

These bloodsucking calls take place all day long.

★

Early one morning the mall gate hadn't even finished rising and the fucking phone rang with a crusty who won't soon leave my retail hell nightmares.

"Good morning, Handbags. Our item of the day is the new Juicy Couture French wallet that comes in bubble gum pink and black, would you like to know more?"

"Is this purses?"

An old lady's voice. I felt a sense of impending doom.

Something very wicked this way comes . . .

"Yes, Ma'am, it's Handbags."

"You say something about juice?"

Unfortunately I did, and now I deeply regret it.

"Yes, Juicy Couture, it's our item of the day."

"Why is juice the item of the day in the purse department?"

I'm not even going there.

"It's not important, how can I help you today, Ma'am?"

"I'm looking for a black purse. Do you have any black purses?"

Does McDonald's have hamburgers?

"Yes, we have lots of black handbags."

"What do they look like?"

Are you fucking kidding me?

"Umm . . . they're black."

"I *know that!* Don't get smart with me, young man! I want a nice black purse and I don't want to pay an arm and a leg."

I was tempted to correct her on the purse word and tell her that she'd better be prepared to pay with at least two of her arms and possibly even a leg. But since she sounded so cranky, I changed my mind.

"Well, we have a great selection. You're welcome to come in and I'll . . ."

"I want you to describe each black purse to me so that I can make a choice."

"Over the phone?"

"Yes, over the phone. How else would you do it?"

I'm thinking e-mail . . . fax . . . courier pigeon . . . stripper.

"Ma'am, we have hundreds of black bags. There's no way I could possibly describe them all to you over the phone. It's best if you come in to the store."

My Super Seller blood began to boil. It may be infected with Boy Scout DNA, but I do have customer service limits at The Big Fancy.

"I want to do this over the phone first. You will pick out ten of your best black purses and describe each one to me. Then you will hold them. Then I will come in to the store in a few days time and then I will possibly choose one."

Possibly *choose one? She's nuts! Why did I answer the Fucking Phone!? I fucked myself good. She'll be a fucking nightmare. FUCK!*

"Yes, Ma'am. I will pick out some black bags for you."

"Make sure you pick ten of them. They had better be nice and I want you to describe the details on each one."

Isn't it time for your medications? What mental ward are you calling from? I'm not describing the ceiling to you, you entitled crazy bitch!

In spite of my errant thoughts, Big Fancy's customer service creed prevailed. Thirty minutes later I had picked out and described ten handbags all under $200 for the old Phone Shopper who said her name was Mrs. Weidlemeyer.

"Make sure you hold them, and they better be in good condition. I'll be very upset if I come in there and find out you have nothing to show me."

"Don't worry, Mrs. Weidlemeyer. Everything will be fine."

I held Mrs. Weidlemeyer's ten black handbags for five nail-biting days. The bloodsucker never showed up.

Maude was not happy that I'd kept them on hold so long, and I got a dirty look from Sharky Sherry as she snatched a DKNY satchel from my hand, saying, "I have a customer for this. Charge Send!" I grabbed six of the black bags to take them back to the floor, stopping to call Phone Shopper from the stockroom.

"Hello, Mrs. Weidlemeyer?"

"Yes, that's me, who is this?" she barked in true crusty fashion.

"It's Freeman from The Big Fancy. I was calling to see if you still wanted me to hold these ten black handbags for you to come in and look at?"

"What black handbags?"

I almost choked.

"The black handbags you called me about five days ago. You asked me to pick them out and hold them for you."

"I don't know what you're talking about. I'm on the Do Not Call list, and you are not allowed to bother me with sales pitches. I'm going to report you immediately."

Click.

Mrs. Weidlemeyer disconnected me.

"I guess you won't be needing these then," I screamed back into the phone, "you bloodsucking nightmare!"

I slammed down the phone, put the handbags away with smoke coming out of my nostrils, and went to drown my Big Fancy sorrows at Cinnabon.

★

Phone Shopper Hell must end once and for all. I've considered many solutions to this problem, some of which involve making them pay with ten years of hard fitting-room labor at a discount store or forcing them all to live in India and work at call centers. The most effective way to deal with these bloodsucking timewasters is to hit them right in the mouth: All Phone Shoppers should be pepper-sprayed.

I will write Congress, George Clooney (because he would agree with me—he sold shoes before stardom), and all the powers that be and demand something be done about people who call stores or businesses and ask ridiculous, dumbass, idiotic questions over the phone. It should be outlawed, and these entitled morons should be brought to justice by having their calls traced and their faces sprayed! The Phone Shopper Police would show up at the door of a horrible

Phone Shopper like Mrs. Weidlemeyer, and as soon as the crusty answered it, she would be pepper-sprayed right in the source of the problem. The police would tell her, "That, Mrs. Weidlemeyer, is for being a bloodsucking Phone Shopper and causing Freeman to miss sales for his Super Seller discount. Don't do it again. *Capisce?*"

I stand firm on my decision.

All Phone Shoppers should be pepper-sprayed.

Entitled to My Blood

"Do you see what I'm talking about?" The crazy custy turned the open wallet upside down in her hands and held it up to my face. "The stitching is crooked if you turn it this way."

And why would you want to turn it that way, you dingbat? Your money will fall out!

Crazy had been sucking my blood for ten minutes over a $55 credit-card wallet that she swore looked different when you turned it upside down.

I don't know why she thought this.

Maybe the track lighting was shining on it differently?

Maybe she was a D Rat and wanted a discount?

Maybe she was just insane?

Who the fuck knows? I'm sure it's a little bit of all of the above.

Happy Fourth of July from The Big Fancy!

The holidays often brought out the wack-a-doodles. The temperature outside was pushing 100 and all kinds of crazy was running inside to get cool.

While the normal people were out burning hot dogs or going to movies, I'd signed up for stars-and-stripes hell duty with Sharky, Jeremy, and Dok. I had no plans, and I really needed the extra holiday pay. Linda Sue had the day off, of course—she rarely worked any of the holidays we were open, somehow weaseling out of them because of family commitments. Maude was also on duty but was bestowed with the hideous assignment of being in charge of The Big Fancy while Satan enjoyed the day off.

Off barbecuing a few salespeople with the Gestapo, no doubt.

Speaking of barbecues, Cammie was also off and going to a pool party in the hills with some mutual friends. I was invited to join her and was seriously considering meeting her there if I had any energy left by the time I finished my patriotic Big Fancy duties.

Little did I know I was about to be drained like a gas tank in a bad neighborhood.

My Fourth of July bloodsucking hell hit right after lunch.

I was innocently colorizing the clearance table full of straw and microfiber that had gone down to 50 percent off and was still collecting dust. My mind wandered, dreaming about what kind of food would be at the pool party and wondering whether there would be any hot dudes.

Suddenly a gravelly voice yelled from the hard aisle, *"You! Blondie! Over here! I need your assistance!!"*

When I turned to see what was connected to the scary voice, I considered lying and delivering the old salesperson's dumping line, "I don't work in this department!" and then running off to shiver and shake in the stockroom somewhere. But I was too awestruck by what I saw. It was a huge freakish-looking woman in a double-wide wheelchair. She had the face of Shrek and the body of Jabba the Hut, and she was dressed like a circus gypsy, with lots of jewelry and a wrap around her fat ugly man head.

She was also sweating.

A lot.

"This store is not ADA compliant!" she roared so loudly that everyone heard, but nobody cared. "You need to assist me and take corrective measures immediately or I will report you and this store for breaking laws."

I saw myself being handcuffed and led out of the store by policemen.

Jail must be better than this.

I wanted to run but was too paralyzed. Jabba Shrek raised a fat moist finger at me, like I was her pet Chihuahua who just peed on the carpet. "This store is very bad! What is wrong with you people? Shame on you! Do you not care about people with disabilities? It's dangerous in here! I'm going to injure myself. Your department is not ADA compliant and you will need to clear a large space to accommodate me or I will report you and this store to the authorities."

Great! Entitled and a bitch all in one! What happened to being nice and saying please?

"Well, why are you standing there staring at me?" Jabba snapped, "I don't have all day, and I need handbags."

Yes, mistress Shrekky, no problem!

I didn't know what Jabba Shrek was talking about. Our department and store were compliant with the requirements of the ADA—Americans with Disabilities Act. Satan had drilled those expectations into us, warning that the store could be fined and we'd be written up if we didn't follow the law. Because our floor was so tight in the Handbag Jungle, we often had to use rulers to make sure we provided enough browsing space as required by law. I always went out of my way to assist customers with wheelchairs, bringing merchandise to them, getting a clipboard so it was easier for them to sign sales documents, and just making sure they were comfortable.

Yes, our aisles in the Handbag Jungle were completely ADA compliant. What they were not set up for was ADA times two, plus four parts pure nasty.

Jabba Shrek's ride was the size of a golf cart, so that meant I was going to have to move a bunch of fixtures and tables just to get her off the main aisle. It would be no easy feat.

And as always at The Big Fancy, things went from mildly annoying to full-blown chaos.

I had barely moved one shelving unit and a table when the Fourth of July party decided to rage in the Handbag Jungle.

Shoppers rushed in from the aisle and instantly we were slammed. Sherry was devouring custys at the register bay and Dok had a few in her teeth nearby, watching me curiously every now and then. I could just hear her thoughts: *That woman so ugly. I stay over here!*

Yeah, you're one lucky shark, Dok. Stop staring before I tell her you're the handbag expert of the department and I send her to you!

With Jeremy at lunch, this meant the two department sharks were going to have a feeding frenzy at the expense of my creepy bloodsucker.

I was Fourth-of-July fucked at The Big Fancy.

By a mean woman who looked like characters from two summer blockbusters.

My floor moving was leaving me as sweaty as Jabba Shrek. I pushed the heavy fixtures aside, rearranging them into a haphazard circle that reminded me of a wagon train encampment. Jabba then rolled her caddy cart into the now-spacious Handbag Jungle and parked it in the center.

The throng of custys shopping on the sale tables and fixtures didn't seem bothered by the new arrangement. Usually when we move merchandise while we're open (even though we're not supposed to), custys will start shopping from the floor.

Seriously, why do we even bother with racks and tables?

One afternoon during a move we sold three Dooney and Bourkes straight from a pile on the floor. I told Maude, "I think we should just leave it!"

"I hope you know your merchandise. I've never been waited on by a man before in a women's section, and I'm apprehensive about you assisting me. My daughter is having a fiftieth birthday party in Chicago," Jabba Shrek said, glaring at me while she wiped sweat from her sizable forehead, ". . . and I need several bags for the trip, a good-size everyday one with lots of pockets and a dressy evening bag for the dinner. And I shall need a tote for traveling. I want this to be my only stop and I don't have a lot of time."

I'm grossed out and scared as hell, but you don't have to ask twice, Shrekky! Boy Scout is off and running.

I had my reservations about waiting on this demanding sea hag, but a sale was a sale, and she wanted *three* bags. I ran all over the department collecting bags for her and dropping them in a pile at her feet.

That was when I noticed the stench.

Rotten tomatoes and baby powder.

Jabba Shrekky didn't need a new handbag; she needed a bath!

Bile rose up in my throat. Stinky tore into the bags I brought her, analyzing each one. She ripped the stuffing from them and tossed it all over the floor, making a huge mess.

Jabba Shrek is a pig, too. How lovely!

She fired questions at me.

"Will this withstand the Chicago rains?"

Sure, if you cover it up like a baby.

"Does this come in another color?"

Yes, the color of my blood.

"Is this evening bag too small?"

What with the wheels you're driving? Hell no! You must have a hundred places there to hide your lipstick.

At one point Jabba Shrek made me lean in close to show her how one of the straps adjusted on a Coach satchel. I took a deep breath like I was jumping into a cesspool and got through it with Jabba ultimately rejecting the strap as too complicated.

Man, was that scary! My throat is burning!

Just then a custy tapped me on the shoulder and began asking me a million questions about a $350 Longchamp bag. Noting that the sharks all had about three custys each, I opened up my jaws and went to work selling to her.

Oddly enough, Jabba wasn't upset and ended up wanting to see the Longchamp herself. It didn't work for her, but I didn't care at that moment. I was thrilled I could excuse myself from the chains of her stinky entitled sweat and go ring up my new custy.

Except that's not what happened.

Like so many times before at The Big Fancy, I thought a sale was going my way and then it did an about-face and I was left with nothing.

"Thank you so much for the help!" said the custy. "Janice at the Jewelry counter is holding some stuff for me and I'm her personal and I'd love for her to get the credit."

I'd love to take that Longchamp and shove it up Jewelry Janice's ass!

The nerve! I'd never let my Shoposaurus loose in a store expecting people on the verge of being fired to help her. (It wouldn't happen anyway. They were all terrified of Lorraine.)

I watched the $350 Longchamp sale walk away with sweaty tears in my eyes.

You'll be getting a call later, Janice, on how to take care of your Shoposaurus!

"Are you going to finish helping me?" whined Jabba. "I think I want to see more Longchamp bags and maybe some of the sale canvas totes. I think they would be great for traveling. I also may want to pick up something for my daughter. It's a special birthday, you know."

No, I didn't know, and I don't care. Just make up your fucking mind and please go far, far away.

It was another half hour before Jabba Shrekky made a decision. Her Sweatiness decided on a $230 black DKNY tote, a red Kenneth Cole satchel for $260, and a Kate Spade fabric bag for her daughter at $335.

The total sale was $825 and it had cost me a gallon of American blood.

My customer service work didn't end there. I had to ring everything up, wrap the Kate Spade in a box with a pretty bow because she wanted it to look nice for her daughter, and then attach everything to her double-wide chair, which took another fifteen minutes because I had to find something to tie the bags with.

I was never so glad to see a customer drive off. In fact, Stinky didn't know it, but I waved from the aisle.

Goodbye, Shrekky! Don't come back now, ya hear!

I wish I could say my horrible bloodsucking tale ended with her rolling off into the mall, but it did not.

Several hours later, right before I was scheduled to leave, the phone rang.

It was Julie from the Pasadena store. "Hi, who is salesperson 441064?"

Aww, shit. A return, right before I go home? Happy Fourth to me!

I confessed to her that it was me and then she presented the bad news: "Dude, this crazy bitch in a huge wheelchair just came in and returned the three bags you sold her two hours ago. She said they were gifts and you talked her into them and she didn't really want them, so we did the return. Sorry."

Jabba Shrekky! You stinky lying whore! I thought you liked me!

That was the thing with many of the custys at The Big Fancy: Their actions always spoke louder than words.

I hoped there was a lot of beer at this pool party because I was going to get hammered.

And then jump in the pool.

I had to get the bloodsucker sweat off me ASAP.

The Sale of My Discontent

The Big Fancy Fall Preview Sale was in full swing. So were my nerves.

The hours of desperation had arrived.

I had become a sales-zombie.

This always happened around 3 P.M. on the first day of any Big Fancy sale, but the Fall Preview created the greatest number of storewide sales-zombies because of its popularity, the weeks-long exhaustion it would deliver, and the great volume of stuff the custys would gobble up.

I was so far gone the track lighting made my bloodshot eyeballs ache.

My pants were wrinkled and dirty, under my dress shirt my T-shirt was soaked with sale sweat, and my dress shoes were slowly eating my feet. On top of all that, my stomach decided to join in with some nauseating whirlpool action. It might have been ridiculous to feel that way about selling *handbags*, but that's The Big Fancy pressure cooker!

Late in the afternoon, when I didn't feel like selling, pushy sales-zombie went into automatic pilot.

Me: "The price on that blue snakeskin bag is great! It goes back up to $155 after the sale. $103 is a fantastic price. You can't beat it."

Custy: "Where's it made?"

Shit. I hate this question.

Me: "Uh. China."

She frowned and eyeballed the bag, rotating it in her hands.

Custy: "It's $103 and it's made in China?"

Me: "But it's really *well* made. They take great pride with stitching in China and it makes the price great too! Many of our best bags are made there. Also, snakeskin is hot for fall. The blue is beautiful. Makes a really great accent color."

Custy: "I don't need blue."

She drops it. Picks up a chocolate brown Perlina handbag and begins digging through it.

Me: "Perlina is a great everyday bag with lots of pockets, and the leather is butter soft."

Custy: "I suppose it's made in China too."

Me: "Yes, but Perlina holds up really well. I have customers who swear buy them. That's all they'll buy. They love the way the leather feels."

Custy: "How much is it?"

I opened the bag and pulled out the ticket that's attached to the inside zipper pocket. It's annoying not to have the ticket on the outside, but when they are, customers just rip them off. Strange but true. If they're not thieves, I imagine they must be artists who use Big Fancy tickets to decoupage their bathroom walls.

Me: "It's $109.90. It goes back up to $165 after the sale. That's a great price!"

Custy: "Everything is a great price to you."

Even though I wanted to hit her after that, she was right. I had probably said that three times while I was waiting on her.

What can I say? I'm a desperate slut.

Me: "You're right. I'm just so excited about the sale. I've never seen such awesome merchandise and prices."

Fucking bitch. I'm too tired for your nastiness.

The crusty put the bag on her shoulder and looked in the mirror.

I am so desperate for a sale and doped up on caffeine that I neurotically hit her with every pathetic selling point I can think of.

Me: "The bag looks really comfortable on you. If the strap is too long, we can have it shortened free of charge. The outside pocket will be great for your cell phone or sunglasses. The gunmetal hardware is great because you can wear it with gold or silver. It zips on top, which is good for security and it is easy to get in and out of because it has a nice wide opening. And you can never go wrong with brown, brown is such a neutral color, goes with everything, and it looks really great with your brown hair!"

Custy: "You can stop now. I'll buy it."

Well, thank God for that!

★

Custy: "Is everything on sale?"

Me: "No, just what's on those counters and those tables."

I pointed to give her directions to the sale's vicinity.

Custy: "What about those bags?"

She pointed to the shelves on the wall.

Me: "No, just what's on those counters and those tables."

Custy: "Are those on sale?"

She pointed to some designer bags in a glass case.

Me: "No, just what's on those counters and those tables."

Custy: "What about those? I like those. Are they on sale?"

She pointed to a rack of regular-price bags.

Me: "As I said, only those bags on the counter and those on the tables."

Okay. Now you're starting to irritate me.

I point again to all the sale merchandise.

Custy: "Are you sure? How do you know they aren't on sale?"

Me: "Because the only things that are on sale have Fall Preview signs!"

I picked up a nearby sale sign and held it up to her.

Me: "This is a sale sign. All of the bags below it or behind it are on sale. Do you understand?"

She stared at me, thinking over the sale sign lesson I had just given her. It was too much information.

Custy: "What about those bags over there?"

She pointed to a fixture full of Coach bags that never go on sale.

Custy: "Are those on sale?"

I didn't answer.

To keep from slapping the bitch, I made a beeline for the counters. Surely someone wanted to buy something over there.

★

I'd been on hold with Big Fancy Credit for almost five minutes. In Retail Years that might as well be five hours.

A woman was trying to purchase a cheap Maxx leather hobo bag for $69.99. A nasty code had appeared on the register and I was waiting for the verdict.

"I think the system is down," said Asshat Richie, walking by on the hard aisle.

"Happy sale to you too, Richie!" I was joking and hating him at the same time.

"Is there a problem?" asked the custy. "I've never had a problem. How much longer am I going to have to wait?"

"I don't know," I responded with a tight smile.

I was just as aggravated as she was because Sherry, Dok, and others were ringing up sales and they weren't getting any codes.

"Well, I don't want to stand here and wait all day," she bitched.

Turning nasty, are we now? Hold your water, honey!

"You'd think they'd have more operators working," she continued bitching as if someone cared. "After all, it is a sale."

Is that what it is? I thought it was dance party. A party to dance for the man!

"I pay all my bills on time. I don't owe this store anything. Why is this happening to me?"

I don't cause these problems, lady! I don't know why you are happening to me. Why can't I just get an easy sale? Why do they all have to involve a root canal into my brain?

"I don't know, ma'am. There must be something wrong with your card."

Or your luck—and it's rubbing off on me.

"But I don't owe anything. How can there be something wrong?"

"Did you move recently?" I asked, thinking of known problems why her card would bring up a code.

"No, not recently."

"I don't know why," I sighed, leaning on the bay, and changing ears with the phone because I'd been waiting for so long, ear sweat was starting to trickle.

I thought of another roadblock and asked her, "When was the last time you used it?"

She paused thoughtfully.

"Must have been about fifteen years ago."

Fuck me with the fucking phone! No wonder, you dumbass bitch!

Finally an agent came on to confirm this. He told me she'd need to open a brand-new account because her other one had been closed due to nonusage.

I suggested she open a new account, and she said, "Umm . . . no thanks, I'd hardly ever use the card. I just wanted to get a sale bag. Guess I don't need it. Thanks!"

And with that she was gone.

Aaaaaaaaaaaagh!

★

When sales-zombie sets in, the last thing you want is a custy raking you over the designer coals. Apparently this Discount Rat got the $600 white Ferragamo Kelly handbag she was carrying on sale at one of the other Big Fancys.

We have the exact same one in black for *regular price.*

Ratty wanted it for the same price as her white one.

I can understand the confusion, and I can even forgive a custy for asking once, but I had to explain to the moron over and over that the reason the black one was not on sale was because we carry it all year round. Ferragamo won't let us put it on sale. It's part of their classic line, which is not on sale. The custy's white bag was seasonal and had been marked down at the end of the previous summer. She was lucky to get it.

I tried to explain it to her, but I might as well have been trying to teach Latin to a sleeping eighth grader. "I still do not understand," she persisted. "I bought my white Ferragamo on sale. This one should be on sale too. They are the same bag," she repeated for the fifth time.

And for the sixth time I told her: "The white was seasonal. Discontinued."

I want to seriously take the Ferragamo and slap her with it! Listen to me*!*

"These two are exactly the same. Do you see that?" she replied, holding her white bag next to the black one in case I didn't believe her.

"They sure are," I answered, trembling with sales-zombie rage. "And that black one is *not . . . on . . . sale!*"

I was in no mood to feed the Discount Rat new markdowns, and I knew Maude wouldn't like me discounting this one because black Ferragamo was one of our hot sellers.

She continued talking to herself as if someone else cared. "See! Ex-act-ly the same."

And you get a gold star! Well done, dumbass Discount Rat!

"They are the same," I reaffirmed, looking around for other customers to approach.

I wished I had a recorded message I could just hold in her face and play over and over.

"That's not right," she responded. "I should be able to buy the same style for the same price."

I was still politely persisting. "But it's not the same. It's a different color."

I'm really tired of saying this. But here I stand. Here I repeat. Should I write it down for her?

"When will it go on sale then?" she started in.

Oh fuck, here we go.

"When Ferragamo decides to discontinue it," I said back, with attitude building.

"When will that be?"

When you're dead, I hope.

"I have no idea. They are still making the style as far as I know."

Ah fuck, why did I say that? I knew it was a mistake. Never sound unsure with a D Rat!

"As far as you know?" she questioned. "So it might go on sale at any second."

"I don't know."

I just wanted her to shut up and leave.

"If I buy it now, can I get the sale price when it goes on sale?"

"We are happy to do adjustments up to a month after purchase."

"Is that it? What if it doesn't go on sale for two months?"

"You don't get the adjustment." I lied, thinking of Mrs. Green's power and how she could get adjustments six months later.

This rat is seriously going to do me in.

"Well, I should get the adjustment," she whined. "You don't even know when it's going on sale, but you told me it would go on sale if it's discontinued. That's not fair to me. I should be able to get the sale price anyway."

I have a Big Fancy Fall Preview Entitled Discount Rat headache.

★

I'd just racked up a juicy late-afternoon sale even though sales-zombie threatened to take me out. *Titanic* tilting in her final upright position before she slipped under.

A custy was purchasing three sale bags and a wallet, totaling $454.32.

Not too shabby. I'll take it!

As I handed her a shopping bag full of her purchases, I said, "Enjoy your new bags."

The custy frowned and did not say what most custys say.

"I don't want that," she replied.

"I'm sorry, you don't want what?"

I really had no idea what she was talking about.

"The shopping bag," she said wrinkling her nose, "I don't want one with the word 'sale' on it." While I totally agreed with her artistically—the words looked nasty, in orange and white—I wasn't completely sure why she wouldn't at least use the bag to carry her purchases home.

"These are all we have today," I answered honestly. "They are larger than the regular ones and hold more."

Entitled Crusty Sale Bitch let her neurotic idiocy spew all over me: "I'm a very good customer, and I want my purchases in a regular shopping bag! I do not want a bag with "sale" written all over it!"

Uh-oh, looks like Sale Crusty is headed to Tantrum Land.

I tried to reason with her.

"Ma'am, you did purchase sale merchandise, and all I have behind the counter here are shopping bags with 'sale' printed on them."

Now there were customers standing behind her, watching. Some were holding handbags, ready to buy. The sharks would show up any second now.

The crusty sale shopper continued, "I'm not walking out of here carrying a sale shopping bag. I won't have people thinking I'm just a sale shopper. I'm a regular customer and I spend a lot of money in this store!"

"I believe that wholeheartedly and truly appreciate your regular customer patronage," I answered.

And then she throws down the ultimatum that would have my tired feet running all over the store looking for a fucking plain Big Fancy shopping bag.

"If you can't find me a regular shopping bag," she replied, sounding like a Disney witch, "then I'll just return everything! I don't want them anymore."

What the hell, lady? Is it two-year-old time? Did you miss your afternoon nap and punch and cookies? How about I spank you with a shopping bag?

I did have a clear plastic grocery-store-style bag that we used for inter-store stock transfers, but I didn't think she'd approve of the see-through aspect. In my personal drawer I also had an Abercrombie and Fitch shopping bag with a cute shirtless guy on the front, but there was *no way* I was giving that up. I also thought about offering her the used Neiman Marcus shopping bag that was on the floor behind the counter—a custy used it for a return.

Now everyone can think you shop at Neiman's! How about that!

I ran to every cash wrap nearby—Hosiery, Women's Shoes, Cosmetics, Men's Shoes, and Accessories. To my horror, no department on the second floor had a plain nonsale shopping bag. Every cash wrap had been fully stocked with sale packaging.

I had no choice: I headed down the escalator to look on the first floor in the receiving dock, where the wrapping supplies are kept. After a frantic scour of the dock, I discovered they were out.

"You are supposed to be using the sale ones," the receiving guy reminded me.

"My customer does not want a sale shopping bag," I told him. "She's an entitled bitch."

Receiving guy's eyebrows went up.

Right about that time, I saw a regular shopping bag sticking out of the trash bin. I ran over and pulled it out.

Slightly wrinkled but it'll work.

Something pulled out of the garbage. Perfect for Entitled Shopping Bag Bitch. I could not have been happier!

Another Big Fancy customer about to be pleased!

★

I staggered around Handbags, sales-zombie pulsing through my veins, but the custys kept coming at me with their dumbass sale questions from hell. I wanted to rip every hair out of *their* heads.

"Do you know the price of this?"

Yes, it's 1 million dollars!

"Is everything on sale?"

If you can outrun the dogs!

"I found it on the sale table, shouldn't it be on sale even if the price isn't marked?"

Shouldn't you just shut your entitled trap and fuck off?

"It's not my fault someone dropped it on the sale table even though it's not on sale. Shouldn't I get it on sale anyway?"

Ma'am, it doesn't work like herpes and syphilis.

"This doesn't have a ticket!"

That's because custys are eating them!

"Can you put it on sale?"

My magical Discount Rat wand is broken.

"Will you give me an extra discount?"

If you buy something extra.

"How much is it with tax?"

Fuck if I know. Do I look like a walking calculator?

"There's a mark on the bottom of this bag; can you clean it off?"

Let's just pretend we did! No one will ever notice.

"Don't you have a fresh one from the back?"

No, I'm sorry, they're not done baking yet!

"Is this the sale price?"

Only if you can click your heels together three times and say, "There's no place like The Big Fancy!"

"Why isn't it on sale? It should be!"

You got that right; it's one ugly piece of shit!

"Can you call another store and get me one in black?"

I could, but I don't want to. I'm currently in sales-zombie mode.

"Is it returnable?"

As long as I didn't sell it to you!

"Will you hold all of these bags for me? I want to come back next week."

I'll be in Hold Prison by then.

"Is that the final price?"

Until the buyers decide to mark it down more.

"Isn't there an additional off?"

Only if you can stand on your head and sing "The Star-Spangled Banner" while eating a mouthful of pretzels.

"Is this all you have on sale?"

Yes, unfortunately. You're shopping in Broken-Down Burbank.

"Why isn't everything on sale? I thought the whole store was going to be on sale."

If it were, my life would be a lot easier.

I may have hated The Big Fancy Fall Preview Sale at times, but I sure did like the paycheck that came with it!

Finally—I can go to a movie!

★

As the third quarter sharky sale days of summer came to a close, we had survived the Fall Preview Sale with a small increase thanks to better merchandise and big designer markdowns. Super Seller was back in sight for a few of us. With a quiet fall moving in, we all found time to get away from the Handbag Jungle. While Maude stayed home and gardened during her vacation and I sat in a theater during most of mine, Cammie took the trip of her lifetime to Ireland with her grandmother and was inspired to start working on her new handbag line. Not to be outdone, Sherry and her family went to Italy for a week. What shocked the shit out of us all was that she came back with presents for everyone. Each of us got three postcards with hand-drawn sketches from a street vendor somewhere.

Umm . . . thanks, Sherry, you're so sweet!

It was the oddest thing ever. Here was this woman who was as cold as ice most of the time, and now she was handing out presents from her vacation!

Cammie didn't even bring me anything!

I threw Sherry's hand-drawn sketches in the trash when I got home. I think Cammie burned hers.

Linda Sue also went on a vacation, only more local, to Monterey. She must have felt competitive because she *also* brought back gifts for the department—a little seashell flashlight for each of us. I didn't even wait to get home to trash that; it went in the can right outside Mount

Fancy. I don't know where Dok went or what she thought of any of it, because *Pretty Flower give me headache*, and I couldn't understand half of what she said.

Just when I thought my summer was going to The Big Fancy sale sharks, Jeremy invited me to Comic-Con in San Diego, and we had a blast! I can also tell the world he is not gay! (No, I did not make a move on him.) The way I differentiate the metrosexuals who might be gay from the ones who claim to be straight is how much they talk about pussy. There is no gay man on the planet who wants to talk about pussy, and it ended up being one of Jeremy's favorite subjects. It didn't bother me—I like talking about any kind of sex!

With our brief respite from handbag hell over, the crew of the Handbag Jungle headed into the bombastic 4th quarter, which always starts out bumpy, with dicey numbers in October. But Cammie, Jeremy, and I felt we were in good hands with Maude; she was our Captain Janeway, and she'd steer our starship safely.

3rd Quarter Sales Associate Rankings

Sales Associate	Year-to-Date Volume
Sherry	$203,457.08
Freeman	$175,930.94
Cammie	$169,401.69
Dok	$168,325.19
Linda Sue	$167,184.47
Jeremy	$110,458.58

The Big Fancy

Freeman Hall
Handbags
Burbank

Dear Freeman,

YAY! WAY TO GO, GUY! I knew you could get yourself
back on track! You made your 3rd Quarter goal by
$976.42! Not by much, but a win is a win! Keep
powering on, and that Super Seller discount will
be within your reach!
One customer at a time!

Sincerely,

Suzy Davis-Johnson

SEASON'S BEATINGS!

It's Not Over Till the Bloodsucker Buys Something

Night of a Thousand NATs

Halloween was still a few days away, but it came early to the Handbag Jungle one Friday.

The Nasty-Ass Thieves (NATs) locked their sights on Broken Down Burbank and swarmed.

And unfortunately we weren't armed with cans of Raid to stop the nasty custys.

There was no predicting a NAT infestation. You never knew when they were going to show up in droves, one shady custy after another, doing questionable returns, stealing whatever they could, and giving salespeople bogus sales that were too good to be true.

Jeremy and I were closing on this fateful NAT Friday night, but we had been scheduled for a lobotomizing three-hour class on new Client Capture features. After that nightmare of listening to Brandi treat us like we were three years old, we took our Big Fancy fried brains and fed them grub to match at the Golden Arches, and then returned feeling like bloated grease zombies for our closing shift.

We had no idea that a NAT swarm was underway.

We should have seen the bad omen.

It was hanging on the DKNY tree.

But it wasn't a DKNY.

In fact, it wasn't even from The Big Fancy's Handbag Jungle.

A NAT had decided she wanted a new bag, so she traded out her old one. The NAT put the stuffing from the new bag into her gross old used one and then hung it on the DKNY tree.

"Uh-oh. This doesn't look good," Jeremy said as we eyed the dirty piece of leather garbage the NAT had left us as a present.

"Fucking NAT," I said, picking it up with my fingertips and heading to the main bay, where Cammie and Dok were barely upright, looking like they'd been run over—our very own Handbag Jungle roadkill.

The minute I walked in the bay, Cammie saw the NAT remains. "What the fuck is that? *Another* Nasty-Ass Thief?"

Apparently it had been a day of them.

Completely overcome with sales-zombie NAT-itis, Cammie unleashed.

"It has been one fucked-up day full of NATs!" she said. "I want to cut all their slimy balls off! I watched some big German douche high as a fucking kite take a Kate Spade tiger print clutch, fold it in half and shove it down the front of his pants! Our only Kate Spade tiger! Rubbing it all over his sweaty nasty balls and cock. Fucking disgusting! Fucking NAT!"

"Ewwwwww," Jeremy and I both said at the same time.

"So gross," chimed in Dok, "I can't even look."

"Yeah, well, I called security and dumbass Steve answered," Cam ranted. "Fat Bastard said he couldn't do anything about it, because *I* fucking saw it. My eyesight is not good enough? Stupid dick."

I understood this part of Security's rules, but it sure didn't help us, and we weren't supposed to chase people either. I guess we were just supposed to stand by and let the NATs take it all. I was glad Maude was off and didn't have to deal with any of this, although we were all used to Big Fancy NAT swarms.

"So Fat Bastard and Tina follow him all over the store, and I guess he was fuckin' wasted and almost took a bunch of suits," she raged. "Then they followed him over to Mervyn's, where they teamed up with the douches over there, and the fuckin' NAT tried to steal a shirt or something. I must have waited on a thousand of the fuckers. I gotta get the hell out of here! Oh, and Michelle from Hollywood called with an alert, apparently they had a grab and run. Some NAT bitch took off with three Coach patchwork bags."

"Ouch!" said Jeremy. "That's like fifteen hundred bucks!"

And with that, Cammie and Dok fled the NAT-infested Jungle, leaving it in our hands for the night.

Immediately the phone lines began ringing.

With NATs.

My NAT wanted to buy the most expensive item we had in the department for his love, and then have it overnighted to NYC. "You overnight, there, right?"

I hung up on him.

Jeremy's NAT wanted to ask twenty questions about returning with only partial receipts.

Within several hours we'd had several NAT-related credit-card problems and at least three bogus returns.

I had a NAT trying to push through a $500 check. After my last expensive noncompliant circle, the last thing I wanted to do was purchase a more expensive model!

I pretended her check wouldn't go through, and then I pretended to call credit.

"Sorry, ma'am," I told her in a few minutes' time, "the register won't take your check. Something to do with the computer and your bank. You need to call them in the morning."

Sometimes bullshit will stick to NATs and kill them.

She fucked right off without a word.

Good riddance, NAT!

While I was celebrating a successful NAT extermination, Fat Bastard Steve walked up and dropped a Kate Spade tiger clutch onto the counter—the one that had been violated by a NAT.

"We don't need this anymore," he said, walking off.

The phones started ringing, probably with more NATs. "What the hell is going on?" Jeremy said.

"The NATs are swarming again," I explained. "Get out your NAT swatter."

It was going to be a long night.

★

A NAT swarm wouldn't be complete if it didn't bring with it an Old NAT up to no good.

An Old NAT who wanted a Lulu Guinness cosmetics case with a poodle on it.

Old NAT caressed the bag, then handed it to me and said, "I have a poodle at home! So cute."

"It sure is. Will that be cash or charge?"

"Oh, I'll pay cash," she replied.

I unzipped the case to retrieve the ticket, and what to my NAT-fighting eyes should appear?

A ticket that didn't go with the case.

Now the sad Discount Rat part here is that the cosmetics case was on sale for only $25.99.

But that wasn't enough for this Ratty NAT. She had to put a ticket inside it that went with an on-sale credit-card holder, for $12.99.

You cheapass Discount Rat NAT!

I often got irritated with these NATs and would scold them.

I didn't hold back with this one: "That's the wrong price. Someone switched tickets. Sorry about that. It's $25.99. I know you love poodles, so I'm sure you'll still want it. Will that be cash or credit?"

Old NAT glared at me and pranced off.

★

A custy approached me with an Isabella Fiore bag that had several pug dogs on the front. It was $500 and really quite stunning if you liked that kind of shit. We only had one, and we'd had for it weeks. There weren't fifty of them in the back, and they weren't blowing out the door.

The custy looked like she was going to buy it, and I was just about to comment on the bag, when she said: "Hi, I'd like to return this. I don't see anything I like, so I'll just get my cash back."

Lady, are you kidding me? How fuckin' stupid do you think I am?

This NAT's mistake was thinking I was an idiot salesperson when clearly she was the dumbass here. She picked up a bag we only had one of to try and scam me! If she'd had even half a brain, she would have grabbed a Dooney, which we have breeding in the stockroom. It would have been harder for me to catch her.

But no, this annoying NAT grabbed a bag from a plastic stand under a spotlight that was now empty!

Seriously? Nasty-Ass Idiot.

I ignored what she'd said and replied, "Isn't that a beautiful bag! Did you say you'd like to pay cash?"

"No, I want to return it for cash," she said, now looking confused.

My game was to pretend not to hear a word she said.

"Oh yes, it's definitely returnable if you don't like it. Just keep your receipts. No problem at all!"

Since I had the bag in my hand, I pulled it closer and clutched it tightly.

No way in fucking hell are you going to take our one-of-a-kind Isabella Fiore pug bag. You can fuck right off, thief!

"No, I want to return it," she repeated, starting to get agitated.

"Like I said, after you pay for it, there's no problem returning it— with your receipts!"

I gave her a big shit-eating shark smile.

Over the next few minutes we kept playing that game: I didn't hear a word she said and pretended she wanted to buy the bag.

Over and over again.

After wiping her out mentally with games, she looked at me like I was crazy and ran off.

I called Fat Bastard to tell him, but it went to voice mail.

At least the Handbag Jungle's only Isabella Fiore Pug had been spared abduction.

★

All night long the NATs swarmed.

Every time we turned around we found tickets on the floor, which was not a good thing during a NAT swarm. It meant they were creating their own prices and possibly going to other departments to find stupid salespeople.

Another price-switcher NAT wanted to buy a brand-new $300 Dooney and Bourke satchel we'd had just gotten in. For $39.99.

We laughed in her face.

Then a Tween NAT showed up and wanted to return a fake Kate Spade with a crooked label.

Tween NATs aren't too smart!

We laughed in her face, too.

The counter saw plenty of NATs passing through: We did several questionable credit returns (with receipts missing), and then a NAT stopped at the counter and wanted to buy a $1,000 gift card. We deduced he was a NAT when his credit card was declined and he'd forgotten his ID in the car.

The credit card probably hasn't been activated by the real owner, you mail thief!

It wasn't until near closing time when the worst NAT moment of the night happened.

Just like in any good scary movie, it's not long after the warning when the monster jumps out of nowhere.

The NAT who was the subject of a region-wide Coach theft alert arrived at the counter for her payday.

"Hi, I need to make a return," the NAT said. "These Coaches. I want my cash back. Thanks."

Whoa, hold up there, Natty!

I was ready for this NAT.

My invisible can of Raid was aimed right at the vermin. There had been too many today, and I'd had it.

"I just need your ID and I'll see if I can get it approved," I told the NAT.

She looked at me skeptically, but tossed me her driver's license, which even at a glance looked *fake as hell.*

"This isn't gonna take forever, is it? Cuz I need to be somewhere."

"No, ma'am," I replied, writing down her info. "Hopefully it'll just be a few minutes."

I handed the bitch back her fake driver's license.

"Good," the NAT huffed. "Then I can get my cash and get out of here. The parking in this place is shit!"

I caught Jeremy's worried look as I left him alone and went in the stockroom to call the temporary store manager, Melinda, the manager of Women's Designer.

She was another longtime manager, and I knew her well. Of course she had also been eaten alive by NATs all night and was relieved when I offered to take care of this bitch. Melinda told me to do whatever I wanted and there had even been an e-mail about the stolen Coaches anyway. I then started the process of having Fat Bastard look her up to see if she had a Big Fancy return record.

Suddenly Jeremy came running into the stockroom and locked the door.

"Dude, she's some kind of freaky bitch! Her boyfriend showed up, and they want to know why it's taking so long!"

"They can fuck right off! We're not feeding the NATs tonight. And it will ruin the department's good day. Not going down without a fight on this whore."

Suddenly there was a pounding on the door.

"Hey! What's going on in there?" yelled the NAT. "Hurry up! Why is it taking so long?"

The NAT yanked at the door. Thank God Jer had locked it. I could hear her boyfriend behind her. "Why it takin' so long? Where are they? I gotta go back to the car."

"Dude, we're trapped!" whispered Jeremy. "I'm not going out there!"

"She's only got two strikes," Steve finally announced into the phone. "It's your call."

Thanks, Fat Bastard. Two is good enough for me! THE BITCH IS DONE!

Although The Big Fancy had strict rules about which custys could be denied, they did keep track of the NATs. They knew the ones who were blatantly bleeding us dry and leaving a paper trail, and if there was enough evidence, they could be exterminated. In cases like this where it was a regional grab and run, the chances were not looking good for the NAT getting her cash.

I slowly opened the door and peered out with Jeremy behind me like a scared bunny.

Maybe the NAT got scared and ran off.

I doubt that.

"Is she gone?" said Jer.

Just then from behind a handbag tree, the NAT jumped out like a skeleton. "So, did you get the authorization? I'm tired of waiting."

Oh, I got your authorization all right, you fucking NASTY-ASS THIEVING WHORE!

When I was a manager and in charge of The Big Fancy some nights, I dealt with hundreds of thieves like this.

Even though it scared me because any of the NATs could rip me to shreds and eat me, I secretly enjoyed telling them to fuck off as they called me every name and insult they could think of.

This NAT bitch was no different.

"I'm sorry ma'am, the return was denied. You will need to go back to the store you *bought* them at. I can't help you here."

"*What? You fuckin' little faggot! I want to see your store manager!*"

I ignored her for a moment and ran to the bay, hearing her call Jeremy and me one name after another. I got the stolen Coach bags off the bay's ledge, shoved them back in the bag, and threw them onto the counter.

The NAT stood there screaming at us and threatening to kill us. The entire Women's Shoe department was now watching. I could see some of the guys walking up behind the NAT.

If this bitch did anything, she'd have a bunch of angry Big Fancy shoe sharks pummeling her in no time.

"Get the fuck out," I said, shaking.

I was dying to add, "You fucking nasty-ass thieving whore!" But I also knew that as a manager, returning their insults only incensed them even more.

No, the only way to get rid of NATs fast is to call the po-po! Then they run like hell.

"Hi, connect me to the police, I have an emergency," I said to The Big Fancy operator, who did no such thing and immediately started asking me a million questions, which I ignored. Unfortunately we couldn't dial 911 from our department phones. Today you'd just pull your mobile phone from a pocket and have the police there in minutes, but back then salespeople often felt unsafe.

NAT wasn't running as fast as I would have liked.

She kept staring at Jeremy and me with her nasty buggy eyes, mouthparts poised to strike her next victim.

"Dude, I don't like the way she's looking at us," he whispered. "Like she's gonna eat us or something."

The operator continued to freak out in my ear because she had no idea what the fuck was going on, and then the department phone started ringing. It was probably Steve wondering whether we were okay.

You better stay there, Fat Bastard, she looks hungry tonight and you could end up being her steak!

The NAT and I had locked eyes for a moment.

And then NAT yelled out for all to hear: "You fuckin' purse-selling faggots. I bet you all were just fuckin' each other's brains out in the stockroom! Hahaha! Fags!"

Sometimes when you deny NAT bitches like that they go and say the weirdest shit.

And I will never forget that one!

WTF? Even if Jeremy were gay and we had the horny hots for each other, we wouldn't have been able take advantage of it because we were too busy dealing with your nasty thievery, you dumbass!

I was considering answering as she turned to leave, but then I caught all the stares and smiles of half the Shoe department. They weren't agreeing with her, but they got how scary funny it was!

But it was my stockroom fuck-buddy who made everyone's night with his response.

"And I bet you'd like to watch!" Jeremy yelled. "Wouldn't ya, honey! Not getting enough at home?!"

The entire Shoe department, along with a few handfuls of spectators who'd caught the early Big Fancy Halloween floor show, erupted in laughter. Some people even clapped.

The NAT stormed out of the store but then stopped right outside.

She was considering coming back in, but we all spotted Mall Police coming in the distance.

After witnessing the altercation on the cameras, Fat Bastard was finally on the scene.

NAT decided she wouldn't win. She flew away to be someone else's Halloween horror.

★

Jeremy and I were exhausted and rattled, but we also felt the adrenaline rush of victory. We actually cried with laughter while cleaning up the NAT-sacked Handbag Jungle. A night of horrors behind us, we hightailed it down Mount Fancy, screaming like sweaty girls running from a haunted house.

Jeremy and I decided there was only one thing to do next. Get trashed and watch horror movies. After all, it was October and we'd just survived a real-life one!

We stopped at Ralph's and bought beer, popcorn, and a bag of Halloween candy. Then we perused Jeremy's vast collection of scary DVDs. Seemingly apropos, Alfred Hitchcock's *The Birds* won out, with Jer saying, "They're just like the NATs!"

You got that right buddy! And they tried to pick us clean tonight.

As we watched birds attacking Tippi Hedren, I thought about how much she reminded me of a young Mrs. Green.

I'd like to see NATS attack her!

"Fucking nasty thieves," Jeremy said. "If I'd had a shotgun, I would have picked them off one by one!"

As Jeremy continued to fantasize about what he would do to the NATs, I fought to stay awake.

Me too, Jer! I'd like to dip them all in honey and feed them to the bees. And then to the bears. But my eyes can hardly stay open right now. Forgive me if I rest them a bit . . .

Darkness swept over. Hitchcock's screeching birds turned into a humming noise.

Almost like bees buzzing.

A blank white page appeared. Then letters, quickly forming words.

A script!

ATTACK OF THE NATS

An original screenplay by NAT Fighter Freeman

FADE IN:

EXT. THE HANDBAG JUNGLE—DAY

NATs are buzzing around the Bag Jungle, picking it apart piece by piece. The NATs are bugs with wings and tentacles, and they come in all sizes and shapes. The big ones have recognizable faces like the German NAT, the Old NAT, and the Coach NAT.

JEREMY and FREEMAN are on top of the Handbag Bay fighting off the NATs by squirting them with bottle cleaner and swiping them away with blue rags. They are protecting the Isabella Fiore Pug bag from the NATs that are taking everything.

                    FREEMAN
        We have to save the Pug! If they take it, we're
        doomed!

                    JEREMY
        I don't know how much longer we can hold them back
        with glass cleaner!

Jeremy squirts the big German NAT and he backs off.

The NATs continue to pick up handbags and fly away with
them. More and more NATs fly up, stripping the place.
Once the bags are gone, the NATs start taking fixtures
and track lights.

Suddenly there is a BIG EXPLOSION and the NATs become
momentarily unsettled.

Out of the red smoke three figures emerge.

                    FREEMAN
        The Exterminators are here!

Wearing NAT Exterminator protective gear, in walks
ANGELINA JOLIE, looking as pissed off as ever, ready to
kick NAT ass.

She is followed by NEIL PATRICK HARRIS wearing his
Starship Troopers war gear and carrying a big-ass gun.

The third NAT Exterminator is an Econo-sized can of
Super Strength RAID.

On the can it says KILLS NATS DEAD.

The RAID immediately begins spraying the NATs.

It does nothing to the NATs and they go into a RAGE,
swarming the RAID can.

They bathe in its spray. Drink it.

The NATs EAT the RAID can.

                    JEREMY
        Dude, we are so fucked!

                    FREEMAN
        Angelina will kill them!

The NATs swarm around ANGELINA like out-of-control
paparazzi, but she does not go down without a fight,
kicking and punching, because she's a badass. They
carry her off.

Neil aims his flamethrower at a bunch of big NATs and
FIRES.

                    NEIL
        Take that, you thieving insect whores!

The NATs swarm him, taking his flamethrower and EATING it!

They ENGULF Neil.

                    JEREMY
        What do we do now? They're all dead!

                    FREEMAN
        I don't know . . .

                    JEREMY
        You're the screenwriter! Can't you just write that
        they fly into the sun or something?

                    FREEMAN
        That's a great idea, Jeremy!

A laptop appears out of the red smoke. Freeman types:
ALL THE NATs . . . FLY . . . INTO . . . TH . . .

Damn.

FREEMAN and JEREMY swat wildly, but THE SWARM OF NATS
ENGULFS THEM.

Darkness and buzzing.

★

I shook awake from the nightmare with a chill. My vision cleared enough to show Hitchcock's birds descending upon on a coastal town.

Enough of that shit!

Jeremy was nodding off, too.

One nightmare about NATs was enough. I averted my eyes from the screen and shook my friend awake. "Dude, we're watching *Freddy vs. Jason* instead!"

Custys of the Runway

One of my favorite things about Broken-Down Burbank was the hard aisle that led into the store from the mall.

It ran right by the Handbag Jungle's thirty-foot-long glass encased counter, which I called the Corral. Whenever I was parked behind it and was prepared to help whoever arrived next, I found it entertaining to watch custys coming down the hard aisle heading into the store.

They reminded me of fashion models on a catwalk.

Custys of The Big Fancy runway!

They didn't always buy, but they provided hours of entertainment.

When I was with one of my pals with time to kill, we'd take a load off our weary retail dogs, sort of lean against the counter (as long as no managers were around), and check out all the custys going down The Big Fancy runway.

It was always full of colorful people, arguing couples, or hellspawn threatening to make us all crazy. We watched store employees make their pilgrimage to the Coffee Bar, as well as all the employees of the mall coming in to shop. Whatever came down the runway came by us first.

The freaks were the most fun to watch.

One was an old man who came in a lot. He was squarely built, with an arm tattoo of some kind of raptor about to strike. His Fight Town baseball cap was set low, and he wore a fishing vest covered with a bunch of NASA and Space Shuttle pins. Although he would only stop every so often and pay a bill, I was frightened of him. Which might have been because he also wore a huge button on his vest that happened to highlight George Bush's ugly mug.

It burned my eyes every time I saw it.

Best not to strike up a conversation with this runway custy!

★

One of my favorite runway custys was a fun, nutty lady in her sixties whom I called Flag Lady.

When Flag Lady came down The Big Fancy runway, it was a spectacle, and if there was a crowd, everyone stopped to watch her dance without music.

That's right, dance.

Without music.

Well, she was wearing an iPod, but no one else could hear it.

Rocking an older dancer's body, Flag Lady had big frizzy platinum blond hair, bright red lipstick, major rouge, and blue eye shadow you could see a mile away. She wore a red leotard; a thick stars-and-stripes belt around her waist; a big, red, floppy sun hat; and red, white, and blue tennis shoes. From her tireless bouncing, I could only guess she was listening to the soundtrack from *Flashdance*.

Although Flag Lady never bought anything, she was very friendly and once came up to me at the counter and told me in a German accent, "You are cute as button! Have a magical day! Stay cute!"

Thanks Flag Lady! I'm on my unicorn riding the rainbow staying as cute as I can at The Big Fancy!

★

I've had people try to sell me all kinds of things on the runway: legal services, insurance, cars, vacations, roses, clothing, jewelry, speakers, beanie babies, candy, therapy, long-distance phone service, and even Bibles. One such custy in search of a sucker to sell to sidled up to the counter and pretended to be interested in a new Coach bag we had on display. I had a feeling there was going to be a problem when my eyes were drawn to an oversized, bright yellow button pinned to her ugly corduroy jacket. The words *Herbal Life* blared at me like a billboard. She asked me basic questions about the Coach bag on the counter, but every time I looked at her, my eyes were drawn to the hypnotically bright yellow button.

The custy gazed at me expectantly, waiting for an inquiry.

I asked her nothing, knowing what came next. Frankly, my handbag-hoisting exercise plan and fast-food habits were none of her business.

"Do you know about this?" she said, pointing at the big yellow button with green lettering.

"Uhh . . . I've heard of it," I responded.

And please . . . I do not *want to know more!*

"You look like you could lose a few pounds," she said, not holding back. "Got a bit of a spare tire around the waist there. I can help you out with that!"

No you can't, because I'm going to rip it off my gut and slap you with it! Seriously, what kind of selling tactic is that? Depress the fat people into buying Herbal Life? Oh wait, that's what they all do!

A few minutes later she had pushed her card into my hand and was ready to sign me up.

I was ready to kill the herbal bitch.

My Asshole Manager went into play.

"I'm sorry, Ma'am, but there is no soliciting at The Big Fancy. I'm going to have to ask you to leave," I told her in a stern voice. "Otherwise I will have to call Security."

That will teach you to talk about my spare tire, you Herbal Whore!

She sputtered like she was going to short out and then headed down the runway to the mall.

But Herbal Bitch's damage to my psyche had been done.

I was so depressed at lunchtime I felt the need to feed the tire with a super-sized value meal at the Golden Arches and a candy bar from See's.

★

Homeless people often came down the runway.

I once sold a bag lady a $125 leather Monsac bag, which she paid for with wadded-up cash.

I knew she was a bag lady because I had seen her on the streets of Burbank. She was soft-spoken and polite, and the whole thing was quite strange because she didn't want to use it, nor did she want a shopping bag for it. (Imagine that! A bag lady not wanting a shopping bag?)

She took the small Monsac satchel, wrapped it up in a plastic grocery bag, and deposited it into the handcart I'd seen her roll around the sidewalks.

Your Monsac will look stunning in the basket! Enjoy it, Bag Lady!

While that is my one and only "helping the homeless" story, the other side of it was not such a positive experience for departments such as Shoes and Cosmetics.

When homeless people wanted attention in those departments, they went to town.

One afternoon I saw a shoe guy spend an hour showing shoes to a homeless woman. In the end she told him her sneakers—odorous, mud-colored Keds—were better suited to her fashion needs.

When complaints were made by salespeople Satan would issue a decree. "*The homeless are people too!* And they deserve your service like anybody else! I expect each and every one of you to wait on homeless people the same way you would any other customer." (We'd get fired for lack of sales, so The Big Fancy didn't actually care that you were doing a good deed by waiting on a bag lady who didn't want to buy.)

And how the fuck do you expect us to sell *them anything? Do you know the secret for squeezing water out of a rock?*

Satan was right from a humanitarian viewpoint, but what was she gonna say when all those homeless people didn't buy and the salespeople had sold zero for the day? We all knew exactly how humane she'd be feeling then.

C'mon, Satan!

★

One of the disadvantages of being next to a runway of custys was the runoff of stupid questions you'd get hit with. The Corral looked like an information booth to some people.

"Do you know where the Ford dealership is?"

It's just up the escalator.

"Are there bathrooms in the store?"

Nope, only Sanihuts!

"Do you have an elevator?"

I'm so sorry. You'll have to use Mount Fancy.

"Do you have that strap that goes around the shoulder?"

No, but I have many that go around the neck!

"Is there another Handbag department?"

Yes, at another Big Fancy store.

"Do you take credit cards?

When I feel like it.

What time does the mall open?

When it wants to.

What time does the Disney store open?

I believe when Cinderella finds her glass slipper.

"Do you know if scones have more than 200 calories?"

I was told they were fat free.

★

One time two dressed-up older women strolled down the runway and stopped at my counter, fawning all over a new collection of Isabella Fiore handbags.

I started telling them about the bags and one of them said to me, "You are so nice! Such an innocent child with amazing light. Doesn't he just radiate, Barbara?"

Barbara answered, "Oh yes, June, I could tell right away he has a bright, bright soul."

I wasn't sure where this was going, but I did sort of feel like Hansel in the gingerbread house. Only there were two witches deciding how they wanted to eat me.

Then Barbara said, "Can I ask you a personal question?"

For a split second, I thought maybe they were going to set me up with one of their gay grandsons.

But I knew better.

"Do you find your Savior in Jesus Christ?" she asked.

I knew it! Right-wing Christian bitches!

I had encountered these types before and knew just what to say. "No, I'm Jewish."

Which wasn't a total lie, because I do have an affinity with Judaism, but what fun it was to watch the Jesus freaks lose their happy fake smiles before Barbara said, "Good for you, dear! That's just wonderful."

And with that the good Christian bitches took off running down the runway.

★

Sometimes NATs provided lots of runway entertainment!

Usually this would come in the form of a NAT being pursued down the runway by Security.

But one afternoon, we got quite the floor show watching stolen credit-card action in Women's Shoes. All that was missing was popcorn.

A woman had grown angry when one of the shoe cashiers had to keep her credit card because of a minor little detail: It was stolen.

Instead of doing the sensible thing and running, this NAT decided she was gonna go for the Oscar and pitch a fit. Things blew out of control quickly, with Fat Bastard Steve and another security agent arriving and refusing to give the card back.

So what did dumbass NAT do? Freaked out and got into it with The Big Fancy agents, calling them names and claiming they'd hit her. In no time they were pinning her to the floor, trying to hold her down while the cops were called.

"Help!!" she screamed in a clearly fake vulnerable-victim voice. "Help me! Rape! I'm being assaulted! Help! Rape! Help! Rape!"

The NAT's freak-out had brought the entire floor to a standstill.

I was already laughing at her as she attacked Fat Bastard with fisticuffs while screaming like she was being mauled.

Jeremy, Linda Sue, and I had front-row seats to a NAT fight in the shoes.

"Holy shit, dude!" said Jeremy. "She's kicking Steve's ass!"

"That is one scary bitch!" added Linda Sue.

As the NAT fought and screamed, Steve and his agent managed to get her to the floor . . . where she passed out!

Or should I say, pretended to pass out.

After a few moments, thinking she was really out, they eased up on their grip. The crazy NAT jumped up like she'd just taken 50,000 volts to the chest and took off down the runway, making a break for the mall.

Only she wasn't a lucky NAT that afternoon.

The bitch crashed into two off-duty vacationing Florida police officers. They had seen the commotion and were striding down the runway.

NAT went down.

And this time, she didn't get back up till she was cuffed.

The funniest part about the whole showdown was how Big Fancy Gestapo members Tammy and Stephanie reacted when they arrived on the scene and the NAT was doing her floor show.

I had been helping a custy, and we were both staring.

"Freeman," Two-Tone said in her fire-breathing-dragon voice, "focus on the customers! Don't bring attention to it."

Bitch, it's FIVE FUCKING FEET from me. I'm not going to act like it's not happening! The NAT might start throwing shoes or something.

They wanted us to act as if we were at Disneyland and everything was calm and happy at The Big Fancy Kingdom? The custys had even stopped shopping.

"Did you want to see another Kate Spade bag?" I asked the custy I was helping.

"Not right now! I want to watch this crazy bitch in the shoe department!"

Sometimes custys like to be entertained too!

★

Since we sold dog carriers in the Handbag Jungle, every once in a while we got visited by a cute furry canine.

When Tinky the black and white Chihuahua arrived off the runway and landed on the Corral's glass countertop, we were all instantly in love. His fashionista mommy had brought him because she was in search of the perfect little dog carrier for him.

Yeah, it was kind of Paris Hilton sickening, but the woman was nice, and we all just fell in love with Tinky. He wasn't your average nervous Chihuahua.

We were all dog people—although not necessarily Chihuahua people—and Cammie, Maude, Dok, and I fawned all over Tinky like he had just become the Handbag Jungle's mascot. The runway custys took notice too, stopping to pet him, especially the kids.

Since we had fallen in love with Tinky, we showed his mommy every bag we thought could work, including several dog carriers by Kate Spade and Coach. And we made sure that Tinky was going to love his new home by letting him test all the bags!

To my delight, Tinky's mom decided on the Coach signature carrier for $500.

Nice choice! Tinky is one lucky doggy!

As I rang up Tinky's new home, the excitement of it all caught up with him.

Tinky tinkled all over the glass counter.

Poor little guy. The look on his face was, "Oops!"

And the response?

All the women laughed and went "Awwwwww!" When you're that cute, I guess it takes a lot to get in trouble.

As Cammie ran for the paper towels, I noted that he had just barely missed spraying a $2,000 Marc Jacobs we had only one of!

That would have been bad! Good boy, Tinky!

Tinky's mom apologized, but to be honest, since she was giving me such a great sale *because* of Tinky, I wouldn't have cared if he had dropped some poo, too.

Fashionista's Dog, Crazy NAT, or Religious Freak, one thing was for sure: Custys of the runway were never short on providing entertainment for us salespeople.

Giving Till It Hurts

"Gooooooooood morning, Burbank!" screeched Satan over the PA like a seagull in heat. "I hope you guys are ready to spend some money!! It's all about United Way, and we need to give back! So we are selling raffle tickets for the auction, and it's only five bucks if you want to join the pancake breakfast! Do you heeeeeeeeeear that, Burbank! Five dollar bottomless pancakes! All you can eat! Yuuuuum-mmy! It's going to be right on the receiving dock during the rally!"

Breakfast on the receiving dock?

Next to the giant green dumpster that smelled like spoiled Big Fancy?

The deranged queen had lost her charitable mind.

No thanks, Satan! I'll just stand in the background and vomit like everyone else.

The infamous United Way campaign was under way at The Big Fancy.

We had all been brought in early to be bled dry and give.

Whether we wanted to or not.

Like so many companies, The Big Fancy chose to be charitable with the United Way, a nonprofit organization that reached out to many communities and did a lot of good. Though they were never around during any of the disasters my family or friends went through, I didn't doubt that they helped many people. What I didn't like about this whole United Way business was how companies inadvertently forced employees to donate if they didn't want to, and how every year the drives got more aggressive because stores wanted to raise more than the year before.

This is worse than trying to beat last year's sales figures!

And let me be clear: Neither The Big Fancy nor United Way put a gun to my head and said, "Freeman, we want ten dollars from you out of every paycheck."

They didn't need guns because they had cards.

The United Way would supply companies with official donation cards for us to fill out.

"Here are the cards," said Maude, passing them out to us at the counter before we went to the big Rally Pancake Breakfast disaster. "Suzy's expectation is that every department participate 100 percent, so I need you to fill it out and hand it back to me because Tammy will be collecting them at the rally."

"This is such bullshit," said Cammie, starting to write out hers. "Like I can afford ten dollars a paycheck!"

"What if I want to choose my own organization, do they still let you?" Jeremy asked.

"Here's the booklet that lists them," replied Maude, handing it to him.

"I don't know," said Linda Sue, "it's good to give back, and the United Way *has* been around for many years, I don't mind doing a dollar."

Such a sweetheart, LSD!

But Linda Sue was right. The United Way had been around for a long time and had done a lot of good (despite some scandals that didn't sit well with me). But the reason I was not on board with the helping hands was because of the AIDS crisis. For me, a young gay man attached to a community dealing with a health crisis, my concerns at the time were for charities connected to AIDS. And United Way was spread thin. None of my AIDS charities were listed in their brochures. Even though I was a poor sales-bitch, I donated time to Project Angel Food and AIDS Project LA, and I did both the AIDS dance-a-thon and walk-a-thon. If I was going to donate *any* of my meager Big Fancy pennies to a charity, it was going to an AIDS-related one; that much I knew.

But I'd had to fill out the United Way cards and collect them many times as a manager over the years, so I already knew the drill and didn't complain the way I had to General Judy back in The Big Fancy day.

"How come there's no box to check if I don't want to participate?" I'd asked her.

"That's just the way it's set up," she replied curtly. "Everyone has to participate."

Or what? You're sent to Siberia? They garnish your paycheck?

The card in question was made out of nice glossy card stock with United Way graphics.

It had no place to say, "I do not wish to participate."

And these were the only choices the card offered:

$100 per pay period.

$75 per pay period.

$25 per pay period.

$10 per pay period.

$5 per pay period.

That's it.

No "Thanks, but no thanks."

No "Not this time, I'm poor."

No "I don't want to, I have to eat."

No "Get lost, I have rent to pay."

No "Fuck off and die."

No nothing!

When I'd voiced my concern to Judy, there wasn't even a spot to make your own amount, which there was on the newer cards that Maude gave us.

Had there been complaints over the years?

I was very alarmed the first time The General told me I had to donate. I told her I didn't make enough money, I couldn't afford to give United Way any of my pay, and I was involved in AIDS organizations.

Well, when I said the AIDS word, Judy backed down. She probably feared I'd go to Two-Tone. She called Tammy herself and explained the situation.

I was allowed to write at the bottom of the card, *I do not wish to participate.*

And that's what I had done for many years until coming back to The Big Fancy and being faced with yet again another donation for the hands that help.

As we were all considering what our pushy United Way donation would be, noisy Gestapo members Brandi and Richie pulled up to the counter, clearly having downed too much coffee. "We've got raffle tickets and pancake breakfast tickets! *Woohooooo!*" screamed Brandi, hurting my ears.

"Get 'em while they're *hot!*" added Richie.

"I take one. I hungry," said Dok. "Come with bacon and coffee?"

"You bet, Dok!" replied Richie, tearing it off. "Orange juice too!"

It also comes with eau de Dumpster! I don't think you will like it, Dok. It's not going to be pretty!

"How about you, Freeman?" said Richie. "You look like you love pancakes!"

Asshat! How about I turn you into one?

"No thanks, Richie," I replied to Ass, "I'm on a diet."

"Well what about a raffle ticket!" he pushed. "They're only a buck and we've got a lot of great prizes to give away."

Last I heard it was half-empty testers from Cosmetics, some of our returned handbags spruced up, a bunch of returned shoes and clothes, and coffee cards. I'll pass.

"I'll catch you at the rally," I lied, knowing I would do everything in my power to avoid the Gestapo there.

I didn't want Maude to catch any grief from Suzy over the 100 percent participation rate. I knew that if I added my own spot on the card that read, "I do not wish to participate," Maude wouldn't have full participation, she would catch shit for it, and my card would land on Satan's desk and burst into flames.

So I checked the box that said "other."

And I wrote: "A one-time donation of $25 to go to Best Friends."

Best Friends was a dog and cat rescue somewhere in L.A. I chose it out of the brochure when Jeremy finished picking out his charity, which was the American Cancer Society. There were lots of great organizations, to be sure. But I still felt coerced by United Way and The Big Fancy into giving, and it bothered me—even more so than if a homeless person had come up and asked me for money, which doesn't bother me half as much as a corporation asking. And if I had it, I'd often give it to the homeless dude because I could see the need in his eyes. It's hard to see that from suits who were already bleeding you dry with seedy commission practices. There's also peer pressure to worry about with corporate giving programs, so it's a good thing I didn't care about what my coworkers were giving. I know there had been fallout in other departments.

I happened to see the cards before Maude turned them in, and I thought it was surprising that Sherry had chosen to give $5 a pay period. I didn't know what her organization was, but $120 was a lot to be giving up on the salaries we made. Even for the head shark.

Maybe she thought it was $5 once?

It was nice to know that under all those ragged teeth she had some kind of heart, even if it wasn't usually on display in the Handbag Jungle.

You are *a good person, Sherry! At least to United Way.*

"*Is everybody hungry!*" screamed Satan out over the store. "It's time to start the United Way rally on the receiving dock! We've got pancakes! We've got raffles! We've got great United Way speakers! And really amazing United Way videos!"

Don't you mean shit that will make us cry and want to write big amounts on our pledge cards?

As always, I would attend the United Way meeting with eyes open, brain in sleep mode, and ears muted.

Hoarders of The Big Fancy

As the holidays approached, along came several big discount events that saved both custys and employees 30 percent storewide. The excitement to buy was at fever pitch.

The handbag stockroom shelves overflowed with merchandise on hold—and not just handbags. It was stuff from all over the store.

Between the custys and the salespeople, the hoarding was at an all-time high.

And so were Maude's nerves.

"I hope to God everyone is planning on buying these fucking holds," Maude said, looking at the stuffed shelves and bags all over the floors.

Not only was there merchandise for Lorraine, Bee, and a bunch of other personal custys, but the employees were hold-hoarding also.

We had our holiday shopping to do as well.

You can imagine what a sale did to people who are surrounded by beautiful new things all day.

We were shopping like billionaires, like the place was Target and our discount was 50 percent.

That box of holiday chocolate peanuts is only $15 and I get 30 percent off! Since my $100 eye cream is part of the 30 percent, I should get two! 30 percent off $500 Marc Jacobs shoes is such a great price!

Yep, we were all smoking The Big Fancy merchandise crack.

Our dreams to own were bigger than our wallets. But we didn't get it. We worked there. The merchandise felt like it was ours. And after a while an $800 handbag isn't all that shocking. Even if you're only making $28,000 at The Big Fancy. You kinda forget that part.

My employee custy Gretchen from Cosmetics sure did.

She went through a hold-hoarding love affair with a petal-pink Marc Jacobs satchel that left me wanting to beat her with it until it turned red.

The bag had been returned 500 times (what else is new!), and I watched her ogle it for days; for some reason I was always around when she stopped by the sale table.

One day she seemed more interested than normal and asked me questions about it.

"Marc calls the color Petal Pink," I told her.

"I just love it, and the leather too," she said, groping it like a fruit. "So cute! I've always dreamed of owning a Marc Jacobs."

Being the hungry shark I was, I couldn't resist telling Gretchen that it was going down to 50 percent, making it still a decent sale for me at $299.99 but also a real bargain for her!

Who says I don't throw Discount Rat bones to the employees! You should thank me, Gretchen!

Gretchen was thrilled beyond belief, of course.

And like any sale prediction, there's always a fifty-fifty chance it won't happen. I had tossed the dice with Gretchen in hopes of reaching two grand that day in sales, but it all went to hell when she replied, "Can you hold it for me?"

Shit! No. I don't want to hold it for you. I hate employee holds! They never come back!

"Sure, I can do a few days."

That was my way of trying to make it end as quickly as possible because I hated holds and employees were even flakier than custys!

"Can I get it on Friday because it's payday?"

She might as well have said, "The sky is falling," because it commenced a long, sordid, hold-hoarding, drama-filled nightmare of dealing with Gretchen and her precious Marc Jacobs sale bag!

Friday came and went.

I called her and she begged me to extend it for a week more—her birthday was coming, and her boyfriend was going to buy it for her.

Gretchen's birthday came and went.

But not the pink Marc Jacobs.

It sat on my hold shelf.

"I promise I'll get it on Tuesday!" she begged. "I have gift cards!"

Big surprise: Gretchen broke her promise.

After nearly a month of this, with Maude telling me if I didn't put the bag back out on the floor, she would, I called the MAC counter to deliver the news that I would no longer be holding her pink Marc Jacobs bag.

To my surprise, Gretchen came running over with her Big Fancy credit card in hand.

Maybe I should have gone hardcore on her sooner?

Of course, it wasn't that easy. She wanted to do part credit, part gift card, part cash, and part fucking check!

Really, Gretchen? Are you trying to make me want to murder you?

And after all that, the bitch's card was declined. I couldn't believe it.

"Maybe you can call Suzy," said Gretchen. "She's approved many of my sales before."

I didn't want to call Satan, but what choice did I have? I needed the sale.

What I wanted do was strangle Gretchen with the pink Marc Jacobs, but I knew that would only bring me temporary joy.

Satan was no problem.

"If it will help you get to Super Seller, you bet I'll approve it," said greedy Suzy.

For once I agree with you! Thank you!

Gretchen squealed like she was on *The Price Is Right* when she heard the good news.

"Can I take it with me to the department?" she cooed.

"I'm supposed to check it in with Security," I replied.

"*Please*? I want to show all the girls," Gretchen replied, taking the entitled employee road. "I'll just check it in myself for you."

Whatever, just go. I don't care. Get out of my sight.

I was done with Gretchen. It was always something with her.

So she went skipping out of the Handbag Jungle to show off her pink Marc Jacobs like it was an engagement ring. I saw all her coworkers smiling and looking happy for her.

Maybe I was being the bitch!

Gretchen was genuinely happy and I did get a sale.

Unfortunately, the douchey vibe I got from her lived up to its feeling.

One Saturday morning a week later I was unpacking a shipment of Longchamp, and a box of transfers from other stores arrived. These were mostly bags we specially ordered for specific custys. They were all wrapped in plastic bags and had forms attached with information.

As I went through them, my stomach turned when I saw a transfer with my employee number, 441064, and the words "return" from the Anaheim store.

The note on the transfer slip said: "We don't carry this, sending it back."

Bitch went and returned it!

I was furious. When I confronted Gretchen days later, she smiled sweetly and apologized, saying it was because she had too many pink handbags and she had too much stuff in general; it was time to clean out the closets.

Sigh. Leave it to me to get a Big Fancy Hoarder in recovery.

The Big Fancy Christmas Miracle

It was December 23 and all holy hell had broken loose.

The Handbag Jungle was a holiday disaster area.

Tags and stuffing littered the floor. The shelf and tower displays were in disarray, with handbags thrown into heaping piles and wallet fixtures looking as if they'd been shaken and turned upside down.

We were trapped at the register bays surrounded by hungry holiday custys; Cammie and Jeremy were at one bay and Maude and I manned the other.

I couldn't tell what was going on at their counter though it was mobbed; between the two of us we had about six people lined up.

All waiting to buy!

I was dying to shout "Please have your credit cards ready. And if you help wrap, that will move the line even faster!"

Normally, I'd be stressed about a situation like this, but it had been a bloody holiday sales battle in the Handbag Jungle, and all I could do at the moment was salivate, turn to the next custy, and announce, "Who's next? Will that be cash or charge? Would you like a gift box?"

This was no dream or fantasy.

I called it The Big Fancy Christmas Miracle.

★

I knew something was different in the Burbank air that morning when a normally Grinchy Satan got on the PA, and instead of bitching and making our ears bleed, she said, "Happy Holidays, Burbank!" She said, "We're coming down the fourth-quarter

245

homestretch, and today is the big one. Pace yourselves and keep Super Seller in your sights! Have a great day and Merry Christmas to those who celebrate it!"

Who kidnapped Satan? And what did you do with her?

Seconds later she came back on said, "Sorry my energy is low, guys! I think I'm coming down with something."

Satan is sick! I think my icy retail heart is melting. I hear angels singing!

Already my December 23 was off to a great start.

Maude, Cammie, and I were opening the Jungle. We were all exhausted from our preholiday slog through the last several weeks, and like everyone else in the store, we were overcome with the sales-zombie virus. Besides attempting to prepare for and celebrate our own holidays, we'd been engulfed by the unforgiving holiday hours of The Big Fancy—we were holiday slave-elves scurrying about, taking care of early-morning markdowns, floor moves, and stock work.

And then there was gift-box hell to contend with. December was all about gift boxes at The Big Fancy. Each custy got a box with their purchase if they wanted, so boxes had to be made around the clock. Even Satan held box-making parties with the Gestapo in her office. I had made so many Big Fancy boxes, I could have done them blindfolded. During the holidays making boxes was the responsibility of every Big Fancy salesperson.

Unless your name is Sherry. That bitch has made hardly any boxes.

Sherry's greed and laziness had gotten to everyone, and I nearly had to take drugs to tell her congrats when the sharking bitch whore made Super Seller at the beginning of the month.

Since the rush began, Sherry had turned into some kind of robotic holiday sales-demon, steamrolling everyone on the floor. She'd done no less than five grand every day in the last two weeks. And don't think we all didn't bitch about it.

Sherry's sharking was the number one topic in the Handbag Jungle.

Yes, the last few weeks of holiday hell had been brutal for sure. The shark fights got bloody and personal, ending up in the stockroom with tears and name-calling nearly every other day. Linda Sue and Dok weren't even speaking to Sherry. Of course Linda Sue wasn't speaking to Maude either. She barely said two words to me, and that was fine, because I had no interest in entering the world of LSD. Cammie had gotten into it with all of them, but normally it was Dok or LSD who ended up in the stockroom crying, and it was usually at the hands of Sharky.

Moments later Cammie arrived with scrumptious-looking peppermint cupcakes she'd made for everyone and then the goodness just kept flowing. Maude appeared from the Coffee Bar carrying two large cups. "Eggnog lattes for my two favorite human beings to work with! We've got a monster day ahead of us!"

And then it happened.

The phone rang.

Three times in a row, to be exact.

Within minutes all the sharks called in sick.

That's right.

One by one.

Linda Sue first.

Then Sherry.

Last was Dok.

When Maude got over the initial shock and panic of losing three crew members on the busiest volume day of the year, the celebrating let loose.

No sharks = More sales for us.

No sharks = No fights and crying in the stockroom.

No sharks = No bitching.

Jeremy was called and told to get his ass in pronto. When Maude mentioned that the gruesome threesome were out, he cheered and said, "Shall I bring champagne?"

"We can totally handle it," I told a very nervous Maude, ready to stand behind the register and ring till my fingers bled.

"I'm getting us a gift wrapper for the day," she replied. "We don't have a choice; we can't do it ourselves unless the Gestapo helps out."

"I'd rather be drawn and quartered," I replied.

And just then, like in the movies, when you talk about the evil villains, they show up.

The Gestapo appeared at the counter wearing Santa hats.

I wanted to barf red fur.

An overly cheery Brandi and Tammy dumped piles of cheap candy canes on the counter while saying, "Happy Holidays! Be sure to check everyone's ID."

The candy canes were nasty, so we left them on the counter for passing hellspawn, but even the Gestapo's moment of niceness stood out.

Was holiday cheer coming to The Big Fancy Burbank?

The jubilant mood continued.

The doors opened to brisk business.

The man custys poured in.

December 23 was the biggest-volume day of the year! And in the Handbag Jungle the male custys were probably responsible for creating most of it. Although I heard the wretched question "Can she return it if she doesn't like it?" over and over, I stayed in the moment and remained grateful for all the sales falling into my hands with no Sharky there to steal them.

By mid-afternoon our Big Fancy Christmas Miracle continued as the floor took on a party atmosphere. Custys were happily buying lots of Coach, Kate, and Dooney, and our friendly custys and personals came by to wish us holiday cheer. Like Bee and Darlene. They dropped off a box of See's candy, which made chocolate-lover Maude very happy. And when my Shoposaurus Lorraine heard we had three sharks out, she showed up with a gift basket loaded with snacks and energy drinks to get us through the day: "You've got to have nourishment to deal with all those cocksucking last-minute pricks."

I didn't tell Lorraine that the man custy was the easiest one to deal with in the Handbag Jungle, but I also knew they could be as bad as the women. I'm sure Men's Sportswear had plenty of man customers bitching about color and fit.

The Big Fancy Shark-Free Christmas Miracle raged on all morning as the four of us rang up one man custy after another.

And more miracles happened as Dina and Daiva from Customer Service surprised us all with several stacks of gift boxes. "I know you're short-handed today, and I hope this helps!" said Daiva.

The Handbag Jungle has elves! Who knew? Thanks, girls. You bet this helps!

Because the sharks in heels weren't there, as well as most of the normal Big Fancy women custys, the bitchy factor was way down.

I'd better savor this holiday moment!

A man walked up and asked if we had a nice black bag and wallet.

"How about a Kate Spade Sam, it has a matching wallet?"

"Will you box it for me?" he said.

"Hell yeah, dude!" I replied.

"Sold!"

Why can't this be every day at The Big Fancy! I'd be rich.

I must have sold twenty Kate Spades that day.

The BF Christmas Miracle had put me in such a good mood I was thrilled to spread my holiday cheer.

A man I'd been expecting came to the counter all frantic and worried.

"I think you know my wife," he said, clutching our accessories mailer from a month ago. "She left this on my desk a few weeks ago with a note that said, 'You better get me this Coach purse for Christmas, or don't plan on coming home.' Please tell me you have the bag. I know I waited till the last moment, but she'll kill me if I don't come home with it."

You better start making funeral arrangements, dude!

Unfortunately the Coach bag in question was the patchwork satchel.

Sold out everywhere.

Oprah wouldn't have been able to get it.

"No, sir. It sold out everywhere weeks ago. That was a hot one. It's two days before Christmas. No store has it. I've heard it's even sold out online."

"You're sure you don't have one hiding in the back somewhere?"

A dumb attempt on his part, but I did have to lie here.

I'd been hold-hoarding this particular Coach bag on my shelf for a good custy. It was the last bag in retail existence and I was not giving it to him.

"No, I sure don't."

"What the hell am I going to do? She'll be pissed! She'll divorce me! She said if I ever fucked up another holiday gift, I was screwed."

I didn't feel sorry for him one bit.

That's what you get! Bad man custy!

"Sorry, dude. Wish I could help you, but I can't. There's a great jewelry store around the corner in the mall. Maybe you could get her something nice there."

Last-Minute Man frowned and sighed, mumbling about how much trouble he was in.

Seconds passed.

Suddenly he was muttering, his last-minute shopper desperation in full bloom.

"Jewelry. She'll have to be fine with jewelry. I'm out of time. Where is this store?"

"It's around the corner."

As soon as Last-Minute Man left, I picked up the phone.

I knew exactly who his wife was.

I had her number, and she'd told me he'd be coming in to buy that bag. She picked up immediately.

"Did you send him to the jewelry store?" she asked.

"Yes, he's on his way there now," I replied.

"Excellent, they have what I want on hold, and they're going to make him think he picked it out. Here's my credit-card information. Send the Coach bag you're holding to me by UPS."

"You won't get it till after the holidays, are you sure you don't want me to just go give it to him?"

"No. I'm gonna make the little procrastinator stew. And jump through a few hoops first."

"Awesome. Shall I put it in a box for you?"

"Absolutely."

★

As my shark-free holiday buying fest continued, with custys buying everything in sight, a Big Fancy Miracle of the Celebrity Kind happened.

I suddenly found myself waiting on the hilarious comedienne Kathy Griffin.

Yes, *the* Kathy Griffin! Right there in my Handbag Jungle!

Kathy was a blast to wait on. Normally it was frowned upon at The Big Fancy to talk like a fan with a celeb custy, but being gay and a comedy writer, I could not let the opportunity fly by. I told her how much I loved her on *Suddenly Susan* and said she should have her own show! (She didn't have one at the time—Bravo came later.)

With her signature WTF? look, she responded: "Could you please call the network executives and tell them that?"

Well look at you now, Ms. Emmy! You didn't need me to call any fuckin' suits!

Kathy bought several Kate Spade cosmetics cases.

And she earned a fan for life.

★

When Maude handed me the phone, all I heard was screaming and crying in the background. Finally a voice made its way through the mayhem: "Hello, Freeman, this is Mrs. Mendelson, you were kind enough to find the Kate Spade giraffe canteen for my daughter's Hanukkah gift. Well, we've had a disaster happen. A candle from the menorah fell over and landed on the bag! It left an imprint from the wax and burned a hole in the front of the bag! My daughter is hysterical because it was her big present and the only thing she really wanted this year. I know you said it was sold out everywhere, but I'm hoping for a miracle! Can you find another one? I'll even pay for it! This was our bad luck, and I sure would not expect The Big Fancy to pay for it."

Did I hear you right, Mrs. Mendelson? You don't expect The Big Fancy to pay for it? I must be dreaming!

I was blown away. Even though (according to my friend Seth) I am only an honorary Jew, I was sympathetic to her plight. But it was Mrs. Mendelson's taking responsibility for her own actions that made me want to become the savior of Hanukkah. I hoped it wouldn't take eight nights and days to perform this retail miracle.

"I'm so sorry to hear that, Mrs. Mendelson," I replied. "I think it's so kind of you to pay for another one, but The Big Fancy will let me do an exchange for free, and I will find your daughter another one!"

Mrs. Mendelson was beyond thrilled, telling me she'd be writing a letter to Suzy!

I knew my quest of finding a sold-out bag would be daunting, but I decided to use her story when I called other Big Fancy stores all over the country trying to replace the menorah-murdered Kate Spade.

"Yes, hello, this is Freeman from Burbank, can you check? I need a Kate Spade canteen in giraffe to replace one that was burned by a candle that fell out of a menorah! And the custy wants to pay for it! Can you even believe that? She didn't blame us!"

Within three calls I had Mrs. Mendelson's giraffe bag. "Oh, the poor baby," said Jane in Chicago, "I'm Jewish, and my daughter loves Kate also. And I've had a few menorah disasters of my own. Tell you what, I have one of those bags hiding in the stockroom. I'll send it to you!"

Another Big Fancy Miracle.

Mazel!

★

Although I felt the need to start wearing a sign that said "We do *not* carry Louis Vuitton, so stop fucking asking," my Big Fancy miracles didn't stop with the festival of lights.

I helped a young couple looking for a bag for Mom. The wife was hiding behind sunglasses and a bit neurotic at times, but they ended up purchasing a $325 Longchamp shoulder bag. They wanted a box and since the wrapper was busy, I decided to do it myself.

That's when the next miracle happened.

While I was at the table boxing up the bag, I casually looked up and saw that the wife was fingering the wallet fixture.

But as I continued to watch her, it became clear she wasn't fingering.

She was straightening them!

WTF?? Is this for real? A custy straightening? Where is my camera?

I wanted to rub my eyes in disbelief.

A custy was cleaning The Handbag Jungle on December 23.

And just then, as if it couldn't get any better, her husband joined in and began helping her at the wallet fixture.

My sales-zombie jaw fell to the floor.

Do you guys want a job? We'd much rather have you than the sharks!

Now they were both cleaning up the wallets, organizing them by style and even color.

Pinch me! I must be dreaming!

I wrapped a little slower, giving them time to finish the bottom row.

When I returned, they had straightened the entire wallet fixture, organized half the DKNY display, and handed me some stuffing and tags she'd found on the floor.

Wow. Just wow. Merry Christmas to me at The Big Fancy!

I thanked her profusely, saying, "That was really kind of you, but it wasn't necessary."

I couldn't think of anything else to say.

"People are such pigs," she replied. "You all are working so hard! It was my pleasure. I worked in retail for many years, and I know your pain."

And there it was.

She was one of us.

Unless you've worked in a store on December 23 and lived to tell the tale, you have no idea just how hellacious it is during the last mad holiday rush to buy gifts.

I ran to the other side of the bay and grabbed some of the candy canes the Gestapo had left. It was tacky, but I wanted to do something to show my appreciation for her Random Act of Retail Kindness.

But my holiday heart grew even bigger in that moment.

I suddenly remembered the Longchamp vendor, Jackie—a real live wire—had left matching key fobs during her appearance last week. We had one left.

So I used it as a thank-you for two awesome custys.

As the lines grew deeper and the man custys wandered around like lost puppies in The Handbag Jungle, lunch hour approached. It became apparent none of us was going anywhere.

"I'm ordering Domino's for the stockroom," Maude said, picking up the phone. "We can have mini breaks in between ringing."

I loved how she said "ringing!"

Ka-ching! Ka-ching!

It just kept getting better.

"I'd like to get this Kate Spade," said a man custy.

"My pleasure!" I said with a shit-eating holiday grin. "Would you like a box?"

Oh how I loved The Big Fancy Miracle.

★

Maude, Cammie, Jeremy, and I were the four highest salespeople in the store that day.

Maude—$19,732

Freeman—$18,894

Cammie—$16,543

Jeremy—$13,975

If only we could have gotten a picture of the sharks when they saw the department totals on Christmas Eve. It would be our little present to them. Cammie talked about putting a bow on the list of sales figures. Linda Sue would probably bitch herself into a blizzard.

Merry Christmas to us!

And Merry Christmas to you, Big Fancy, you crazy old store!

★

As the 31st arrived, custys buying last-minute evening bags for New Year's Eve wasn't the only excitement going on at The Big Fancy. It was also the end of the Super Seller contest. The final day had arrived, and if you weren't at most ten grand away from your department goal, chances are you would not be one of the lucky Big F salespeople who'd get to shop with a 31 percent discount and buy Gucci, Marc Jacobs, and Cole Haan.

"*It's your last chance, Burbank!!! Woooohoo!*" screamed Satan over the loudspeaker. "*Work it! Push it! Make it happen!* I want to see all of you buying from your coworkers, getting close to achieving Super Seller! Let's help them out, Burbank! *Woohoo!* The store has a *huge* goal today! Three hundred and ninety thooouuuusand dollars! It's up to us today, Burbank! Get out there and get shopping!"

And then what, Suzy? Do we all file for bankruptcy or just return everything?

Since Cammie and Sherry had made their goals during the holiday rush, all eyes were on me to make the Handbag Jungle's Super Seller win a three-way. Yeah, I wanted the discount, but could I afford it? Many of my coworkers and custys were more excited than I was. Like the final scene of *It's a Wonderful Life*, where all of Jimmy's friends and family fill up his basket with money, one by one, all of those close to me at The Big Fancy made their pilgrimage to the register I was trapped at.

Maude bought a new toaster and coffee maker. Cammie had to have new boots to party in. Jeremy bought a new Roar shirt and jeans for a hot date he had with one of the Cosmetics girls. And Bonnie from Customer Service picked out a Coach bag. My personal custys who knew about Super Seller were also showing up to support me. Bee bought a $75 clutch, and Darlene even joined in, grabbing herself a credit-card case for $25. Jabbermouth Virginia stopped talking long enough to pick up a sale Isabella Fiore she had been eyeing for some time.

But even with buyers lining up all day at the register attempting to push me into Super Sellerhood, if it hadn't been for my Shoposaurus, I would have fallen short and never made it.

"I'm gonna buy this whole motherfucking store!" she said with a wild, hungry look in her eyes. "I need outfits for my nieces' birthdays—they're ungrateful little whores and return every fuckin' thing I send them, but I'm keeping the fuckin' receipts and tags this time so my Frayman won't get dinged. The spoiled little cocksuckers will just have to wear the shit I give them!"

Or go to The Big Fancy and throw a tantrum until they get a refund!

"I'm sure they'll still be able to return," I said with confidence and relief that I wouldn't be getting a monster return.

"I also need gambling wear and housedresses for my mother, and how about another motherfucking handbag? Frayman, you can't be a Super Seller without a cocksucking bag purchase from me!"

You got that right, my little Shoposaurus! Spend big!

And that she did! Lorraine dropped nearly six grand. The bag of her choice was a special-edition fashion Ferragamo Kelly made out of wooden strips. "It looks like a motherfuckin' birdcage!" Lorraine howled. "I fuckin' love birds, I'm wearing this little bitch to Cirque du Soleil's KA! It's fuckin' perfection. Everyone will love it!"

I had no doubt Lorraine would be the belle of the Vegas Ball. She always was.

As The Big Fancy was about to close and ring in the New Year, I was exhausted from the buying frenzy and doubted I'd be seeing any balls dropping over Times Square. Somehow I had managed to pull off Super Seller, hitting sales of $12,658 in one day—a number I'd normally only see at Christmas or during a huge sale. But I hadn't reached my goal because of brilliant sales skills. It happened because of caring coworkers and personal connections I'd made with my custys who cared about my handbag success. They were all watching my Big Fancy back and wanted me to win. I had become a Super Seller.

Now that The Big Fancy store was mine for the taking at 31 percent, what would I buy?

4th Quarter Sales Associate Rankings

Sales Associate	Year-to-Date Volume
Sherry	$345,652.92
Cammie	$335,698.35
Freeman	$326,050.94
Dok	$305,369.30
Linda Sue	$301,236.67
Jeremy	$240,369.25

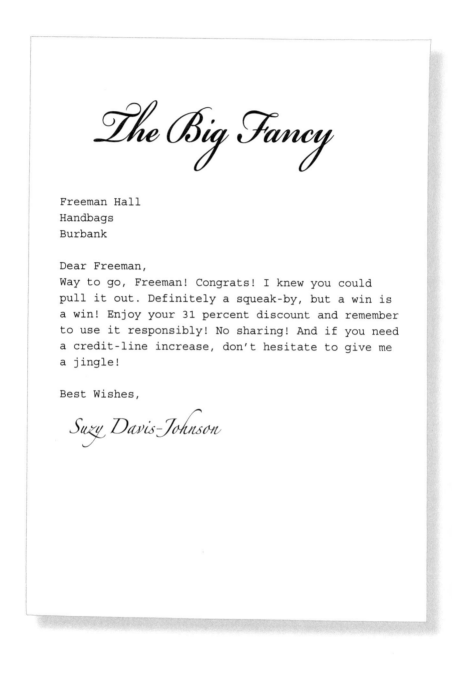

The Big Fancy

Freeman Hall
Handbags
Burbank

Dear Freeman,
Way to go, Freeman! Congrats! I knew you could
pull it out. Definitely a squeak-by, but a win is
a win! Enjoy your 31 percent discount and remember
to use it responsibly! No sharing! And if you need
a credit-line increase, don't hesitate to give me
a jingle!

Best Wishes,

Suzy Davis-Johnson

Hard Times at Big Fancy High

I am in my favorite section of The Big Fancy surrounded by all the trendy men's clothes that I love. I'm grabbing everything—$250 jeans! $150 shirts! $100 T-shirts! My Shoposaurus is leading the way, throwing clothes at me. "I know you want this cocksucker," says Lorraine. "It has a motherfuckin' skull on it, and I know you love the fuckin' skulls! Personally, they creep the shit out of me." Lorraine has turned into my personal shopper and we're being followed by a cute sharky salesman carrying a tower of clothes and shoes that my Shoposaurus helped build. I can't stop grabbing everything in sight! Lorraine is at my side admiring the Marc Jacobs shirt I'm trying on. "It's fucking gorge, you need that cocksucker, take the black and white also . . . you can never have too many!! You need extras, you hate doing motherfuckin' laundry!" As the shopping rampage continues, Lorraine finds a $300 Gucci sale shirt and yells across the department, "OMG . . . Gucci for Frayman . . . OMG . . . Fraaaaaaaaaaayman!"

"Freeman?"

Oops.

Gestapo bitch Brandi caught me fantasy-sleeping with my eyes open.

I was standing with a group of Big Fancy salespeople in the register training room. We were surrounded by sleek new registers that had big screens that responded to the touch of a finger.

The Big Fancy was going even higher tech! I just hope none of us get so pissed that we accidentally punch the screen instead of gently touching it.

"It's your turn to read aloud," said Brandi.

Of course it is! I forgot I was at Big Fancy High remedial reading class.
Thankfully, this new register-training hell only lasted a few minutes more. I read my paragraph about only cleaning the screen with a damp cloth, not our beloved glass cleaner, and hightailed it out of there because the store was about to open.

I collected the money bags and headed down the escalator to the Handbag Jungle.

There was no rally, but Satan was not in a good mood. There had been a complaint.

I took the escalator down while she screamed about a bad custy complaint over the PA. I didn't quite catch the whole deal but the custy was not happy with the way one of the salespeople looked.

"We need to take better care of ourselves!" pleaded Suzy Davis-Johnson like she was Dr. Oz. "Have makeovers! Whoever doesn't want to work here and have a makeover, come up to my office, knock on my door, tell me you don't want to work here anymore, I will gladly walk you to the Employee Entrance, kiss you on the cheek, give you a hug, and wish you a fond farewell. If you do not want to be here, you are all disposable, and I don't want half-assed-looking people working in the store. We need increases! We need better-looking people to attract better customers!"

Seriously? Makeovers? Have you been talking to Dok? She'd like nothing more than to see everyone instantly turned beautiful!

I tuned her out.

You had to; otherwise she could make you drop to the floor in the fetal position, covering your ears. And Vomit would follow.

Another year gone by at The Big Fancy.

Just like that. In the blink of an eye.

It was January all over again at The Big Fancy.

This is how you get trapped in retail; the hell just blurs into itself!

Scan Gun Inventory was right around the corner, and then came the difficult months, when misfires would run rampant as soon as the custys decided to take a break from shopping. Some would not survive The Big Fancy's chopping block. Things were going to get ugly.

But they already had.

We weren't even a week into the new year when a shocker swept across the Handbag Jungle.

★

"Get in here fast," Maude said, calling me at home and waking me up from a good sex dream. "I need you to cover Linda Sue's shift."

"Is that bitch sick again?" I groaned, not wanting to get out of bed.

"No!" Maude said. And then she covered the phone and whispered, "She's getting canned right now!"

I jumped out of bed fast and hightailed it to The Big Fancy to witness the show. After sprinting up the mountain, I reached the hallway where Satan's office was, and sure enough, the blinds were closed. And no one was in HR. Which meant they were all in Suzy's office.

With Linda Sue!

Oh, I could just imagine the high drama that was going on in there.

I was sure she was crying. Even though she could be a nasty bitch, I had seen her break down at the drop of a hat in the stockroom.

When I got down to the Handbag Jungle, Maude greeted me with a latte, and I followed her into the stockroom.

"Cheers!" she said, handing it to me. "Thanks for coming. Well, shady Miss NAT was apparently returning a lot on 1s. And she did it to a secret shopper."

I was stunned.

But then again not so much.

LSD, you are a shady lady!

As a manager I'd lost three people for the same type of theft.

I didn't really see them as NATs or bad people, even though they were completely shunned from the store, humiliated in front of their peers, and usually prosecuted.

Like so many other salespeople of The Big Fancy, Linda Sue had gotten tired of fighting the paycheck-killing returns. She would do returns on 11111 instead of her number. That way she'd keep her commissions.

Well at The Big Fancy, *nobody* got to keep her commission on a return.

And if you did, you'd committed the crime of the century.

So a secret shopper caught Linda Sue processing a return with the 11111 number because she was tired of fighting. Or maybe she was afraid of misfiring?

Whatever the reason—no more Linda Sue.

Just like that.

I couldn't say I'd miss her.

★

"What do you think of this one?" said Maude, looking at a black Kate Spade messenger bag that had been returned slightly used.

We were going through a big box of them. Kate was one of our top vendors, so she was also one of our top returns. Although it was a short-lived shopping party, at the time, Satan let us buy used custy bags at a 75 percent discount before they were sent to charities. A Kate Spade could end up costing twenty bucks!

"I think it would be great for your trip to Europe!" I replied.

"That's what I was thinking," she said trying it on her shoulder. "I can't wait to get the hell out of here. I'm gonna miss you, Cammie, and some of my friends in the store, but I'm ready for a new adventure."

That housewife who had lost interest in cooking so many years ago had now lost interest in The Big Fancy.

Maude was retiring after Inventory.

She took me to lunch at Pizza Kitchen to celebrate after she formally told Two-Tone. I was really happy for her. She'd given so many years to The Big Fancy, and I didn't want to see them do to her what they had done to so many. What Maude brought to The Big Fancy every day was lost on them. The Big Fancy never truly appreciated anyone's passionate commitment.

If they did, they would fire most of us.

"I'm just tired of it all," she said. "It's becoming a different world, and even though Linda Sue is out of the picture, I want to get out of this store and spend time with my family."

Maude was lucky to be leaving The Big Fancy on her own.

There were others who wanted to stay but were spit out by Broken-Down Burbank and Satan. Like Jose the Receiving manager. Two-Tone's hours cut did him in, and they forced him out. No retirement party for Jose! And the same was true for Maggie, a sweet woman in her sixties who worked in Lingerie. She'd been with the store for two decades and had survived many managers. She didn't survive Satan flooding the Lingerie floor with sharks.

Maggie reminded me of Lisa from Hosiery the year before.

Heads will always roll in the springtime at The Big Fancy.

They don't know how to survive it any other way than to point fingers at the unlucky and start firing.

I was chatting once with Big Fancy CEO Don McCormick and Suzy Satan, and another department manager interrupted to talk with Don about an ongoing problem her number one Super Seller salesperson was having with a new register procedure.

I kind of knew what his response was going to be; I just didn't expect it to be so harsh and mechanical.

"We were here before her and we will be here after her," he said, as if he'd blurted it out a million times before. "If she feels we're mistreating her by spending millions of dollars on technology to help her make more money for herself, then she is welcome to leave. The mall doors are to the right of her department. That's all I have to say about it."

And there was the truth right there.

Even though he was right from a business sense, and this associate needed to accept the procedure, it was a harsh response to give one of your top producers. It's stayed with me, because it's basically the voice of every corporation: "You are replaceable."

He walked off not saying another word, leaving the stunned manager to go deliver the final decree to her Super Seller.

At The Big Fancy you were only as good as your last sale.

And if you kept those sales up, your reward was a 31 percent discount.

★

But there was something else of greater value that employees of The Big Fancy were able take with them in the end. The friendships.

There was—and still is—no doubt in my mind that I'd remain friends with Maude, Cammie, and Jeremy, as well as many other people from The Big Fancy. Our experiences, good and bad, had bonded us together, just as they do at any job.

When The Big Fancy isn't there for you, it's the people you work with who are.

And as long I wasn't working solely with crazy or heartless sharks, there were always moments of laughter and fun that eased tension in the Jungle.

Like when Cammie, Jeremy, and I tried to explain to Dok what the sexual meaning of Pearl Necklace was (if you don't know, Google it—but don't say I didn't warn you about the R rating).

"I not get. What you mean?" said Dok, trying hard to understand. She was no prude, and we had all enjoyed hours of sexual-harassment-rule-breaking fun. "What go on boob? Necklace? I not get."

Jeremy had no problem spelling it out for her in black and white.

Dok blushed when she understood, and there were rounds of laughter.

We thought that was the end of it, but apparently not.

Within five minutes the phone was ringing.

Gestapo Richie was calling because a custy had just complained that we were talking about graphic sex acts on the floor.

I nearly wet myself right there.

This would not end well if I didn't deny it to the end. "I don't know what you're talking about, Richie," I replied.

"She said, you guys were talking about . . . um . . . the pearl necklace thing."

Poor Asshat Richie.

"Pearl necklace?" I repeated loudly, catching the attention of everyone. "Jeremy has one on hold for a customer, and we were talking about how to tell the difference between the real ones and the fake . . ."

I stumbled with my lie slightly, but it was met with approving nods and thumbs from my fellow Jungle Bag People.

"Oh!" Richie said, buying it hook, line, and sinker (or should I say boobie?). "She must have misunderstood. Thanks for clearing it up."

Anytime, Ass.

At The Big Fancy there were also plenty of those we all wished never to see again.

★

I had just returned some shirts because my Big Fancy card was over the limit and in need of a payment, when I ran into Satan near Customer Service.

"Hey, Freemaaan!" she said in her I-want-something-from-you voice. "So, guy, have you thought about it?"

I knew what she was getting at.

I was actually afraid to answer, even though I needed the money.

"Now that Maude is retiring and Linda Sue has left us—thank god!—there's a lot of opportunity down on that handbag floor, and I have no doubt you are the man to take the ball and run with it this year."

"Well, it's intriguing," I dodged the question, coy, but terrified.

"I'll let you hire another guy!" Satan added in desperation.

I guess I was holding on to some shred of possibility I might return to writing. But the only writing I'd done was in my Big Fancy nightmares.

"So what do you say?" said Suzy Davis-Johnson, smiling at me like she was about to take hold of my balls and squeeze forever. "Handbags needs a new captain!"

And I needed to pay for more new clothes and shoes.

All aboard the Titanic!

God help me.

Acknowledgments

Fans of my first book *Retail Hell* should give Karen Cooper and Victoria Sandbrook a standing ovation for bringing this next tale to life. Seriously, tweet them your undying thanks! Without their dedication, passion, and belief in my retail stories, *Return to The Big Fancy* would not have become a reality. And of course the doors to The Big Fancy would not have opened again without my badass agent, Holly Root, so tweet her your thanks too!

I knew the retail gods were smiling when Jennifer Hornbsy came into the picture to perform her magic as my editor. Little-known secret—she was the awesome copyeditor for *Retail Hell*! How lucky were we to get her amazing skills and humor again for this second ride!

The Big Fancy tales are endless and none of mine would be complete without inspiration from Nancy Foster, Vanessa Schafer Brown, and Jeff Swan. This book is as much theirs as it is mine.

I also want to thank my former hellmates Krystine Chaparo, Christiana Glasner, Dr. Janna Segal, Bronte, Dianne Hansson, Misha Behbehani, Lida Movahedi, Carolyn Meister, Melinda Filardo, Michael Jameson, and a hoard of other retail slaves who have crossed my path over the years that I am unable to list here. You know who you are!

My descent back into The Big Fancy would also not have been possible without the man who has my heart, Dane Lenton—his love and light were with me every step of the way.

The journey back also brought me love and encouragement from my family; Michelle Quevedo, Billee Burchett, Davia Venckus, Pamela Vallandingham, and Beach Weston.

I want to also thank Lady Gaga for being my musical minister. She taught me to "marry the night," and get past my obstacles. Everyone needs a fight song and a remix of that one was mine.

I thank my comedy heroes, Trey Parker and Matt Stone, whose work continues to teach me so much about writing satire. Thanks also to my other mentors that have helped me in some way along this trip: Augsten Burroughs, David Sedaris, Michael Tonello, Kathy Griffin, Stephen King, Tom Hanks, Steven Spielberg, Jennifer Saunders, Michael Patrick King, and Louise Hay.

Thank you to publicists Julie Nathanson, Teri Weigel, Beth Gissinger-Rivera, and Lauren Miller, and to my film and TV agent Brandy Rivers. I also want to give props and heartfelt thanks to everyone at Adams Media; it takes more than just me and a few others to get a book out in the world.

And even though they are not writers, publishers, or former coworkers, there were people who kept me lifted up and on track every day during the journey: My three yentas: Bonnie Denenburg, Jane Summer, and Denise Livker, Rabbi Eliahu Shalom Ezran and Ora Ezran, Kari Del Mastro, Danusha and Walt Kibby and their son Walt, Connie Franco, Everyone at Ralphs #198, Kerry Daley, Benjamin Kissell, Ken Arlitz, Julie Darling, Calindy Mann, Gina Mae Temelcoff, Patrick Miller, Joe Flynn, Terry Everton, Tony Salazar, Leyla Mutlu, Dina Oxenberg, Jordan and Carol Weiss, Craig Questa, Andrew Zeiser, and the Friday Night Tufts House Band: Dane Lenton, Bert Wood, Michael Lenton, Marty Shalders, Mike Lance, Jim Ruble, and Gio Valladares. Music does soothe your soul and it's even better when it's live!

Lastly I want to thank all of my Monster Bloggers and RHUers on the Retail Hell Underground. Your voices and stories have kept me inspired, aware, and laughing. Continue to spread the word about corporate and custy injustices. Speak your truth and stay strong!

About the Author

FREEMAN HALL is the author of *Retail Hell* and *Stuff That Makes a Gay Heart Weep*. A twenty-year survivor of retail and other service-related jobs, Freeman created the popular blog RetailHell Underground.com, where people in the service industry go to rant, laugh, and support each other. Freeman lives in Los Angeles.